I Need to Tell You

I Need to Tell You

Cathryn Vogeley

E. L. Marker
Salt Lake City

Published by E. L. Marker, an imprint of WiDo Publishing

WiDo Publishing
Salt Lake City, Utah
widopublishing.com

My story is told to the best of my recollection. In order to maintain their anonymity, in some instances I have changed the names of individuals and places.

Cover design by Steven Novak
Book design by Marny K. Parkin

ISBN 978-1-947966-58-1

To my sisters in loss
and
all who suffer society's injustice

Can you understand being alone so long
you would go out in the middle of the night
and put a bucket into the well
so you could feel something down there
tug at the other end of the rope?

The Abandoned Valley by Jack Gilbert

Part I

❧ 1 ❧

My eyes squeezed shut while the ting of metal instruments broke the silence. As if my chest had lost its elastic, I breathed in short, tight spurts. The ceiling tiles with their tiny holes looked down on me as my chin tilted upward.

Exam gloves snapped; metal wheels moaned across the cold floor.

Dr. Franklin stood from behind the sheet.

"No doubt about it. You're pregnant."

As if I'd been slapped, I cried, "Oh, God," and covered my face with my hands.

❧   ❧

It was 1968, Pittsburgh, Pennsylvania, when the sanctity of virginity still bumped against the emerging culture of free love. In a city of blue-collar workers and Midwest values, an unmarried pregnant girl was labeled "tramp." My first year of nursing school was coming to a close, and I hadn't yet turned nineteen. Gavin and I were each other's first love, dating over two years, eventually having guilty sex in his father's Cadillac convertible. Always in the front seat, because moving to the back made me complicit. I preferred to think of myself as Scarlett O'Hara in *Gone with the Wind*, ravished by Rhett Butler, rationalizing that sex wasn't my fault because he had talked me into it. What a pain in the ass I was, behaving as if I didn't want it, enjoying the turn-on, but then telling him "No" when he unzipped my shorts. When I said, "Stop," he nuzzled my ear and neck, moving his hand over my bare back until my shorts were off. The sex was spectacular, but afterward, I cried even as he lay over me. It was my job to make him stop, and I never did. He was a guy; it was natural for him to want sex. The girl was supposed to say no and make it stick.

Pregnancy constantly worried me. He used a condom only once. It took away the romance. I didn't like seeing his penis or waiting while he rolled the rubber in place. He said it was too much trouble and never used one again. Rhythm was our method of birth control: watch the calendar, count the days from the last period, no sex during the week of ovulation; a good Catholic's choice.

Dr. Franklin and his assistant lifted my ankles from the stirrups. The young nurse kept her head down, gathered instruments together, and whispered to the doctor. She swished out of the room, followed by the door's thud, then stillness. Dr. Franklin touched my shoulder, and I opened my eyes to his downturned, droopy expression that mirrored my own dread.

Many years before, Dr. Franklin had delivered similar news to my mother with congratulations. A baby was a blessed gift from God. Even when, as in Mom's case, there were three babies in three years and two more after that. Never mind that she cried constantly when I (number three baby) was young or that she was overwhelmed with expenses and the work of taking care of children. The important thing was that pregnancy was a gift, unless outside of marriage.

I would be a despicable embarrassment to my family. Mom knew nothing of my condition or the appointment that day. It seems foolish now that I chose her doctor to confirm my pregnancy, but I'd thought of little else since I'd skipped my first period. I'd never had a pelvic exam and the idea of it repulsed and scared me. This doctor was someone my mother trusted, so it made sense to see him.

I took the doctor's hand and sat up, with my legs dangling over the exam table's edge. Barely able to breathe, with my head hung low, I curled into myself.

"Does your mother know?"

My head barely moved. "No. Nobody does."

"You know the father, I presume?"

The question cut at my already suffering pride, even as I pushed the anger down. Walking in there pregnant and not married. Did he think I was a whore, someone who got laid, asked for it—like a stupid, dirty girl? This wasn't my fault, I wanted to scream. *I'm the one who always worried about getting caught. And now look where I am—a stupid, dirty girl.*

Dr. Franklin washed his hands, wiping and wiping with paper towels. He crumpled them into a ball which he then fired into the wastebasket. He turned to face me, hands in coat pockets.

"What are you going to do?" he asked.

"I don't know." I closed my eyes, shutting out the room, and took in a deep breath.

"Are you going to tell your mother, or should I?" he asked, hands still in pockets.

"I'll tell her."

"You're sure?" he asked, as if he were in charge.

"Yes. Don't worry. I'll tell her. You don't need to," I said, my voice barely audible.

He treated me as if I were no more than a child who'd written curse words on the blackboard. But his attitude fit the era when decent girls did not go *all the way.*

Or so I thought.

I felt split in half, since my first time with Gavin. I was an impure girl who went to Mass every Sunday, taking Holy Communion and Confession, putting ashes on my forehead at Lent, acting saintly. The congregation chanted: mea culpa, mea culpa, mea maxima culpa. Through my fault, through my fault, through my most grievous fault. Catholic teachings were clear about human imperfection. We are born with sin on our souls and must make it up to God by following the Commandments and doing good deeds.

The rain had stopped before I left Dr. Franklin's office. Dazed and dodging puddles, I trudged back to the dorm; my shoulder-length, auburn hair fell across my face and I didn't have the energy to push it away. Water filled the imperfections on the sidewalks of Pittsburgh's Oakland university district. Tree branches sagged and rainwater dripped onto my beige shift and into my platform shoes. A couple of long-haired guys wearing tie-dyed T-shirts and bell-bottoms passed me with the blank expressions of untroubled souls, like I'd been no more than a month ago.

Earlier in the day, I had worked on the med-surg floor with my fellow freshman nurses, scrubbing dentures, holding my breath while emptying bedpans, lifting and wiping and sprinkling cornstarch under heavy sagging breasts. When I left the area that noon, I was still free of this reality, able to hold onto hope. But now everything was turned the wrong way.

At the stoplight, I stepped off the curb in front of a rumbling Corvette. Tires screeched as I jumped back, heart racing. A woman in huge Jackie Kennedy sunglasses crossed the road toward me, screwed her face tight, and said, "You better watch it. Next time you might not be so lucky."

Luck? Mine had run out. My safety, or the safety of the child, or of anyone else, was of no concern to me. My parents would have to be told. Nothing else mattered—not good grades, favorable clinical reviews, working after-hours as a babysitter, playing forward guard on the school basketball team. I was eighteen, but I felt like an eight-year-old in big trouble.

Mom had names for women who had sex before marriage: "loose," "slut," "tramp." She married Dad six months after meeting him, because they couldn't wait. "Couldn't wait" to me as a kid meant they were so in love they wanted to marry. But now I understood the meaning—as well as her reason for telling me this. Abstinence had been honored by my parents, and I must follow in their footsteps. Mom left out the parts about nature's design of sexual desire and how healthy it is, what precautions to take. Her message was the opposite. Nature wasn't discussed, except to stress sinfulness of the body, that sex was bad, and that anyone having sex was disgusting. Unless married. I would rather die than admit to Mom that I wasn't a virgin. But she'd soon know, and whether I wanted to or not, I'd have to get married.

❧ ❧

Gavin and I first met in the gymnasium of Central Catholic boys' school, where every student was Catholic. Along with the other wallflowers, I stood self-consciously on the perimeter and refused to join them. Move away, I thought. *Do anything but stand here like a paper doll.* And so, I shouldered my way through the dimly lit crowd of slow dancers. About halfway to the other side, a guy in the requisite coat and tie faced me and said, "You want to dance?" He was muscular, a few inches taller than me; I agreed, overjoyed at the chance to stay off the wall.

His broad hand with a hint of callus on the palm was more like that of a man than a high school kid. The herringbone sport coat felt scratchy against my cheek. As we danced for the first time, there was a faint scent of aftershave, a musky, aphrodisiacal fragrance. The gym was overly warm with so many bodies radiating heat after dancing to fast songs like "Hanky Panky" and "Wooly Bully." My new outfit, a teal wool skirt and matching sweater with pearl buttons, seemed like a good choice at home, but now I worried about my deodorant failing.

He offered to take me home, and we bumped against one another's shoulders as we strolled through the parking lot while dry leaves clicked over the pavement. I wasn't certain if I liked him or not. We were opposites—me with blue eyes, freckled skin, auburn hair; him with the Mediterranean Omar Sharif-type good looks, deep-set eyes, and tight, wavy, black hair.

The way he talked was different, too, with his quiet, serious voice, like a grown-up.

"Did you say your brother goes to Central?" he asked.

"He used to. He graduated already. Maybe you didn't hear me before." *You already asked me that, bucko.* Small talk: I was glad to be talking regardless, anything to lasso my nerves.

"Oh, no, I heard you. I was only checking to see if you were telling the truth."

I stopped and looked at him. "Telling the truth? About my brother gradu—"

Gavin interrupted, "How long have you been coming to the dances?"

"Oh, this is my second one. Hey, isn't that something, us both alone on the dance floor? I mean, it's so incredible, don't you think?"

"I saw you before you went into the crowd. I decided you looked like someone I wanted to meet."

"You walked onto the floor to ask me to dance?" I faced straight ahead, trying not to show how much this pleased me.

"Uh, huh," Gavin said.

Yeah? Now that is saying something. He saw me first and came for me. And with that, I walked a little taller.

Toward the back of the parking lot, away from other parked cars, streetlights reflected on a midnight blue Cadillac convertible, a half block long and shining, as if it were on a showroom floor, waiting for a customer.

"This is your car?" No one I knew had a luxury car.

"Yeah," he answered with the matter-of-factness of a kid who covered himself with cool confidence.

"No way. Seriously? This is your car? Are you kidding me?"

"Well, it's my dad's car."

"Wow, and he lets you drive it?" I'd never ridden in a Cadillac. This boy was different. He held his shoulders straight, upper body slightly back, with a bit of a swagger.

I was sixteen but didn't have a license. Before my sixteenth birthday, at the dinner table where Dad sat at the head, Mom at the opposite end, and my siblings along the sides, I asked Dad if I could get my learner's permit.

He did not turn toward me but kept his eyes straight ahead. He took another bite of meat and continued chewing until finally he said, "Why?"

The question took me by surprise. I wanted a license because that's what you did at sixteen. That's what my brother and sister did, and my friends were getting theirs now. But I knew that was the wrong answer.

"Um, to, to drive?" I said, stuttering.

Still, he looked straight ahead; then he said, "What are you going to drive?"

Again, I wasn't expecting this question and managed to squeak out the words, "Your car?"

"No, you're not," he said.

And that was the end of it. I wouldn't consider arguing or begging or using any other means to change Dad's mind. He was a tyrannical parent, prone to unpredictable rages. He physically abused me and my siblings, showed consistent disapproval, and withheld affection. I seldom communicated directly with him and learned to hide when he came home from work. I grew up nervous and afraid. Not having a license embarrassed me, but the choice had not been mine.

"I'm a good driver. Besides, I earned it," Gavin said.

He opened the passenger door. I slid onto the burgundy seat, inhaling the earthy sweet aroma of leather. *Wow, this is nice.* I twittered inside, ran my hand over the leather, put my fingers to my face, and breathed the scent. Gavin came around the front of the car, got in, and rotated the key. The smooth engine purred. I wondered what I should do.

"You want some music?" he asked and twisted a dashboard knob. The radio's dim red light glowed. He looked at me. "Hey, what are you doing over there? C'mon, slide over here closer to me. I want to make sure I know the way to your place."

I moved across the bench seat next to him, like in the movies when a girl sat close, and felt pleased with myself.

I'd had a few dates by that time, but they were flat, boring. I had to do the talking, trying to make them comfortable. Not like with this guy. He was self-assured and grown up. Gavin talked only when he had something to say. My insides fluttered, but I tried to match his calm.

The long car floated onto the street, smooth as a magic carpet. Inside was silent with only the sound of the radio. My feet rested unevenly—my left on the hump in the center of the floor and my right off to the side, creating an inelegant position.

"Do you ever put the top down?" I asked, keeping my voice casual.

"Well, yeah, but not when it's thirty-five degrees out." He paused, then said, "So, Cathy, are you a senior?"

"I'm a junior. You?"

"I'm a senior. You go to Bennington? Isn't that a new school?"

"Uh huh. My sister Corrine goes to Cathedral, so she doesn't have to go to Wilkinsburg. You know. Not so nice down there. Hoods and everything." I fluffed my hair out from my collar and adjusted my back more comfortably on the seat.

"What's that supposed to mean? Black kids? Foreigners? Kids that look different than you? You have something against them?" He spoke without taking his eyes off the road.

"Oh, turn left at that next light." I pointed and he signaled to switch lanes. "Actually, to be honest, I don't know anyone like that. My mom and dad don't want us to go there. I guess it'd be scary."

"Why? Why would you think it's scary?"

The engine had warmed up by then. Gavin reached over my knee to the heater control, and I jumped, moving out of the way. We each pretended nothing happened, but there was this energy, like a heightened electric charge that comes when two live wires are close together.

I pushed my hands under my legs for a moment, then laid them on my lap. "I don't know. It seems rough, I guess. You know. From things you hear."

"I don't see how you can decide if you've never known anyone in that area," Gavin said as he eased the car to a four way stop, leaned forward to see out, then pulled ahead nice and easy, attentive as if he'd been driving forever.

"Well, one time when I was a kid, I was at a playground near my aunt's place around where some kids were playing. I was only about eight or nine. I guess I was staring at this one kid. I didn't mean anything by it. I never saw a Negro in real life." I tucked my hair behind my ear, wondering if I'd said too much.

"You're kiddin' me," he said, genuinely surprised. Gavin kept his eyes on the road.

My world was middle class suburbia with neighbors, teachers, priests, friends who were versions of me. Public places had segregated restrooms. I wasn't snobbish or racist, only naïve. My parents led insular lives, conveyed prejudice in their words, although they never used racial slurs, they were clear in their message that people who looked different were best avoided.

The turn signal ticked a low, smooth sound, oddly pleasant.

"No, seriously. Anyway, before I knew what happened, the kid I'd been staring at came at me like a torpedo—punched me right in the gut. It hurt so bad I almost fell down." I began to relax. Talking to Gavin felt easy, like talking to my sister, Corrine.

He smirked and shook his head. "Sucker punched you, huh? Right in the solar plexus. Lucky you. Did you hit him back?"

"Are you crazy? NO! I wouldn't even know how and wouldn't want to anyway. He'd probably knock me out. It was such a shock; I wanted to get out of there."

"I'da flattened that kid if he hit me." Gavin sounded so grown up to me, so powerful and certain of himself.

"Yeah, well. I doubt you'd stare at him. Plus, you wouldn't have given him a chance."

"Wait, I thought you said you didn't even see it coming."

"Oh, all right, yes, that's what I said. But if it had been you, I could imagine you'd see it coming."

The car turned onto a ferociously steep but short road that connected to my street.

"Uh huh. I wouldn't be standing around with my head in the clouds. You have to pay attention. Take care of yourself."

"Over there on the right. The house with the light over the door."

Gavin guided the car along the curb next to my front yard where the pin oak's leaves had turned bright orange and begun to fall. I expected that he would ask for my phone number.

"Thanks for the ride. It's nice of you to drive clear out here," I said, unsure if he would walk me to the house. I hesitated, ready to open my side and say goodnight.

He turned off the engine but left the radio on. I waited. He loosened his tie and skootched down a little in the seat, leaned his back against the door, and put his arm around me. *This had never happened on other dates.*

A song came on that didn't play on pop music stations, "Could This Be Magic," by another doo-wop group—one of the many oldies my older brother and sister listened to on Terry Lee's *Music for Young Lovers* evening show.

Could this be magic, my dear, having your love, if this is magic, then magic is mine.

"Oh, this song," I said. The porch light shone bright and steady above our steep front yard. My curfew was eleven o'clock. Sitting in a car with a boy was something new for me. When Corrine had sat outside too long, or past curfew, Mom had flashed the porch light. Out of the corner of my eye, I glanced at the dashboard clock. Ten thirty.

The radio played. Gavin's elbow rested on the door. He absentmindedly touched his necktie. I felt nervous sitting there, quiet. I had to talk.

"You know, my brother Evan used to wear a tie to classes every day. It must be uncomfortable and complicated. Do you hate it? At Bennington the boys don't have to wear ties."

"Hate what? Tying a tie?"

"No, having to wear one every day."

The song ended, and Terry Lee spoke in a low voice, "This next one is for all those young lovers listening tonight."

"Nah, it's no big deal once you get used to it. Tying it is pretty simple. You just have to know how. Here, I'll show you."

Gavin tugged down the knot on his tie. A slippery sound, silk against cotton. He slid it from under his collar.

"For Your Love" came on. Slow, full of angst and a dreamy saxophone.

"Here ya go. Sit up a little," he said.

I leaned forward. He reached over me and positioned the tie around my neck.

With one arm around me and the other one manipulating the tie, his tweed jacket sleeve brushed my cheek.

"First, you make sure it's a little longer on one side than the other. See? Like this." He leaned closer to see the tie's ends; serious, concentrating on getting it right. The scent of mint on his breath.

"Now lay the wider end over the skinny one."

"I can't see. It's too dark."

"Here, lean over this way more; get in the light," he said, helping me move closer. The porch light shined through the driver's side window.

"Okay, I can see now."

"Bring this part underneath," his voice feather soft. "Put this end across."

His lips brushed my ear lightly. His cheek touched mine, barely, enough to sense his warm, smooth skin. I pretended to take in the knot-tying lesson. My breathing shallowed, then deepened. My heart galloped; my eyelids weighed down. I felt dizzy.

"Take the wide end up and through the loop around your neck."

"You Belong to Me," *another love song.*

"Take the wide end through the knot in front," he said as he tried to straighten his vantage point to make the knot straight. His lips touched my neck. I melted to him, intoxicated by his body's warmth, the scent, music.

"Last step, tighten it and pull up on the knot." His voice stayed low and easy.

"Now you try it." He released the tie. Like a parent teaching a child to tie shoes, he added, "Go ahead, I'll help you."

"Uh, okay. I don't know if I can." I began with the wide end over the skinny one. "What's next again?" I asked.

He leaned to me, his hand on my face, delicate, his lips on mine, his breath sweet. My eyes closed, Gavin's hand, rough against my skin. His thumb slid to my neck, barely touching. A kiss, then his cheek to mine, warm breath delicate in my ear, lips brushed my neck and back to my mouth.

"Your skin is so soft," he whispered.

We stayed in the car until my curfew, kissing only, no hands below the neck. I was sixteen; he was seventeen.

Gavin and I, with that kiss, slid into that magnificent part of life when two people fall in love for the first time, an experience that would never come again in that innocent way. This self-assured boy from the other side of town, son of Greek and Italian parents, whose dad owned a bar. More different from my family than anyone I'd ever known. He swept my heart away.

Between songs, I learned his last name was Makis and he lived in the Pittsburgh city limits, in an older and more ethnic neighborhood than mine. Gavin worked at the tavern after school, loading and unloading crates and mopping floors.

We dated every weekend, usually going to interesting places: Phipps Conservatory for the flower show; sometimes to a movie; or on a Saturday afternoon, we'd go to the zoo, Frank Lloyd Wright's house called Fallingwater, or the library, where we worked on homework together. We talked about religion, work, school, war, and love. Usually, we ended a date parking at North Park or some other out-of-the-way place. Making out was the dessert. Dinner gave the appearance of normalcy. A meal without a sweet finish would be wholly unsatisfying.

৵   ৻

Gavin's grades were high in math, science, and philosophy. He said he could be anything he wanted and considered engineering, law, or medicine. But Mom didn't like his cocky attitude. She said his family lived in a seedy part of town. It was true that they weren't like us. Gavin's dad was a rough-talking guy; his mother was ambitious, sarcastic, and usually orchestrated the business of bartending. My parents were the opposite: repressed, angry, judgmental, and afraid.

Gavin refused to talk about our future. When I brought it up, he'd say, "That's a long way off." Gavin and I sometimes argued about religion and Catholic rules. He saw the teachings as part of a requirement to conform with school and his Catholic family. My belief was simple: I had to follow the laws or go to hell.

More importantly, I fretted about pregnancy. If I cried after sex, Gavin reassured me with, "Everything will be all right. Stop worrying. Nothing's going to happen."

2

Back at the dorm, I collapsed onto the bed. A large window next to me faced a wing of the hospital across the sidewalk. My eyes fixed on the building's brick wall, then to the space above, where barely an aisle of sky was discernable between the buildings. A sky, not white or black, but a sickening opaque gray. *I'm so tired. I want to sleep. Why am I so tired? Get up. Get up.* But I didn't get up, nor did I sleep but turned away from the window.

My giant panda, Babbu, stared from across the room with his black plastic orbs for eyes. He still wore the embroidered smile as if nothing had changed since the day he was lifted from the game booth shelf.

It had been late summer at Kennywood, Pittsburgh's historic amusement park. Gavin and I spent the day riding our favorites: every roller coaster, the Ferris wheel, the Rotor, Laff-in-the-Dark, bumper cars, Noah's Ark. End-of-day sunlight flashed through a slit between rides and made long shadows on the pavement. The day had been hot, but now the temperature dropped and made me wish for a sweater to cover my bare midriff and shoulders.

Loud cheers came from a game booth. A kid and his date walked past us, muttering, "That sonofabitch is rigged. It should've busted when my pitch hit the middle pin."

Gavin played a lot of softball and had a decent pitching arm, so he decided he'd give it a try. He told me to pick a prize, because he'd win the best one. When on the third pitch he hit it exactly right, the whole pyramid crashed down. I was jumping around, pumping fists, cheering like a sports fan.

"So, which prize do you want?" Gavin asked. "Anything on the shelves." The black and white mega-panda on the top shelf sat looking straight out. It was the only prize that didn't look junky, so I chose him. Gavin doubted it would fit in the car, but together, we stuffed it in the back seat. On the way back to the dorm, I turned to look at the panda, a massive child sitting behind us with arms stuck out like he wanted a hug.

"Hey," I said, "let's name him Babbu."

"Sure," Gavin said, "whatever you want."

❧　　❦

I turned away from Babbu, who symbolized all that was good between me and Gavin: the laughter, teasing, necking, studying, dancing, riding with the top down, listening to music. *What now?* I had a sudden vision of an army officer with his hand raised in front of my face, commanding with a shout, "Halt."

Life as I knew it was over.

The desk clock ticked, annoyingly. I could not be still and walked from my closet to the bed, up again to the mirror, to the bathroom, to the window. *What if Gavin is excited to be a father?* He was sweet with my little sister, Jeannie, taking her for piggyback rides and playing in the swimming pool. I pictured an infant in his big hands and how awed new daddies can be. *But what if he isn't happy? No one will be. The timing is so wrong. But he loves me. He'll love this child.*

Finally, it was five o'clock, when Gavin usually got home. I dug into my wallet for change. In the hallway phone booth, the glass doors clattered and banged under my push. In my mind, I had a picture of what would likely happen. Gavin would take the news the way he did everything: quiet for a minute. He always had to think about things. But he wouldn't hesitate for long. He'd say, "I guess we better get married. It's a little inconvenient. But it would've happened sooner or later. Married. Or pregnant, then married."

On the ledge beneath the black pay phone, an index card lay covered by doodles of hearts, and in swooping circles, someone had written the name *Bobby*. I lifted the receiver, my hand shook, and the change bounced on the floor. I leaned down and could barely move for the tension, as if my entire body had cramped. My head felt pressured and aching. I picked up the nickels, the coins rattled and dinged into the pay phone, then a dial tone. The cord had been twisted and tangled by the last girl in the booth, probably Bobby's girl. I held the cord and let the receiver dangle till it stopped spinning. I dialed Gavin's number.

He knew I'd skipped. He knew I had the doctor's appointment. Gavin answered on the third ring.

"I'm pregnant."

"Ah, Christ." A sigh. "Are you sure?"

I didn't answer.

"Cath, maybe you should see another doctor. You know. Get another opinion. There's such a thing as mistakes, you know."

I didn't answer.

"Listen, this is too much to process right now. I'll call you back later," Gavin said, his voice sounding deadly serious.

I knew he'd need to think. But what I wanted was for him to say that he loved me and not to worry. Like he had all those times in the car.

"Bye," I said and placed the phone in the metal holder. It thunked and the coins jangled through. Any other time, I'd flip out the change cup, one of those mindless habits you do to finish up a phone call, in case someone before you had forgotten to pick up their money.

I sat motionless on the curved wooden plank, feeling stunned. Finally, I rose and pushed through the squeaking folded doors. I didn't check for money.

～   ～

I went to classes, where we prepped for our final exams. The year was winding down, but we continued with normal hours at the patient's bedside, passing medicines and giving baths. My greatest relief was time with friends at meals where we made fun of the mean instructors. We reminisced about the time we slept in the clinical lab. It was a prank, something to do to say we'd done it. Three of us snuck in the dark, dragged mannequins from the beds, and took their place. I'd actually fallen asleep when suddenly the lights snapped on. I lay still with eyes closed, listening to the sounds of wastebaskets being emptied, water running, then click, the lights went out. We thought it was hilarious and felt so mischievous, wondering if the janitor thought we were the dummies.

With the girls beside me, I blocked out my problems as we sauntered back from the cafeteria. I pretended I was no different from them. My uniform buttons still laid flat around my twenty-six-inch waist. Two senior students walked by on their way to night shift, wearing their nurse caps. My class would be awarded caps at the start of our second year. The uniform was a big attraction for me, and I could hardly wait to wear a cap that would make me a real nurse. But in the fall, I'd be five months pregnant. *Could I stay in school if I married?* You couldn't in high school. But this was different. A girl in the class soon to graduate had married and was now largely pregnant. She didn't live in the dorm, but she managed the clinical experience and classwork the same as everyone else.

It'll be okay. I can do that, too. I'll get my cap and graduate.

～   ～

At each day's end, I hurried to my room, hoping for a note on my dorm room door. But again, there was no note saying Gavin had called, and three days had passed. I closed the door behind me and stripped out of my uniform. It dropped to the floor and

I left it there, too tired to pick it up. The double knots on my white nurse shoes refused to yield, and anxious as I was to get them off, I put toe to heel, then wiggled my foot without untying. Trapped in my own clothes, I struggled against the stupid shoes, incapable of slowing down or picking apart the knots as I had done dozens of times before. Eventually, with painful twisting, the shoe released. *Why does everything have to be so hard? What is Gavin up to?* Inside I seethed. We'd never had a day without talking unless one of us was out of town.

I'd made Gavin my confidant and my world. Every minute we were apart was merely an interval until we were together again. He made me come alive. And now I felt as though I was sealed in a soundproof box, waiting for Gavin to let me out. I had no intimate friends to confide in, only him.

Corrine might have understood, but since she had married, we had little in common. She was eighteen months older than I was. As sisters growing up, we fought over toys, jacks, closet space, and everything else until we reached our teens.

Corrine always looked like a magazine model when she went on a date. One Saturday, when we were in high school, I sat on the bed watching her get ready. She pulled up sections of hair, and with the other hand, ran the comb toward her scalp until it stuck out everywhere. Aqua Net hairspray made the sound of fine sand in a tin can as she shook it. Corrine closed her eyes and took in a deep breath, then sprayed her hair for nearly a minute—over the top, sides, and back. Her cheeks rounded as she let her breath out, then after waving the spray-filled air in front of her face, she set the can down, smoothed the mass into a bubble shape, checked the back using a hand mirror, and with the rat-tail comb, picked up any flat spots.

I said, "Gosh, I wish I could do that."

"Do what? You mean tease your hair?" she asked.

I nodded.

She bit her nail, one of her bad habits, and said, "I'll do yours, come on." She picked up the comb. "Wait, let's go to the bathroom. I can reach your head better if you sit on the toilet."

That afternoon, she gave me a makeover: hair, make-up, and nails. Mom disapproved. Said I was too young to look like that.

Corrine not only looked good, but she had rhythm, too. She tried teaching me to swing dance on Saturday afternoons to Dick Clark's *American Bandstand* on TV. But my timing was off, and I'd twirl the wrong way. I'd never be as cool as she was.

Corrine married the unambitious stock boy from Dad's office right after graduating high school. She wasn't even pregnant. The marriage disappointed Mom and Dad, but they celebrated it regardless. Corrine followed the rules, and that's what mattered.

Telling Corrine was out of the question. Saying the words out loud was too much for me.

ᔧᔧ   ⤚ᔧ

Chattering noises came from the hall outside my dorm room, a familiar clang of the water fountain's foot pedal. I gathered my textbook and notes, and sat at my desk in my white slip. A buzzing hairdryer, elevator doors, laughter breaking out, a repeated *btttrrriiing* of the telephone. For days, I had jumped when it rang, rushing to answer, but no more since every time it had been a false alarm.

"Cathy. It's for you." Loud knocking, then, "Are you in there?"

"Hang on a minute." I bolted from my chair and threw a robe around my shoulders. But then I sat down again, closed my books, held my head, elbows on the desk, steeling myself for what might come.

I slipped into my bedroom slippers and moved down the hall, dragging my feet along the linoleum.

The receiver waited on the phone's top platform, and as I sat on the tiny wooden bench, I picked it up and nervously spoke into it. "Hello?"

"Cath, hi," Gavin said in his soft whisper voice, not drawn out, more clipped.

"How are you doing?" he asked.

"Okay," I answered. "Tired. Everyone around here's excited about finals and taking off for a few weeks."

Down the hall, a dorm room buzzer signaled that someone waited at the reception desk. A classmate hurried past, dabbing at her lipstick.

"Are you still there?" I asked.

"Ah, yeah. Sorry. I was thinking."

"Thinking? About?"

"I don't know. Look, Cath, I know what you're thinking."

"What am I thinking?"

"You're probably thinking we ought to get married." He said "married" with a Pittsburgh accent, it came out "murreed." I flipped the pay phone's metal change cover, letting it chink against the stop. My foot slipped on something white: it was the card with Bobby's girlfriend's doodles. It had been walked on and was dirty with shoe prints.

"What are *you* thinking?" I asked.

"Well, look, Cath, I don't know. I don't know if I can do that right now."

A sudden flush of adrenaline, my heart raced, my breath caught.

"What are you saying? Seriously? You've got to be kidding. You don't know if you can do that right now? What the hell, Gavin? I mean, come on." I spoke quickly, hardly believing what he'd said.

"Okay, listen. I don't know. There's so much to think about. I need some time. I have to finish school. I don't know how I can do that and take care of a family."

Those words hit me in the gut. I didn't feel ready to take care of a family either. I was as qualified to manage a family as to pilot the Apollo spacecraft. My world was turning upside down, rolling topsy-turvy. *What is happening? We are in love, aren't we?*

"Well, you just think on it then," I said. "I have a final to study for."

Gavin sucked air in a deep breath. "Okay. See ya."

I ran to my room, pushed the door closed, and slammed onto the bed; I cried into my pillow, wrapping it over my head to muffle the sounds. Doors boomed shut, toilets flushed, voices called out to each other. In the hallway, my friends Holly and Margaret sang a duet, each taking a separate part. "Hey hey Paula, I want to marry you . . . we've waited so long for school to be through . . ." Margaret answered, "Hey Paul, I've been waiting for you. Hey hey Paul, I want to marry you, too . . ." A familiar routine of theirs. I turned onto my back. My hands went to my belly, low, where a small grapefruit of firmness had begun. My breasts hurt. *What am I going to do?*

Laying on my bed under the window, I stared up at the space between the buildings again. I squinted, trying to see nothing but the sky, obliterating the massive barriers. But I still saw the bricks. Finally, I held up my hands, blocking the walls, pretending they weren't there.

According to Catholic Church teachings, premarital sex was a grave sin. Mom's weird attitude about sexuality confirmed what I learned in school: that sex was forbidden, disgusting. Mom labeled young women in form-fitting clothing as *cheap*. Her reaction to Marilyn Monroe was tsking and eye rolls. Mom's attitudes represented our society, as far as I was concerned. These were incontrovertible truths, unchangeable, biblical.

An idea came to me. I'd get away, take a "vacation." Go to Florida and stay at Nana's and Papa's. Other girls were planning trips on break—why not me? I called the airline and reserved a seat to Fort Lauderdale. In two weeks when summer break would begin, I'd get as far away as possible.

No one in my family had married because of pregnancy. No one I knew had a baby without being married. I doubted that my parents would stand behind me if I didn't marry. Unconditional love wasn't a "thing" in 1968, when it was a bad idea to tell children that no matter what, you'd always love them.

Our extended family was polite, smiling, and restrained. Family gatherings were subdued, and no one argued or criticized openly, even though Mom gossiped the whole way home from family visits. The ugly side of my immediate family stayed within our home: Mom and Dad's rages, intolerance, tension. *Present your best self. Hide everything else. We are a happy, respectable family.* I couldn't tell Nana and Papa. It didn't fit with who they thought we were.

The corner lot was in a neighborhood with flat, winding streets and generous yards with pastel-colored stucco houses that were prim and perfect; palm trees and a live oak grew in the weed-free, precisely-edged lawn. I thought my grandparents' home, which was a light pink tulip color, was the prettiest on the block.

I followed Nana into the house; Papa trailed behind having taken my suitcase from the trunk.

Inside, the walls and furniture were beachy colors—whites and tans, pastel floral patterns on cushions and pillows. The main room felt airy. The house lacked the oversized mahogany furniture, clutter, and tension of home. I sensed the clean spaciousness as too perfect, not what I was used to, although to myself, I insisted it was beautiful and I should love it.

I remembered a summer when Mom and Dad loaded the five of us in the station wagon and drove three days from Pittsburgh to Fort Lauderdale. We visited for ten days, and during that time, Nana accused us of wrecking the place. One day, I used alcohol on my mosquito-bitten feet, slopping the liquid on the pale blue toilet lid, leaving marks. Another day, Nana discovered an oil stain on the light carpet from one of us spinning in Papa's swivel chair. It was a vacation to remember, as we'd never seen Nana upset prior to then, or after, for that matter.

Nana was tall and always wore shift dresses, earrings, and nail polish. She kept her gray-white hair short and swept back, never messy or out of place. Nana had retired from modeling years before. She was narrow hipped with long, slender legs. Over time, her figure had become thick through the middle, and her belly stuck out as if under her shift she held a sea turtle's shell that made her look six months pregnant. An odd look, but likely it was related to a corset.

Papa's ears were too big, his height too short; his face was droopy as if made of melted wax. Most evenings, my grandparents would take a stroll around the neighborhood after dinner, holding hands, chuckling now and then, making an occasional comment, nodding to neighbors. I never heard a cross word between them. They were the ideal model of a long, happy marriage, an example of mutual admiration and respect.

⤚   ⤚

At Nana's, I intended to have a good time, forget about my life at home, pretend everything was as it used to be on our visits, and keep up the charade with a polite smile.

But the day after arriving in Florida, I crouched over the toilet, flushing repeatedly to cover the sounds of morning sickness. In the evening, I fled to the bathroom to get away from the mosquito truck's toxic fog.

The next day, Nana called, "Dinner's on the table!" She had made a place for me at the oblong Formica table in the kitchen.

Papa arranged aluminum chairs with cherry-red padded seats. Metal legs banged against each other. He moved them this way and that until finally satisfied with the setup, then he motioned for me to sit across from him. His thick white hair, still full even in his late sixties, was slicked back with a hair dressing that smelled of peppermint.

I was uncomfortable. It occurred to me that I'd never been alone with my grandparents. That day, having no one else at the table, I felt like I was ten years old again and my family had gone off somewhere without me. My time with Nana and Papa, which amounted to an annual ten-day visit, had always included my siblings. The tightrope I walked on, trying to appear happy and at ease while turmoil roiled inside me, only made my self-consciousness worse.

I split my potato and scooped out the flesh, mashed in butter, and added salt. The milk had an oniony flavor, the halibut strong and fishy; I'd never had such a strong sense of taste.

"What made you decide to come down now?" Papa asked. He chewed with his mouth open and smacked his lips. A tiny piece of potato flew out when he talked. At home, if I talked with my mouth full, Mom would yell at me. I felt embarrassed for him.

Before I could answer his first question, Papa said, "Now, what's this about you leaving nursing school?"

Before I'd bought my plane ticket, I told Nana that I was feeling the pressure of school and wasn't sure I wanted to go back after summer break. I knew that if Gavin and I were going to marry, Nana and everyone else would know the truth. On the other hand, if I had to make other plans, then who knew what would happen. I couldn't think past the fact that I was in trouble.

"Oh, I don't know," I said, avoiding his eyes. "The term's over, you know. I'm not sure it's what I want to do."

"Don't you like it? What don't you like about it?" Nana asked. I chewed my food and gestured: *one moment.*

Papa reached for his iced tea and said, "Listen, Cathy, anything worthwhile is difficult. Sometimes we have to build up determination. Life is tough." He swirled the sweating glass. "And to get anywhere, *you* have to be tough. You know that, right?"

"Yeah, I guess," I said but still could not meet his eyes.

"Look, I know you're here to think about things." He wiped his mouth with a napkin. "Spend some time thinking about this. Ask yourself, *if I can't get through nurse training, what am I going to do?* You think something else will be easier? If it is, it won't be worth much. Buckle down and give it all you've got. Lots of people go through worse than this."

Oh, God, if he only knew.

Nana said, "That's right, Cathy. Learning is never easy. In nursing, you have to not only learn the books, but *do* things to people. That must be hard. I say, think about it and do the best thing. Give it time. If it's not right, it's not right. Maybe do something else and go back to it when you're a little older."

That's exactly what I'll do, I thought.

On June sixth, after a few days in Florida, I had the house to myself while Nana and Papa went out. A thick layer of clouds covered the sun and made the air unusually wet, like a bathroom after a hot shower. I flipped on the television and stretched out on the couch.

"*We interrupt our regularly scheduled program for this special news bulletin. Robert Kennedy has been shot. I repeat, Robert F Kennedy gunned down right after midnight Eastern Standard Time, by a single shooter as he was leaving a campaign rally . . .*" I sat up. An agitated broadcaster described the shooting in detail. Sirhan Sirhan, the gunman in shackles. Robert Kennedy, bloodied and motionless on the floor of the Ambassador Hotel's kitchen. Interviews, commentaries. Distraught Americans on the streets and city sidewalks crying, unable to speak to the reporters. This was unbelievable. *Not another Kennedy.*

The news made me feel queasy. Warm tea—maybe that would settle my stomach. I boiled water and found the tea bags. As I stirred the light amber liquid, I thought about Gavin. He was probably working at the bar, stacking crates, maybe going to softball practice later in the evening. I wondered if he was thinking about me—and what it would be like to be *married.* The word made me cringe. I wasn't ready. Marriage sounded much too grown up.

Back in the living room, I watched the newscaster lamenting and repeating the same details. Bobby Kennedy on the floor, a frantic scene. That potential. Those children suddenly fatherless. I knew I should feel sad, but the scene before me had absolutely no effect on me, as if emotions were stored in a finite container; my bin was empty.

My plane landed in Pittsburgh on a humid ninety-degree day—similar to Fort Lauderdale, but without clear sky. That afternoon, the temperature dropped, and blue-gray clouds gathered over the hills. Fleeing to Florida felt like a prison escape. Now I'd been caught, and soon the sentence would be handed down.

I wanted to call Gavin but waited until Mom and Dad left for the store. When the house was empty, I carried the phone outside and sat on the concrete stoop for privacy, a trick I'd learned from Corrine.

My eight-year-old sister, Jeannie, played out on the dead-end street with neighbor girls. The girls watched for traffic, each holding their own rock near the hopscotch. Jeannie threw down a stone. Her long braids jumped as she hopped from block to block and made it to the end. I wanted to shout, "Good job, Jeannie," to let her know she was noticed and appreciated. I didn't though. My tension squeezed at my throat.

Jeannie turned around and began hopping back onto each section. She deftly stood on one foot and picked up her stone, victorious at the end. *Oh, to be a girl again, playing hopscotch, worrying only about stepping on a line.*

I dialed Gavin's number.

"How was Florida?" Gavin asked.

"Fine. I got sick a few times, and it was hot, a little boring. But good to be away, I guess. Did you tell your mom and dad?" I asked, my voice low.

"Uh, yeah, I did," Gavin said.

"And?" I pressed the phone tight against one ear and plugged the other ear with my finger.

"And they're pissed. They want to talk things over with you," he said, sounding as if he had his hand cupped around the receiver.

"What kind of things?" I asked.

"I don't know. They said, we need to sit down together and talk about this."

My ear had begun to sweat under the phone, and I switched it to the other side.

Jeannie shrieked, "Not fair." Laughter, and the game went on.

I inhaled and let the air out. Gavin's parents, one more worry.

"Great," I said with sarcasm. "We can work that out tomorrow after . . ."

I peered into the house through the storm door window. Still no one around. I turned away. In a low voice, my hand around the mouthpiece, I said, "I'm going to tell Mom we want to meet with her and Dad after church tomorrow. We're usually back by noon or twelve-fifteen. One o'clock should work." I thought of the movies where a criminal waited under a guillotine. *Let's get it over with.*

I pictured Gavin's cheeks inflating, then blowing out with his eyes closed, as I'd seen him do so many times.

"I don't know if that's a good idea, Cath. I think it would be better for you to tell them without me there. Then the four of us can meet later or one day this coming week."

"Ohhh no. Just because you decided to tell your mom and dad on your own, doesn't mean I have to."

The kids moved to the curb; a muscle car rumbled over their game. The radio blasted Elvis singing, "I'll Take Love."

"Okay, okay," Gavin said, his tone conciliatory. "We'll do it your way. I guess I'll see you at one o'clock tomorrow. Listen, I got to get going here. My dad's on my back to get rid of the trash."

We said goodbye, and I hung up.

Such a brief conversation after a week away. We could have been two children who smashed a window, guilt ridden and afraid, about to be discovered.

In the distance, thunder clapped as big raindrops splatted on the pavement. The kids screamed, "It's raining. Hey, it's raining." The chalked hopscotch washed away. Jeannie and the girls took off toward a neighbor's house, leaving the game stones in the middle of the road.

⮞   ⮜

After Mass, I told Mom, "I need to tell you something. Gavin and I want to meet with you and Dad this afternoon."

She frowned and said nothing for a moment. "Why? What's this about?"

"Mom, don't ask me a bunch of questions. Just tell Dad, okay?"

She turned away without saying another word.

At one o'clock, a rap rattled the aluminum screen door. My anxiety pushed me down the steps to Gavin, waiting outside. "Come in," I yelled before I reached the door. He stood straight; his chest was broad, abdomen flat. He was clean shaven, wearing a short-sleeved pullover shirt and trousers. His forearms were tan, shaved too, because of the sport tape he used on his wrists for softball. Gavin touched my upper arm, two seconds of contact between us. It used to be, he couldn't keep his hands off me. Now I made him uncomfortable.

"Hey. How are you doing?" he said in a low voice.

"C'mon in, let's sit in the living room."

⮞   ⮜

My childhood years were a mix of fun and terror, though I never knew which way things would go or why. Dad was the quietest man on Earth, most of the time. Every night at five-thirty, he came home from his accountant job at a rubber band company. Passing silently through the kitchen and dining room, he headed to the closet to hang up his overcoat. Gripping the doorknob so as to hold the catch until the door was closed, he soundlessly eased the latch in place, as if trying not to detonate a bomb.

The slightest bit of commotion lit Dad's fuse. But even without provocation, when I least expected it, when I felt safe and relaxed, the bomb exploded. As kids, before dinner, Corrine and I would rest on the living room floor watching the *Lone Ranger*. Then we'd hear a sudden thundering, a terrifying and familiar sound, coming from another room as the floor vibrated. Before I could react, Dad's foot hit hard in my side; the startle was as fierce as the pain. His entire body shook, and his face reddened with a severe expression.

He shouted, "Get up. Wash your hands, help your mother. What in the world is wrong with you? Get going, move!" When I was too slow, he pushed me down or into the wall. Cries received warnings of, "Shut up. I'll really give you something to cry about." Evan was three years older than me and had the knack of disappearing. Roger was a baby, and Jeannie wasn't born yet. Corrine and I were Dad's targets.

My sister and I found solace together during those times, comparing bruises and sniggering behind the closed bedroom door. Dad had the hearing of a bat. After lights out, our whispers brought him flying up to our room, bursting through the door. The room went from black to blinding light. He raged, "Shut up and go to sleep. What's the matter with you? Keep your mouth shut and go to sleep." He'd rough us up sometimes, yank one of us by the arm. Dad's rage terrified me, and after his angry visits that shut us up, we did not make another peep. But when things were calm on another night, we'd laugh and talk in the dark, make fun of him. Our secret name for Dad was Pickle Ears.

Mom would tell us that his bad temper was because of his mean boss at the rubber band company. "Really, I mean shut up about it," she said. Mom's temper was only mildly better than

Dad's. Her way was screaming derisions and spankings. But at least with her, I mostly knew when it was coming.

My parents were always present, food on the table, a roof over our heads, holiday celebrations, Sunday car rides for entertainment. They did not drink, swear, gamble, or carouse. But the uncertainty, the feeling of walking across a minefield anticipating the next explosion, constantly made me sick to my stomach.

ↄ   ⋈

That Sunday, I didn't know what to expect. I laid my hand on the wood banister at the bottom of the steps. The railing's brace was attached to an area of patched plaster from the time Dad knocked the banister clear off in one of his out-of-the-blue eruptions.

"Mom," I called up the steep narrow stairway. "He's here."

On cue, Mom walked down the steps with her wedding ring skidding along the handrail. Her orange and brown knit top patterned with sharp-angled shapes covered her hips over Bermuda shorts that showed off her pale thick limbs. Those legs she bragged about as a young woman, now covered by long dark hairs that grew sparsely over a roadmap of purple spider veins.

With a dull voice, Mom said hello to Gavin and called toward the kitchen, "Ed, he's here. We may as well sit down."

Mom led the way into our main room that was the length of the house from front to back and narrow as a box car, with about eight feet between the sofa and chairs across from them. Two armless accent chairs filled one long wall, a lamp table between them. Gavin and I moved slow and silent, as if meeting with a funeral director. We sat next to each other on the couch but left space between, aware of what touching meant. As if that might somehow make a difference.

From the accent chair, Mom gathered up the Sunday newspaper: the funnies, Women's Wear, The Parade, and the ads. She dropped the stack carelessly onto the footstool. Half of the pile slid to the floor and scattered. She ignored the papers and sat on the chair opposite Gavin and me.

It was the room where I'd learned to walk. The room where I'd hid behind the drapes and delighted in the sound of each succulent leaf as I broke it. Snap. Snap. At three-years-old, it was a satisfying feeling. The room where I'd enjoyed eighteen years of Christmas mornings, Easter Sundays, Halloween nights dumping out candy on the floor, where my First Holy Communion party was held and from where I looked out to see bright red pin oaks or the white new-fallen snow. The room where Corrine and I spent Saturday afternoons dancing the Twist and the mashed potato. Now, to that list I could add the room where I told my parents, "I'm pregnant."

"This weather's something, isn't it? Hot as Florida," I said, too worried to keep quiet, afraid I might lose my lunch.

Gavin sat on the edge of the cushion and picked at a callus on his palm.

Dad appeared in the doorway, blank faced, like he was barely alive.

"Oh, here's Dad," Mom said.

He and Mom exchanged a look. In social situations, Dad took cues from Mom. She nodded toward his reading chair with a barely detectable head flicker. He sat nearest the hallway so that we formed a triangle with him at the pinnacle.

Dad's arms rested on the chair. He reminded me of the Abe Lincoln statue. Large metal-framed glasses covered the upper part of his face. His thin brown hair combed over the balding head, mouth set flat.

Since the day at Dr. Franklin's office, I'd thought of little else, and now here it was. Time to speak, but my mouth wouldn't work, my shoulders felt like wood, and rubbing my clammy hands across the cotton shorts only made me more nervous.

Mom leaned back slightly and crossed her arms. "So, you've got us here. Now, what's this about? What's going on?"

A fly buzzed on the window behind the patterned drapes. Dogs nearby fought, growled, and then barked.

There are moments in everyone's lives that never truly end, and this was one of mine, a moment that rang on and on.

I said, "Well." My throat thickened. I breathed in deeply and let it go. "I'm pregnant."

Instantly my father and Gavin stood in the middle of the room, face to face. Dad grabbed Gavin by the shirt, hauled him close, spitting and hissing, his face crimson and his voice shaking.

"Why, I oughta flatten you," Dad snarled.

Gavin's muscular body on high alert, feet spread, arms straight, hands fisted about a foot away from Dad.

Mom got up, too, and grabbed Dad's shoulders.

"Now, Ed, calm down. You'll give yourself a heart attack. Stop it, both of you!"

She shoved Gavin and Dad apart, but they kept staring at each other. "Everyone, calm down. Fighting won't solve anything. Be reasonable. Sit down," Mom shouted.

My entire body felt restrained by an emotional straitjacket as the drama played out. I stared in silent disbelief. *Dad going after Gavin as if this were his fault.* I expected Dad to grab me, not Gavin.

Dad and Gavin sat, then Mom took her place on the chair beside the fallen newspapers and fiddled with the garnet ring on her right hand.

"Cathy, are you sure?"

"I went to see Dr. Franklin and he confirmed it."

Mom gasped. Her eyes widened, she held her hands up to her head, her mouth dropped open. "You went to *my* doctor?"

"Mom, I didn't know *who* to go to. I knew his name and that you liked him," I said, matching her shrill tone and throwing my hands up.

"Well, that was awfully thoughtful of you," she snapped.

"Sorry, Mom. I didn't know *what* to do."

She tsked and shook her head, then leaned to the disarray on the floor, grabbed the pile and laid the papers on the footstool. She slammed the big Webster's on top as if to say, *there, that should take care of it.* Jeannie opened the front door and burst into the room, yelling about the rain. Mom barked at her to go up to her room and close the door. "And don't ask any questions." She waited till the bedroom door clicked. "So. What's next? What are you going to do? Get married, I suppose?" Her words were clipped and biting.

No one spoke. Then, Gavin, "I have to finish college."

"You want to finish college?" Mom asked, harsh and quick. "Then transfer to Pitt. You can finish there."

"I'm not sure, Mrs. Vogeley. I really want to graduate from Notre Dame." He leaned on his forearms, looking at the carpet between Mom and us, then out the back window.

"Sacrifices have to be made. Go to Carnegie Mellon then. Or Duquesne. They're places to be proud of, too."

"I want it to be Notre Dame," he said, sitting up, hands on his knees, arms straight.

Mom's words came faster. I knew that sign. On the brink of "I have *had* it." She said, "Go on home and think about it. In one week, come back here with your decision."

Dad hadn't spoken since he confronted Gavin. Once again, he became the Lincoln statue, except for his flaring red face.

Gavin and I stood and walked out the door without saying another word. We trudged to the car and stopped before opening the car door. Gavin said, "Tomorrow?"

I took a deep breath and let it out. "That was awful. Were your parents that upset?"

"They were pretty upset, all right."

We faced each other; my hand touched his thick upper arm. He looked away.

"Okay, tomorrow then. What time?" It was another dreaded meeting. I couldn't fathom how that one would go.

"I'll pick you up at two." The corners of his mouth were down, eyebrows up. That face made him ugly. I'd seen it before when angry at his dad.

❧   ❧

Later, I found Mom alone in her room and tapped on the door. I whispered, "Can I come in?"

She motioned me in but did not turn to me; instead, she kept on folding towels.

"Is Dad mad at me?"

"No. He's not mad. Disappointed, yes; very disappointed." The rest of the day, Mom kept to herself, unusually withdrawn. We did not talk about Gavin or the baby. I felt as though a major earthquake had broken walls and dishes, furniture and roof, and no one had even noticed; a devastation ignored.

❧   ❧

Gavin had known for weeks that I was pregnant. Why did he need another week? It's a big decision, I reasoned. *Our lives.* He'd said, "Don't worry. Everything will be all right." I knew he'd keep his word. I wanted to appear in control, grown up, to keep some dignity, be strong, not desperate. And so, I didn't press him or make demands. I knew he'd be there for me.

❧ 5 ❧

Gavin was his parents' stake in the future, their crown jewel. He was a sophomore at a prestigious university and the oldest of three boys. This pregnancy must have been an unwelcome interruption in their plans for him.

I'd been to Gavin's house only a few times and never to hang out. I doubted that I was liked any more by Gavin's parents than he was by mine. Maybe I was too quiet and inhibited for them? It hardly mattered. Nothing could be as bad as the scene with Mom and Dad where there was nearly a fistfight.

The small house was a story and a half. The front door opened directly into the squarish living room. High up in the main room, short curtains framed a small window. That day, the front door was open, and the screen door allowed plenty of sunshine in. A baseball bat and catcher's mitt leaned against the wall near the door.

The house was quiet, I wondered where his parents were. Gavin had gone out the back door looking for them. A black swivel ottoman sat in front of the living room couch, and since it was the only place free of newspapers, pillows, and books, I took a seat there. The madras plaid blouse I wore had begun to pull across the chest. I yanked the front, gave it a hard tug, and tried to keep my shoulders forward. My white shorts still had the sharp crease from being ironed the night before. Over my thigh, I pulled the crease between my index and middle fingers, then smoothed it flat and pulled it together again.

Gavin returned and said, "They're coming." He sat on the sofa, leaned forward with arms crossed in front, head down. I stayed put on the ottoman, unsure where the best spot would be. Gavin didn't invite me closer. His father, George, stepped in through the front door and walked past us to the kitchen without speaking. A beefsteak tomato of a man, clean shaven, with a circle of curly dark hair around a bald center. The blue knit shirt covered his thick middle and hung down over dark rumpled pants. The few times I'd been around George, I'd found him intimidating: sarcastic, vulgar, direct. He appeared in the living room again and faced us, his back to the door. With the light in my eyes, I couldn't make out his features. He moved around and turned to look out the open door, walked away, then went back to the door again as if he weren't part of our meeting.

Gavin's mom, Irene, came in last, lit a cigarette, shook the match, and threw it in a nearby ashtray. Her features were classic Mediterranean—long straight nose, full lips, dark shiny hair that came to her shoulders in curls. She held her head back in a lofty way, like Gavin.

She sat in the chair closest to me. "Anyone want a Coke? Cathy? Want anything?"

"No, thank you, I'm fine." I twisted to see Gavin behind me. He shook his head, no.

George walked away from the front door again, into the adjacent dining room, then back to the door.

Agitated. Nervous. We were all nervous, except maybe Irene. She was always confident, like a sergeant major.

"Okay then, let's hear it," Irene turned to me.

"Uh . . . What?"

"Gavin says you're pregnant. Are you sure?"

"Ma. I told you, a doctor confirmed it," Gavin said, exasperated.

George's back was to us now, wide and boxy, his hands resting on hips.

Irene said, "How do you know Gavin is the father?"

My head jerked. The verbal slap turned my cheeks hot. "How could you ask me that? I have never been with anyone else. Ever."

"Okay, okay, settle down. It's a fair question, I think." She took a drag and waved the smoke away from her face. The cigarette tip glowed bright red with a rough black edge formed between the white paper and its fiery tip. I thought of a war movie where a prison guard mashed his lit cigarette on the prisoner's forehead.

I wanted to say, "It was your son who talked me into it." But I was too upset to be that honest.

"And what do you think you two should do?"

"I guess get married. I mean, I don't know what else to do." I stared past her; as she inhaled, the cigarette glowed again.

"Have you thought about abortion?"

The prisoner screamed; another cigarette burned his face.

In my world, the word was never uttered aloud. Abortion was against the law. I'd heard tales of back-alley abortions where women were butchered, maimed for life, killed even.

"No," I said.

"No? How come?"

"For one thing it's illegal . . ."

Irene interrupted, "Well, but there are places . . ."

I glanced at Gavin sitting on the couch to my right, his head down, arms still propped on knees.

"I'm not going to do that," I said. I believed that life is God-given, and to take that life is murder. No matter what happened, abortion was not an option for me.

George turned away from the door and faced me, now part of the group.

"What the hell do you want to marry him for?" his words booming like a cannon. His foot now rested on the seat of a straight-backed chair. He leaned on his forearm, as if to say, *c'mon, my friend; be reasonable.* The guard had recruited reinforcements, one with a different tack.

"He has nothing. He'd be a terrible husband." George put his foot down and stood up. "I mean, look at him," he said, flinging his arm out. "He's not trained for anything. Why, the only thing that kid can do is get a hard-on."

"Dad!" Gavin hid his forehead on both hands.

Irene said, "Maybe you have the baby, and once Gavin graduates, you get married then. How about that?"

This made no sense. Women simply did not keep a child without being married. It wasn't done. Children born out of wedlock were labeled bastards and ostracized.

I shook my head. "I don't think that'll work."

Irene inhaled deeply, then pushed the cigarette hard in the ashtray. She stood and smoothed her skirt. No shouting or attacks, but clearly the meeting had ended.

Gavin said, "Well, I guess that's it then. Come on, Cathy, you ready to go?"

❧ 6 ❧

A week later, Gavin and I said hello to each other at the door. No small talk, hugs, or tears. He moved into the living room and sat down. Mom and Dad sat nearby, silent and foreboding. Last Sunday's drama hung in the air.

"Gavin? You've had a week to think everything over," Mom said, edgy with authority. "So, you'll transfer to University of Pittsburgh and get a job around here?"

Gavin sat leaned forward, elbows on his thighs, hands together, head down, eyes to the floor.

"Well?" Mom pushed. "What are you going to do?"

After years of hikes, horseback rides, roller coasters, algebra II tutoring sessions on the lawn of Carnegie Mellon University, drive-in movies, graduation parties, visits to Notre Dame, formal dances, holidays, and softball games, it came down to this one moment.

Gavin looked up, and he said, softly, ever so quietly, "I can't get married now."

In an instant, Dad blasted out of his chair. Mom shot up, shrieking, "Get out. Get out. And don't you *ever* come back here."

I felt pain, as severe as the sucker punch on the playground. I thought of that story I'd shared with Gavin the night we met. He'd said I should have been watching out for myself.

❧   ❧

As a little girl, I dreamed of being someone's princess, a woman of worth and beauty for whom the world awaits. I thought I was that princess to Gavin. A childish fantasy born from romance movies, Miss America pageantry, Mom's fascination with Hollywood. I was unaware of my power, my very selfhood, my importance as a human being, my own majesty as a young woman. Following in Corrine's footsteps—and many other young women at the time—I thought I needed a man's hand in mine to make me whole. And the thing is, no one told me otherwise.

That afternoon, after the world fell in on me, things went on as usual, except that I skulked about the house, avoiding my father. If he was coming in the front door, I went out the back. I couldn't face him, but this time it was because of shame, not fear.

The evening was on the cool side for June. Dinner dishes were finished. Mom hung up her apron. "Cathy, it's time to go for a walk." She threw a nylon jacket around her shoulders and jammed into gray walking shoes. I pulled a sweatshirt over my T-shirt. Mom called out to anyone within earshot, "We're going for a walk. Be back in a bit." The walk idea wasn't a surprise. Mom typically asked for a walk when she wanted a private discussion. Usually with Dad.

Mom walked ahead of me past the car in the driveway. I skirted the errant rose bush whose thorns threatened to hook a little flesh or a piece of fabric. Mom stopped and turned her gaze up the street and to the left, down the street.

I said, "Which way, Mom? Right or left?"

"Let's go down the street this time," she said and turned left. A minute passed. "I can't believe he walked out on you."

"I can't believe it either."

"Gavin never loved you, or he couldn't have made that choice. He's a waste. He used you, and now he's gone." Her opinion agitated out of her, in a barrage of insults. "I have to say, and don't be too hurt, but I doubt you would be—hurt I mean—but I have to tell you this, Cathy. I never liked him."

"Mmm. I kind of figured that."

"I tried, because I knew he meant something to you. But I thought he was a smart aleck, and Dad did, too."

My hand reached her forearm as I stopped. "Why? Why'd Dad say he's a smart aleck? Dad never even talked to Gavin!"

"Gavin has been around long enough, coming to pick you up, coming to the house for a picnic. Dad's seen enough to know."

The road turned upward. The steep angle slowed us down. My breaths quickened; my heart raced. A neighbor—young, slender Mrs. Marten—held a watering hose over newly planted marigolds. She caught sight of us and called out, "Hello there. Cathy, don't forget about Saturday after next. Seven o'clock. The boys are excited you're coming!"

I yelled back to her, "See you then. Don't worry, I won't forget."

Mom continued, "Back to Gavin. Think, Cathy. His father makes his money off a *bar*."

"So?" My breath shortened.

"He probably does the numbers," she tsked.

"What's *that* mean?" I asked. Mom seemed to revel in the worst parts of people.

"It means gambling. And it's illegal."

"You don't know that, Mom." I stopped walking, hands on my hips. I needed to catch my breath. She stopped, too.

"They're not good people," she said. "I'm telling you. Gavin is from a no-good family, or they would have made him get married. I'm glad we found out his true colors. Better now, instead of after you end up married to the guy."

I said, "Let's turn around," and we did an about-face.

"I know it's hard, but here we are. You're doing the right thing by not pushing to get married. Someday you'll thank me."

∾ ∽

As the curriculum year ended, the seniors graduated, and the summer break began. The timing was perfect for me to disappear. I notified St. Joseph's Nursing School of my withdrawal, but with my classmates, I behaved as if I'd return the same as everyone else. I told no one that I would not be back. I waited past the final date to clean out my room so that I'd avoid seeing anyone.

Mom informed me that my brother Evan would drive me to the dorm. "He's not going to say anything, Cathy. We may need him to take you more places than school." It was the beginning of many decisions Mom made without including me. Evan said nothing to me about my pregnancy, even though he was my only sibling that knew. He seemed to live in another dimension and my problems were never part of his.

The day I planned to move out, Evan parked outside the building and said he'd wait. Men weren't permitted in the dorm even though it was empty.

I gathered the cardboard boxes and rode the elevator up to my floor. The empty corridor echoed my footfalls as I walked past rooms whose beds had been stripped and furniture left out of place, past the phone booth and bathrooms, finally to the single closed door in the hall. I put my key in the lock and turned it for the final time. My room hadn't been touched and felt oddly set apart from the others, as if I could wave a hand and bring the rest of the dorm back to life. I froze at the sound of voices from down the hall. A pair of workmen were patching plaster in the lounge. It took a few trips to clear out my first year of nursing school. Finally, I made one last trip to wrestle Babbu to the elevator, wondering what should be done with him. I considered dumping the panda in the trash. *But he looks so happy, smiling with a red bowtie around his neck. Maybe I'll set him on the ground next to the dumpster. He'll be out in the sun and rain, alone, but it's better than in the garbage.*

On the way out, I passed a young woman in the lot who gushed over the panda bear.

"Where'd you find that adorable bear?" she asked.

"Won it at Kennywood," I said and remembered how I'd felt the same way at one time.

"My little girl would love that," she said.

"Here you go. It's your lucky day." I handed the giant stuffed animal over. "Consider it my gift."

The woman fussed about not paying for him. "I mean, we're strangers."

"Knowing your daughter will enjoy it is payment enough. Take him, he needs love," I said.

It was me who needed love although the thought never occurred to me. I deserved nothing.

7

Mom arranged a meeting with her priest cousin, Father Ed, to talk about "the problem." Edward was a familiar face only because he showed up at large family get-togethers: baptisms, weddings, and funerals. As a ten-year-old, I attended his ordination into priesthood. It sent Mom and her extended family chittering like excited birds. There was a big celebration, as if he'd become a saint, chosen by God. He was a big deal, and the most he ever said to me was, "Hello, good to see you. How tall you're getting."

Before the meeting Mom and I folded clothes from the dryer; each of us worked on opposite sides of the bed, facing one another. The blinds were down, because of the afternoon sun. Our second-floor ceilings were low, the air oppressive, the walls too close. I snapped a towel to shake off loose threads.

"What's Edward supposed to do anyway? I don't get why you dragged him in on this," I said, annoyed that she hadn't asked me before making the call.

Mom turned away and carried the empty laundry bag that she'd made out of discarded blue denim to her closet. "We really don't have much choice, do we? I mean if you're not getting married, what else is there?" Her irritation shot tiny arrows at me, toughening my skin with every hit.

"Choice?" The towels I folded were threadbare. "Mom. Do you really want to keep these?" I held one up.

Tiny droplets of perspiration beaded along her hairline. "I suppose not. That one's done for. Throw it by the door, and I'll use it for rags. Anyway, back to Edward. There's a home for unwed mothers where you can stay when you start to show."

"Then what?"

"Oh, for Pete's sake, I don't know. That's why we need to talk to him."

Collaboration, meeting of the minds, sorting out problems, and considering options were not how Mom and Dad operated. Our family was a monarchy. The queen had spoken.

❧   ❧

We met in the evening at Edward's parish office. Mom, Dad, and I sat shoehorned in wooden chairs as tight as a row of airplane seats. I ended up next to the wall, since I sat first. Edward's over-sized ornate desk nearly filled the small, paneled room, so that our chairs were squeezed between it and the wall. Behind the desk hung a depiction of Jesus in the garden of Gethsemane, kneeling in red robes, looking up to a beam of light, hands together in prayer. To my right, a tall, leaded-glass window framed by heavy drapes opened out to a garden and school playground. Photos covered the wall on our left. In the largest of them, a group of children posed on bleachers, flanked by a nun on one side and Father Ed on the other.

Mom commented on the school photo. She stood and stepped around Dad, then moved to the wall of pictures. She leaned into the photo and said, "I can't tell what this is. The kids look about the same age, so it must be a grade school photograph." Arms folded across her front, she examined each wall hanging, unable to sit down and be fully present. Dad moved his legs together to one side, as if to show her he'd heard. I switched around in my chair, feeling claustrophobic. Mom's barbecue ham dinner sat poorly in my stomach. *At least I don't look pregnant yet.*

Edward walked in smiling, his teeth too big for his mouth, obviously a relative of Mom's. At six foot four inches, he towered over everyone and made a formidable presence in a black suit with the clerical collar. Edward wasn't handsome, but he had the most beautiful black hair that he wore long on top and combed back with the hint of a wave over his forehead.

Both arms out to Mom, in his distinctive baritone voice, he said, "Mary, how are you? So good to see you." They hugged and kissed on the lips, something Mom's side of the family always did. *Gross.*

Dad stood and reached out to Edward's extended hand for a brief, solid handshake. "Hello. Nice to see you," Edward said.

Dad kept his light jacket on, as if he intended for this meeting to be short. He sat down and, as usual, waited for Mom to do the talking.

"Cathy, good to see you." Edward leaned over Mom and Dad. Too far away for a kiss, my hand on his coat sleeve, we air kissed.

Mom and Edward talked about finding the address, about traffic on the trip across town, about the photo of the children on the wall. "A gift from the CCD class," Edward said.

He pulled the desk chair back, opened the drawer, and took out a roll of Certs. He peeled one from the end, put it in his mouth, closed the drawer, and sat. Edward went from smiling cousin to priest. His expression changed to serious, and he leaned forward, hands folded together on the desk.

"Cathy, I understand you're here to talk about things," he said.

On the thigh of my black jeans, I noticed a spot of dried barbecue sauce. I scratched at it, small as it was, thinking I could pick it off, but the mark spread and lightened, more obvious now. I've made it worse, I thought, and laid my palm over it.

The picture of Jesus behind Edward held a brass plate on the frame labeled "The Agony in the Garden." Jesus, the night before his crucifixion. The words from Lent came to me, "Heavenly Father, if it is possible, let this cup pass from me."

"Well, you know Gavin, right? You've met him at dinner a few times," I said hesitantly.

Oh, my stomach. I should have asked for water.

He said, "Go on . . ."

The words stuck in my throat.

"I'm pregnant." Pregnant, like the ultimate profanity, f-u-c-k. "And not getting married."

Edward's gaze was steady on me. He remained still. I wondered what Mom had told him. Was this entire meeting choreographed ahead of time?

He said, "You've talked to Gavin, I'm sure? What does he say?"

Dad moved in his chair and cleared his throat. Suddenly the walls and furniture and books and drapes and lights and parents and priest closed in. I had been holding my breath and took a deep inhale, surprised that I needed air so badly.

"He says he needs to finish school. He can't get married right now." Hearing my words only deepened the humiliation. He can't get married *to me* right now. *To me.* Somewhere down inside, I thought that if I was prettier, thinner, and smarter Gavin's devotion would have overcome his ambition.

Through the window, from the playground, a kid shouted, "I hate you. I'm gonna tell Mom you cheated. Mom!"

Edward sat back and stared at the desk. Voices muffled through the heavy office door. The receptionist and someone else, then laughter. The kids' sounds disappeared. In the background, the crickets' high-pitched steady rhythm, accented by katydids' short file-scraping.

Edward said, "Do you want to keep the baby?"

Want to keep the baby? I couldn't imagine raising a child on my own. Mom and Dad never talked about *keeping* the baby. Mom's shame was crystal clear. Raising an illegitimate kid wasn't her style. She wasn't fond of kids anyway.

"Cathy?" Edward leaned forward. "Do you want to keep the baby?"

Mom and Dad on the chairs to my left. Were they holding their breath? Again, sounds from the playground, a basketball bounced, a momentary young voice, then silence. The night creatures stopped at once.

"I don't know how I can take care of a baby on my own."

It was so quiet that one might hear lint hit the floor. So many unuttered words hummed in the background. Mom or Dad might have spoken up right then, stood up for me and their grandchild, offered practical support. But the fact was, neither of them spoke. I knew better than to ask for their help, better than to confront them with the painful request to which I already knew the answer, as their child in their home where the noise and expense of children was intolerable. To ask for help outright would force the spotlight on them in front of Edward and embarrass them as they answered, "No, we won't help you."

"So, no. I guess not," I said.

"You want to put it up for adoption then?"

Put it up? I hated those words; they reminded me of putting an out-of-favor possession up for auction. Or putting Babbu on the ground. I didn't want to hand my baby over to strangers and worry if it would be okay, if an adoptive couple would be loving. I needed to stand up. I tried to stand, but my chair couldn't move, wedged between the wall behind and the desk in front of me. I sat back against the chair in defeat, taking deep breaths, my mouth tight, unable to answer.

Distant relatives had two adopted children. I met them only twice, little boys I think, so young that I had no contact with them. I was a preteen at the time, and to me, they were a curiosity. I wondered how the children were found and where the real parents were. But Mom had said to keep quiet about it. When pressed, because I couldn't understand what happened to the parents, Mom told me to stop asking so many questions.

Edward's eyebrows shot up. "Cathy?"

Mom said, "Yes, she wants to put the baby up for adoption."

Edward rocked back, and the spring of the massive wooden chair groaned under his large frame, elbows on the arms of the chair, hands tented and fingers tapping together.

"Cathy?" he repeated.

"I guess that's what I have to do. I mean, I don't see any other way." And there was Jesus frozen in prayer, begging to be spared his agony.

Mom said, "So, what's the next step?" She held her hand high on her chest, fingers rubbing her neck, a habit she had when she had to pay attention.

Edward looked at me. "Cathy, I want to talk to you alone for a few minutes. How about if you wait here while I show your mother and dad to the sitting room."

Mom and Dad stood and stepped sideways between the chairs and desk. Edward followed them into the hallway. He said to the receptionist, "I'll be about ten more minutes."

Mom's voice talking and laughing in the sitting room as if this was a church social.

I moved to the middle chair, a more balanced and comfortable space than next to the wall. I scratched again at the spot, but it got bigger and lighter on the black denim jeans. *It was little more than a speck before I messed with it. Now, look. Big as a dime. What does he want?*

Edward strode in again, turned, and closed the door.

"Getting warm in here," he said. He arched a shoulder and pulled off the black coat. His fragrance struck me, light and pleasant. *Did the Catholic Church workers use a special MADE IN HEAVEN laundry soap to turn nonbelievers toward God?* The nuns' habits had a similarly pleasant smell that I loved. Edward held the jacket by the shoulders and hung it over the back of his chair, then sat. One hand to his chin, index finger tapping his cheek, the other arm rested on the desk.

"Cathy. Is there anything you want to tell me?" he asked in a confidential tone, like Corrine and I would use at home behind closed doors. But he wasn't Corrine, and I was uncomfortable.

"I just want to know what to do. And I don't want anyone to know about it."

He slumped back in the chair so that it twisted and rocked slightly. Moments passed. "Cathy, did you want to get pregnant?"

My throat tightened; it was a corroded pipe with debris collecting in that dark spot—now nearly obstructed.

How dare he ask me such a thing? I'm the one who constantly worried about pregnancy. Gavin was the one who refused to use a condom.

In a controlled voice, I said, "No, in no way did I want this to happen." The question, which I took as an accusation, was appalling. I wanted to scream at him and everyone involved, "Dammit, this was not my choice. I did not want to get pregnant." What I wanted was to get out of there. But in typical closed-off and polite Vogeley style, I stayed, not moving. "I'm grateful for your help, thank you." These words had worn deep tracks in my mind over years of saying thank you.

Edward sat forward and stood. "Okay, that's it then. Let me bring your folks back."

I moved back to my seat by the wall. Mom and Dad sat, but neither spoke to me. Mom straightened her skirt. She said to Edward, "Your receptionist seems so nice. Is she married?"

Edward ignored her question. "Let's talk about Roselia, Cathy. It's a home for unwed mothers where you can stay until the baby's born. It's very private. It's a wonderful place."

"What does it cost?" I wanted to know, certain that I'd have to pay for this myself. It would be considered 'extra' as in beyond food, clothing and shelter. Extras were up to me to cover.

"Let's worry about that later," he said. "In some cases, when a girl can't afford it, there are charity funds. But for now, let's have you talk with a Sister over at Roselia and see if there is room for you and if it appeals to you. What do you think?"

"Okay, I guess. It sounds okay."

Father Edward stood, came around the desk, handed Mom a paper. "Here's the number. Call and make an appointment for a tour."

We said thank you and goodbye and walked in twilight to the car with Dad in the lead. Mom and I joked about Edward's small office, for such a big man, and the wild kids on the playground. We talked and laughed like nothing had happened. We shut out our problems and avoided reality.

❧   ❧

A week later, my parents and I made a visit to Roselia. Dad waited in the car while Mom and I went inside. I followed behind Mom and the nun, feeling as invisible as a shadow. Girls were not accepted to Roselia until the start of the seventh month. Privacy was a high priority. Twenty-two hundred dollars covered everything: housing, hospital birth, and post-partum care. We didn't think to ask about possible extras such as Cesarean section.

Mom decided Gavin should pay for Roselia. He shouldn't get off scot-free, she said. Twenty-two hundred was a lot; the average annual income was $7,700. I didn't have the money and knew that Gavin wouldn't have it either. Mom said it was his responsibility to come up with it, not something we needed to worry about.

8

During the summer, I learned that my former chemistry teacher, Deborah Bloomberg, had relocated. As a high school senior, I'd watched over her kids while she took night classes. Being a divorcee, she was on her own to care for and raise the children. Her apartment had been small, spare, messy, dark. I didn't like being there, but Deborah was the best teacher I ever had. Deborah could be the answer, and so I called her.

It was a relief to talk to Deborah about my pregnancy. She welcomed me to stay with her till November, offering her sympathy and support. When I asked about the kids, Deborah said they were adjusting well to their new place and finding new friends, although that was slow going since they'd moved after school ended. She said not to worry about Jay and Peggy Sue knowing about my pregnancy. "No judgements here," she'd said. "I'll explain everything to them," she'd said. For the first time, I felt no shame in the telling.

I found Mom in the kitchen, working flour and Crisco into a pie crust. "Well, that was easy," I said. "Mrs. Bloomberg said I'm welcome to stay with her in Lexington till November first."

Mom kept her head down, her index finger working a tablespoon of water into the mixture. "The less you touch a pie crust, the flakier it'll turn out. Always remember that."

I waited.

"Keep going around with your fingers until everything sticks to the mass, and then make it into a ball." Mom wiped her hands on a towel and looked up. "Oh, did you say something?"

I repeated that I could go to Lexington until November first. After that, I'd be seven months along and then Roselia would take me, if I had the money.

She stopped working the pie crust and faced me. "Is she going to charge you?"

"Charge me? For what?"

"Room and board. You don't get a free ride in this world." It seemed that Mom's mantra never stopped. I have to take care of myself.

"She said I'd be paying her in babysitting and housecleaning. She doesn't like taking care of a house; said it would be good to have some help."

Mom mashed the dough in her cupped hands like a baseball pitcher. "Well, then. Everything's falling into place, isn't it?"

Mom's attitude surprised me. I thought she would be pleased that I had come up with a plan and put it in motion on my own. But she never let on that she was in any way proud of me. "I guess you could say that."

She worked the dough on a pastry cloth and set the wooden roller to it, saying nothing more.

Mom behaved like she was navigating over a snow-covered icy road, holding tight, calculating the distance to home and angry at the car for sliding. She'd focused on cost and concealment as if bringing up my feelings might cause the car to slide out of control.

Only Gavin, our parents, Evan, and Edward knew about the baby. Even Corrine didn't know the truth. I told her I'd taken a job as a receptionist in a dentist's office in Ohio. I told her I wanted to get away from home, experience life. It was a random idea, but it related to health care and seemed more convincing than anything else I could think of. Corrine and I squabbled over it. She had been married for two years by then and knew the freedom of life outside of home. "There's life here in Pittsburgh,"

she'd said. "You don't need to go to Ohio for an experience."
I told her my mind was made up and besides, I wouldn't be leaving until September.

∼   ∽

September was a long way away, so I found a job for the summer
as a caregiver in a charming Victorian that had converted the
second floor into an old folks' care home. An ornate stairway
led up and directly into the main room where the residents took
meals and watched television.

My duties included bathing, dressing, and feeding seven
women. Some were stroke victims who had lost the ability to
speak or walk. There was one woman, Annie, whose trouble
was old age, as she was a sweet birdlike woman, delicate and
weak, but alert. There was also Alice, whose disease dimmed
and destroyed her brain, while physically she remained a pow-
erhouse of strength with meaty hands and sturdy legs.

I was in my fifth month by then and wore loose tops to hide
my thickening middle from everyone. It was August and hot.
The air felt close. No air conditioner. No fan.

The nurse said I was in charge and left the building for a fifteen-
minute break. Six of the patrons were settled in their recliners
facing the TV's afternoon soap opera, *Search for Tomorrow,* with
its opening credits and organ music. I knew the program well
from summers at home, with Mom watching it and *The Guiding
Light* right after it. She loved the dramas and never missed an
episode. Through the storylines and her reactions, I learned how
life worked: a woman's world revolves around a man; men give
money, things, and attention; women manipulate men with their
sexuality; a woman's worth is in her looks.

Now a Spic and Span commercial showed a pretty young
lady with styled hair and a full skirt, a sponge mop in hand,
and a voiceover: "Simply wipe over your kitchen floor one time,
takes off dirt and grime, even heel marks!" The program's organ

music began, and I took a seat behind the others, grateful for the break.

Alice cursed. "I'm not watching that shit." She heaved herself up and stomped toward the stairway. "I'm going out."

I kept my voice low and calm, but my heart bounded. As if approaching a hurt animal, I walked toward her casually, keeping my voice steady and light.

"Alice, they're painting the entryway. It's not a good time. You can't go out now. Wait till later, okay?"

Alice turned and growled, "I don't give a goddamn. I'm going for a walk."

I stepped between her and the stairs with my arms out. "No, no. Alice, you can't go out. Come on, sit with me and take a break."

She raised her hands and pushed me. I grabbed a hold of the banister. She began to pound my chest and stomach. I turned away to protect the baby, raised my arms, warding off the blows; I kept her fists away from my stomach.

"Get out of my way," she shouted. "I don't give a goddamn what you say. I'm going out."

The front door clattered. The nurse rushed up the steps, shrieking, "Stop, Alice! Stop this!" She grabbed Alice's arm and shook her, breaking through her rant. Then with both hands to Alice's shoulders and with authority in her voice, she led Alice toward the medicine room, where Alice's tranquilizers waited for times like this.

The nurse spoke quietly to Alice as she escorted her back to the main room and helped her settle in a restraint chair. I waited behind the residents, rubbing my arm.

The nurse said, "You okay?"

I nodded, "Yeah, I guess. Just kind of shook up."

The nurse said, "If that ever happens again, just let her go. We need to be safe here. Remember that."

"But what about Alice? What if she gets hit by a car?"

"Don't worry about that. Her family will be told about this and we'll go from there."

I checked for bruises that evening with the bedroom door closed. One deep purple mark circled by blue on my arm and another on my shoulder. *That purple one will end up big and gross.*

Nothing as bad as the time when Mom beat me up with both fists for talking back. She said I made her do it; that it was my fault. She reminded me that it was a sin for making her so mad.

I turned sideways to check my hip. When I twisted again, something happened inside my belly, like trembling. It lasted a few seconds and might have been gas. But the quivering happened again as I washed up for bed. A mysterious quickening that I learned later was my baby's first movement.

9

Mom had the TV turned up so loud that I could hear the show's intro music as I stared at the empty suitcase on my bed. My underwear, big tops that still fit, shoes, make-up, magazines, pajamas. *What else would I need for Ohio?* I wanted to sit down and watch TV but kept filling the suitcase. Applause and more music. It brought back times when Corrine and I giggled and sparred during the *Miss America Pageant.*

"Live from Atlantic City! We bring you the Miss America Pageant," blared Bert Parks on stage in his black tuxedo. He stepped back and swept an outstretched arm toward the beauties gliding along the runway, each one adorned in a full-length dress with their state sash. I sat with rapt attention, gawking at the fairytale gowns and sparkling diamond crowns.

I was ten years old, had dressed for bed, donned pink metal-framed glasses, and gathered my hair in a ponytail. Dad and Evan were holed up in their bedrooms, most likely reading. They never watched *Miss America.* Six-year-old Roger slept in the upper bunk above Evan's. Kid number five, Jeannie, was several months old at the time, asleep in her crib.

I called down from the second floor as I pulled on my robe, "I get the couch!" and raced down the steps. Before I made it to the bottom, my eleven-year-old sister Corrine shouted, "Too bad! I'm already sitting on it!" She and Mom took up the entire couch. Corrine hogged the afghan, and Mom sat sideways with her legs up on the cushions and her back against the arm of the sofa. In our family of seven, it was "first come, first served." I took a spot on the floor a few feet back from the television.

A slip of cool evening air leaked through the living room drapes, easing the heat I'd worked up in my attempt to win the couch. The faraway, high-pitched sound of nighttime bugs hummed outside, but I barely noticed. Eight and a half million TVs across America were tuned to the same station that evening. I dreamed of someday being on that stage.

Bert Parks called out the semifinalists, then as the rejects left the stage, it was time for the tricky poise questions. "If you were proficient in tennis or golf, would you beat your partner, or let him win?" I thought, of course, I'd let my partner win, unless it was a girl, and then I'd leave her in the dust. Boys need to win, that much I knew.

"What do you think is the world's greatest invention?" Hmmm. I guess I'd say the telephone. Mom would die if she couldn't talk to Aunt Nancy the entire day on the phone.

Next, the talent contest. I pushed my glasses up and twisted around toward Mom.

"What could my talent be if I ever get to try out?"

Mom huffed, "Well, Cathy, I don't know. But I doubt you'd be qualified."

"How come? Do you have to be rich to enter the contest?"

"Oh, I'm sure. Rich, and more than that. Just enjoy the show. These people aren't average, everyday girls like you."

I turned back to the TV. I didn't care. I wanted to be on that stage someday. But I had what Corrine called rabbit teeth: the central incisors were larger than the rest, and gapped. No one in the family was particularly handsome. Corrine had fat lips and space between her teeth. Mom was by no means a dreamboat with her enormous ears that managed to stick out through her hair no matter what the style, along with a convex-shaped nose, overbite, and a receding chin. I hadn't acquired a woman's shape yet, but I wanted to look like . . . no, I wanted to *be* Miss America. I didn't yet know that I'd look like my parents when I grew up.

The beauties performed their chosen talents: a violin concerto, a square dance, a cowgirl who roped a pretend cow, another who shot arrows at a bullseye. Mom never commented on the performances except to laugh now and then. In fact, she took advantage of the boring talent contest and went to the kitchen for some ice cream.

Corrine said, "I want some, too!" She sprang up and followed Mom. In a flash, I scrambled to the couch in her place.

The bathing suit segment came near the end.

I shouted toward the kitchen, "Bathing suits, Mom! Bathing suits are on."

She yelled, "Okay," from down the hall.

Finalists strutted on stage and lined up, each with a hand on one hip, wearing high heels and modest one-piece suits. One at a time, they stepped forward, turned side to side, and strutted down the runway, while Bert Parks announced her height and weight, bust, waist, and hip measurements.

Mom and Corrine hustled in, each with a little bowl of vanilla ice cream. Corrine stood between me and the TV.

"My seat!"

"Huh, uh. You left. It's mine now! Get out of the way!"

"That's right, Corrine. You didn't call it when you left. So, now it's Cathy's turn on the couch."

Corrine gave up and sat on the floor. I snuggled into Mom's softness, slipped my arm under hers. I reached for her hand, pale and soft with the ever-present oval garnet ring on her right hand. She leaned forward, looking closer at the contestant on screen.

"Oh! A perfect ten!"

"What's that mean?"

"A perfect ten means your proportions are exactly right."

"Right for what?"

"For beauty. If you want to find a husband someday, you have to be attractive."

Another set of measurements were given.

"Uh, oh, not a perfect ten," I said.

But Mom said, "Wrong-O. That's even better. She has a very small waist. Lucky her."

The next woman paraded down the runway. Mom said, "Her rear end is flat! She will never win."

The finalists were full lipped with bright white, even-toothed smiles, and well-proportioned noses. Not one contestant wore eyeglasses. I decided I could try out without my glasses. I knew I could be a contestant if I worked hard enough. Sit-ups, jumping jacks, and leg lifts like on the Jack LaLanne show. The right haircut, the right clothes and shoes. These would make me beautiful, like them. I'd be so proud and marry a wonderful man. I'd be like a princess, with kids and a beautiful house.

Before the commercial, the women lined up shoulder-to-shoulder. "Oh," I crooned, "I want to be *that* one!" I chose a girl with flowing hair and a smile that made dimples in her cheeks.

Corrine crawled to the TV, "Which one are you talking about? Not that ugly one!"

"No! I mean that one next to her."

Corrine said, "Okay, then I want to be Miss Ohio. She's the prettiest. And Cathy, you are that one," she pointed to the so-called ugly one. The girl had fuzzy hair (probably red, but the TV was black and white).

I said, "Okay then, you're that one. She's fat! And your name is Guenther!" I fell sideways on the cushions, giggling at my clever choice of names.

Mom held her cupped hand behind her ear. "Girls! Shut up. I can't hear what they are saying."

The winner cried and quivered as the crown was fastened on her head.

Corrine and I spent the next few days waving a right hand in the air, swiveling the forearm while keeping a big smile—showing teeth, lifting chin up and down slowly while looking over our adoring crowds, and imagining the adulation, the smell of the enormous rose bouquet, and the crown, heavy with diamonds. As in the final moments of the contest, the crown would slip sideways, and I'd imagine an assistant at my elbow resetting the pins to make it straight on my bouffant hairdo.

Every September, we watched the pageant, glued to the TV, commenting on the contestants' appearance, unaware of the contest requirements: single women in good health.

⮞ *10* ⮜

The train ride from Pittsburgh to Ohio was my first time in a railroad coach. The car gave off scents of cigarette smoke, old lady perfume, and something else—that of old library books. My seat with its rough upholstery had gone soft from decades of passengers. The wheels clacking and the car's rocking motion lulled me into a limbo between life at home and the one ahead. Out the window, rows of corn took on animation, like shuffling playing cards.

The engine's whistle sounded, and moments later, we passed cars queued up behind hinged gates. Speeding by the stopped traffic felt like a privilege after the many times I waited for a train in the back seat while Dad huffed and gee-whizzed about the delay. Sometimes we'd waited as long as twenty minutes. *Imagine, life interrupted for only twenty minutes.*

⮞   ⮜

Houses, neighborhoods, and stores came into view as the train slowed and rolled to a stop. The conductor called, "Lexington, Lexington." Those around me rushed to gather their belongings. When I stayed motionless in my seat, a middle-aged man stopped and asked if I wanted to go ahead of him. I shook my head, no. I wanted to stay where I was, in that seat on a smooth ride to the end of the earth. To a place where women like me were welcome instead of hidden or pitied. The car emptied and the conductor announced, "End of the line. Everybody off." He stopped at my seat, "Something wrong, lady?"

Lady. First time anyone called me that. "No, nothing wrong. Sorry, I'm just tired I guess." I lifted the suitcase and shuffled to the exit.

Deborah waited on the platform, while Jacob and Peggy Sue sat on plank benches against the wall. She and I said our hellos with a stiff hug, but when I turned to Peggy Sue and Jacob, they looked down and away, answering "good" or "fine" when I asked how they were doing. We climbed in the faded red Chevy for the short drive home.

Deborah was a small woman with straw-like hair worn in a page-boy, held in place with spray, and plastered to the back of her head. She craned her neck and sat forward, looking over the steering wheel. "We've been here a couple of months, still finding our way around town. Like I said on the phone, the house isn't big, but we'll make a place for you. We still have the cats, by the way. Puffy and Tiger. Remember them?" Her words came out gravely, with a rasping sound, and ended with a squeak. She took one last drag on her cigarette and flicked the butt out the window.

"I don't remember them too much. They stayed in Peggy Sue's room when I used to babysit."

On my lap was the pile of manila folders that had been stacked on the passenger's seat. Mints and gum wrappers filled the dashboard's nooks and crevices. Not like Dad's spotless car that he cleaned every evening—his favorite pastime.

"I can't thank you enough for allowing me to stay with you. You're a godsend."

"The house is a duplex, not much bigger than the apartment we had back in Pittsburgh."

"I'm sure it's wonderful. Thank you again. I don't know what I would have done without you."

"Don't mention it. I'm glad to do it. In fact, you'll be a great help here. I'm gone sometimes in the evening. The kids will be happy for the company." Eyes to the rearview mirror, she said, "Won't you?"

Thirteen-year-old Jacob, who went by Jay, and eleven-year-old Peggy Sue occupied the back seat like silent phantoms, looking bored. Deborah ahem-ed, clearing her voice, asking them again, louder this time.

"I guess so," Jacob said, looking out the window, definitely not wild over having a visitor. Peggy Sue said nothing. I knew them to be shy, rarely laughing, unwilling to carry on a conversation.

Deborah turned onto their street. Scrubby treeless yards, no flowers or shrubs, no cars or walkers, no pets or children—even though it was a wide, level street. The neighborhood of single-story duplex homes built close together reminded me of a post-apocalyptic fifties movie where nothing remained except bare houses. Depressing, but it was only till November. *I'm free for the time being.* Well, not exactly. But I could skip the lies here and stop worrying about showing.

The car rolled to the curb. Jay pulled the door handle. "Jacob! Can't you wait till I'm parked? Close that door."

"Mother, I'm not getting out yet. I'm getting ready to get out."

Peggy Sue said, "Yeah, sure Jay; I saw your door open. Don't be a liar."

"Yeah? Look who's talking. Don't you be a snitch, you little weasel!"

Peggy Sue resembled Jacob, but girl-sized with a mouth as small as a bottle cap and lips like two lines. She drew the corner of her lip up, her eyes nearly disappeared into her forehead, and she shook her head at Jay.

Mom would have yelled at us if, at that age, we misbehaved.

Jay hopped out, acting like the car was on fire. Deborah parked the car and turned off the key, paying no attention to Jay and Peggy Sue's antics. The car doors slammed, I trailed behind, holding my pillow in one hand and suitcase in the other. Deborah walked with quick, short steps, quiet for a moment. "Having you here is a real help, you know. The kids are alone so much."

She dragged the aluminum front door over the concrete step, making a loud grating sound. The entrance opened directly into the living room, which was a dark cluttered space with a low stippled ceiling. I stepped inside, and the fetid pungent smell of cat litter hit me at once. Peggy Sue schlumped behind Jay to their respective rooms, and one by one each door slammed.

The room was spare with a green vinyl cushioned couch facing a portable television and its whacky rabbit ears. A half wall divided the living room from the kitchen, where used plates were haphazardly scattered on the counter.

Deborah tossed her coat on a chair and headed straight for the kitchen. "Cathy, make yourself at home." She opened a kitchen cabinet and reached for a bottle of aspirin. The faucet ran. "I'm making a drink. Do you want one?"

"Yes, I'd love something. Water?" My stomach churned. I let my mouth open a tad and used my tongue to block air from my nasal passage like in nursing school.

"Sure, what do you want in it, besides ice?"

"Just water, thanks. Hang on a sec," I said. "I think I left my scarf in the car." I spun around, rushing outside, trying not to hurl. The door shut, and on the other side, I inhaled deeply. The air was cool and damp with a gray lid above, but so fresh. I leaned forward, hands to my knees. I remembered then that when I babysat at Deborah's place in high school, it smelled like cats and was horribly messy. But in my rush to find a place to hide out, I'd discounted the fact that living somewhere for six weeks was far different than staying six hours. I didn't like the smell and the clutter, but I had no regrets. It felt like she'd extended a lifeline to me, and I accepted it gratefully.

A young woman drove past the house, watching me. She might wonder what I was doing. I reached to the ground, pretending to pick something up, then turned and went back inside before anyone else caught me.

"Did you find it?" Deborah chirped and rocked the ice in her glass.

"No, I must've left it at home. No big deal."

Deborah leaned against the counter strewn with sandwich plates, cups, and glasses; old food; and a pan full of water with SpaghettiOs stuck to the sides. Splatters of dried red sauce covered the stove top. She said nothing about the day-old food and dirty dishes around her.

"You'll be on the couch for the time being. Go ahead and put your things on the other side of it. We'll figure out better arrangements later on." She spoke with authority and moved deliberately with her spine straight, still my high school teacher. Deborah sighed and commented that Peggy Sue's jacket needed to be put away. "She shares my room," Deborah said. "Of course, Jacob has his own room."

"Okay, that's fine. You told me the house was small," I said.

Mom's and Dad's house was small and crowded, and usually cluttered. But the kitchen and bathroom were usually clean. Even so, home wasn't calling to me. I wanted to be anywhere but home. There was no animosity between Deborah and me. It was easy to accept whatever she offered, even a couch for a bed. Two months wasn't terribly long, not like it was the rest of my life; but at Deborah's, I felt out of place, bulky, and uncomfortable. More so than at home, because there I had a bedroom to hide in.

Deborah finished her drink and made another. She handed a water-filled glass to me and said, "This headache's getting bad. I think I'll go lie down. I may have a migraine coming on. Let Peggy Sue know if you need anything."

Deborah's bedroom door closed behind her. Moments later, Jacob sneaked out to the hall, looked both ways, and walked to the living room. Skinny, dark haired with a shadow of a

mustache and blemishes, self-conscious, he kept his eyes away—
like he worried that looking right at me would turn him to stone.
He flicked the TV on and adjusted the antennae. I pretended to
read the newspaper, ignoring him at first until I couldn't stand
being quiet any longer.

I said, "Oh! Hi again," and wrapped my loose sweater across
my front, hiding the obvious.

"Hi," he said, staring at the TV, turning the dial.

"What's on?" I gave him the couch and sank into the beanbag
down on the floor.

"I'm looking." The channel landed on *Lassie,* and he moved
back slightly.

"Such a pretty collie, Lassie," I said. "Did you ever have a dog?"

"Huh uh. We have cats."

"Oh, true. Sometimes people have both." He did not reply. We
watched *Lassie* together in silence.

✎　✎

After everyone had gone to sleep, I made up a bed for myself
in the living room with sheets and blankets. I'd brought my
feather pillow, an old friend, always there when I lay down at
night. It held my head through summer sunburns with a fresh
pillowcase dried on the clothesline; saved the sweet fragrance
of orange shampoo after a bath; cradled my wide-awake excite-
ment through Christmas eves and through the nights before
my birthday. Through earaches and fevers, stomach aches and
nightmares.

The streetlight came through the deformed venetian blind,
hitting my eyes, bright as a laser. I rotated so that my head rested
at the couch's opposite end. The heating duct blew in my face
from the ceiling. I put the blanket over my head. The three cushions dipped at their edges, where the heavy parts of my body
made a cave-in. My belly's roundness had grown, and the baby
lay still while I rubbed my palm gently over it, thinking how the
baby moved very little at night, the two of us asleep, together.

Deborah was gone during the day and busy in the evenings. But her moods were steady, and she kept us in food and toiletries, checked on the kids and their schoolwork. She generously ferried me to the Catholic church for Sunday Mass and came back to pick me up. I kept the house neat and cleaned the kitchen and bathrooms. After a few times doing kitty litter clean-up, I asked if Jay could take care of it, and Deborah agreed.

Jay and Peggy Sue kept to themselves, stayed in their rooms or watched TV. Most of the time Deborah stayed out after her workday, which meant I was the cook. Mom cooked the suppers at home, and I had almost no experience. Food was frozen dinners or macaroni and cheese, frankfurters and fried baloney. Now and then, I made steak and corn. But the steak was tough and needed a lot of ketchup to wash it down.

One day I checked the box at the end of the short driveway. Inside were a few things for Deborah, a catalog, and a white envelope with Dad's small, precise script and his preprinted return address label on the upper left. I imagined him writing my name and the Lexington address. Dad never licked a stamp, choosing instead to use a small, moistened sponge. I turned toward the house when a hawk caught my attention, gliding above in wide circles. I stopped and admired the enormous wings stretched out, unmoving yet carrying it aloft, majestic and free.

Back in the house, I laid the letter down unopened, went into the kitchen and washed an apple, then made a cup of tea. Finally, I felt ready to connect with whatever Dad wanted to say. On a short note, on plain white stationary, he wrote: *Hi Cathy, your mother and I have been thinking of you every day. I'm sorry you have to go through this. I admire your courage. I don't know that I would be as strong. Nothing lasts forever, it will be over one day. Take care of yourself, Cathy. Love, Dad.* Who was this father? Someone different than the one I knew who'd never given affection or compassion. My throat thickened, and tears blurred my eyes.

I hadn't heard from Mom.

&   &

I had been in Lexington for a month, and by then, the baby moved constantly. After my shower, I noticed stripes forming on the underside of my belly and along the sides. White translucent strips where the skin looked very thin; gross. I didn't know what they were, except they didn't itch. Deborah would know what to do.

The rain was letting up, but my mood was low, and I couldn't make myself go out for my daily walk. After I'd made the beds, put on my jeans, the zipper all the way down, loose T-shirt, I picked up the maternity dress from home that only needed to be hemmed, an easy task. The house felt cold, my fingers looked thin and purplish. The navy-blue Notre Dame sweatshirt was my warmest top and still fit, loose as it had been. I yanked it down over my bulky shape. A recent issue of *Glamour* magazine sat on the bar between the kitchen and living room. I picked it up. On the cover, a fair-haired, blue-eyed model smiled out at me, her perfect white teeth and goddess-like beauty saying to me, "You, too, can be beautiful if you try." On one side of the cover, the contents were listed:

50 IDEAS TO MAKE THE NEW FALL FASHIONS
WORK FOR YOU

HOW TO SHAPE UP YOUR HAIR FOR FALL

WHAT YOU CAN LEARN ABOUT TUMMY STRENGTH

The phenomenally thin, handsome models twisted in their bell-bottoms, showing tiny midriffs. *After the baby's born, I'm going to get back in shape, do my sit-ups, and really work hard.*

The mailbox clanked. Daily mail had become an important part of my days, only because it added structure, something that I could expect, an interaction of sorts.

I pulled a few bills and ads from the crooked mailbox. In the back was a business-sized envelope addressed to me. Gavin's handwriting, a combination of print and cursive, words written with a pen held tight enough to depress the paper receiving the ink. My heart sped up, and the world moved a centimeter off its axis, as I held the envelope in disbelief. I must have walked into the house, but I didn't know how I'd gotten there. I slid out a yellow, legal-sized page, the same as he used to send when I was in nursing school and he was away at Notre Dame. The paper crinkled in my hands. I could feel the words he'd written. The note covered a small fraction of the paper.

Dear Cathy,

I'm sending the money as you asked. I want to let you know that it's a hundred percent from me, from the work I did in the evenings loading boxes onto railroad cars. No one gave me any of it. I earned it. Sorry about all of this.

Always, Gavin

A check fluttered to the floor and landed face up. For a moment, I didn't move. Two THOUSAND TWO HUNDRED DOLLARS; pay to the order of: Cathy Vogeley.

My chest felt heavy as I lifted it and stared at the figures.

I didn't want this. Not the check, not the baby that I couldn't keep, none of it. Nothing was the way I wanted it. It was only last year that Gavin and I were teasing and laughing, like the day at Carnegie Mellon University in my senior year of high school when Gavin was home from his first year at college.

"Hey Gavin, this looks like a good spot. Let's put the blanket here."

"You want to lay on a hill? Seriously?"

"Sure, why not? You won't have to hold your book up so far to read it lying down."

The day was full of spring wonders. Bright green lawn, blooming cherry trees, clear crisp air, college kids playing frisbee, and kids like Gavin and me on blankets with books on their laps. He'd picked up a summer course, and I had final exams coming. Algebra II was clear as ink to me. He put down his textbook and rolled onto his side toward me.

"Let's see what you got there, Cath," he said.

Gavin had helped me with a term paper that earned an A for that period. He helped me study for that final exam, too, that won me an A. After studying that afternoon, we played miniature golf and then went to North Park, put the top down, and listened to music.

This all seemed so unreal. We still loved each other. Neither of us had cheated. We hadn't even broken up, not really.

I read the note over twice more, as if I might find words written in invisible ink. The letter had been in his hands right before mine. He'd held the pen, put it to the paper that I now held. The money must be kept safe; so much money, more than I'd ever seen. On the bedroom floor I found my purse, the repository for the few valuables I had. The folded check was shoved in the pocket, and as I laid the purse on the dresser, the mirror reflected an average-looking girl. A girl who ended up like she'd begun—unplanned, unwanted.

Emotions balled up and grew into sadness, confusion, and then anger. *How dare he leave me.* I gripped the letter in my hands, folding and folding, then went into the bathroom, tearing and tearing and tearing, ripping it into minuscule bits and flushing it down the toilet.

"I hate him, I hate him, I hate him," I cried. I wished I could tear up the check, too. I wanted nothing from him.

❧   ᣰ

Deborah was seeing a man named Walter who worked as a salesman covering the Ohio and Pennsylvania territory. I remember him in powder blue polyester pants and a white belt, with a cocktail in hand and little to say, even to Deborah. He kept his thinning gray hair slicked back; he had a short nose, wide mouth with narrow lips, and squinty eyes that made him look reptilian, like a lizard. Or a snake. When the time came for me to enter Roselia, Walter offered to give me a lift back to Pittsburgh, and even though I barely knew him, I was grateful for the offer. I gladly accepted.

The trip between Lexington and Roselia was about three hours on a mostly flat highway. It was the early part of November, and the roads were dry under a slate gray sky. I felt like cargo being shipped from one place to another and this was one more step toward the destination—freedom—when I could resume my life. The car was silent, which was okay with me since I was accustomed to riding with my nonconversational father. I watched the bare fields pass, apple orchards with lines of leafless trees, and barns with dairy cows stepping in mud on the way to the milk parlor.

At seven months my belly had grown beyond what I thought possible, and I'd begun to feel uncomfortable after sitting for a long time. I turned toward Walter, about to say that I needed to stop for the bathroom. My breath caught. He rested one hand on the steering wheel and with the other hand, he'd taken out his dick and masturbated to a flabby erection. *It's his car. And he's doing me a favor.* I looked away, mortified, and said nothing.

11

Roselia and my nursing dorm were similar, except Roselia had a chapel and religious icons, a crucifix above each door, and side altars where votive candles burned—evidence of prayer offerings. Daily Mass was an option, not a requirement, but I went often. I prayed for forgiveness. I asked God to bless my child with parents who would show affection. I'd begun to think of the baby as a girl by then. I prayed that her parents would let her know how precious she was, teach her how to be whole.

∂⟩   ⟨∂

By Christmas evening, I'd spent almost two months with pregnant girls waiting out their time. I'd spend the evening in the chapel where I'd prayed for forgiveness, for strength, and for my baby's future. After my prayers I walked into the empty, dimly lit dining room. Silver garland draped around the door and window frames. Paperclips stuffed into the ceiling panels suspended red ornaments and paper snowflakes. On a shelf above the big metal sink, a circle of holly surrounded a tiny plastic baby Jesus resting in a manger. In one corner stood a Christmas tree with yarn dolls, cardboard ginger men, and sequin-studded Styrofoam balls. Ornaments gifted to us at the foundling home by children doing a good deed at Christmas.

Almost everyone left for the day, except a few girls whose families lived out of town. I didn't know or care where the girls who stayed were or what they had for dinner. My dinner was a slab of baloney on white bread and hard-boiled egg on a paper plate next to a dish of plain red Jell-O. I pulled out a chair and sat. The cold metal felt puny under me with the added baby weight. On the green table was a small square frame of plain paper napkins beside a stainless rack with two loops for salt and pepper. The pepper shaker had been recently filled, but the rack's other side was empty. *No salt allowed here, it makes you swell up, and that can push up your blood pressure.* Hypertension caused serious pregnancy complications, they said.

I bit into the sandwich and moved the bland processed food over my tongue. I thought of Christmases past when the house filled with the rich baking fragrance of peanut butter and Toll-house cookies during the week leading up to the twenty-fifth. Mom would lift each cookie with a spatula and flick it onto a flattened brown paper bag, chocolate chips in moist puddles on sugar patties. The peanut butters lined up, overlapping rows, each one with the crisscross pattern made by pressing a fork into the dough.

"Go ahead, you can have one," Mom said to me.

A rare treat, this warm cookie. (And before dinner!) I considered each one.

"Oh, come on now. They're all the same. Take one," Mom said, the cookie sheet clattering against the stainless-steel sink.

Finally, I picked one and lifted the biggest, most perfect, honey-colored cookie.

I recalled another Christmas memory as I sat in the dining room, alone. I must have been six or seven the year I poked a hole through the gift wrap. A disorganized pile of Christmas presents balanced on the buffet. While Mom was in the basement doing laundry, I checked each tag, taking care to avoid an avalanche. My breath sucked in. A small squarish package with my name: *Merry Christmas to Cathy from Mommy and Daddy.* I pulled on the box, careful not to tear the red and white paper.

I pushed and prodded the gift-wrapped box. Maybe this isn't the Mickey Mouse watch, I thought. On Christmas eve, Santa brought unwrapped toys. And he hadn't been here yet.

I touched the box whenever I could. A few days passed. I thought of nothing else. That package held sway over me as if magic were hidden inside. Finally, I poked a hole in the paper. Mickey's ears! Thrilled, I jumped around inside my head. I pushed the paper together, tried to repair the damage, but the tear was obvious. I'd be in big trouble. Carefully, I pushed the box back into the cave of presents. Inside, I held tight, afraid. I worried for days until I didn't want the watch anymore and wished it to disappear.

On Christmas eve, my siblings and I each picked a spot on the floor, ready to stack our gifts for the next morning. Mom divvied up the presents, called each name, and one by one, Evan, Corrine, and I went to Mom, took the item, and placed it on top of the last one. Finally, Mom picked up the box with torn paper. My breath stuck. *Would she say:"Go to your room. What did I tell you? No touching the presents. Now get up there and not another word."* A spanking? I fought back tears.

Here it comes.

Mom said, "Someone's been into this. Cathy?"

Already guilty, I added lying to the crime.

"I, I, I didn't do it."

Mom held it out, and with a hint of smile, passed it to me. Not bothering to stand, I wobbled on my knees back to my place and stuck it under the other things.

Sitting in Roselia's kitchen that night, I thought of how much I wanted the watch and how I ruined it for myself. And how guilt cut into me, even as a little girl.

The baby turned and kicked. I put my hand over my side and felt a bulge. *Maybe it's a foot? Or an elbow?* A bite of sandwich, a drink of milk. I swallowed the last bit of cratered egg and sucked down some cherry Jell-O.

Twenty minutes away, on the other side of town, my family gathered at the dinner table. Christmas tree decorations twinkled in the living room. Torn gift wrap piled up by the door. Shirts, ties, sweaters folded inside tissue paper in covered boxes. A roasted turkey with homemade stuffing, mashed potatoes, cranberry sauce (clear gel, from a can. Dad wouldn't eat it with anything in it) and rolls. Forks and knives clanking, Corrine talking about who knows what. If I were there, I'd be euphoric over Mom's pecan pie. My parents smiling and everyone commenting on how good the dinner tasted.

The judge in my head tormented: *Go on, feel sorry for yourself. You're not at that table, are you? You're alone with your pathetic Christmas dinner. You deserve it.*

"I know I do." I couldn't hurt enough to satisfy my need for retribution.

The remainder of the evening, I went back to the chapel, knelt, and prayed. Not praising or thanking. Not for the poor starving people of the world. I prayed for forgiveness.

⤙　⤙

The calendar turned to 1969, the year the first draft lottery in my lifetime was instituted. Men whose birthdays fell between 1944 and 1950 were assigned a random number according to their date of birth. Gavin was born in 1948, but college undergrads were exempt. Not that I cared.

Every morning since my due date passed the week before, I woke up thinking, *today's the day*. Time dragged. The doctors told me, "The baby's in position; you're starting to dilate. You'll go soon; don't worry."

During my stay at Roselia, I met periodically with Mrs. Chau, a social worker assigned to my case. Probably in her thirties, bespectacled, pudgy with a faraway look about her. Or maybe it was me who had the faraway feeling, because she spoke only broken English. We struggled to communicate. To me, the meetings were a waste of time, another frustration, a sad roll of the dice that my counselor was a non-English-speaking therapist.

She asked about adoption. I decided, on my own, that my baby should be parented by a couple with a similar heritage to her birth mother and father. I spelled out the difference between Gavin's Greek-Italian background and my German-Irish lineage. I wanted my child to match her adoptive parents so that she would fit well and be spared the inevitable questions about her parents being "real." If Gavin and I couldn't bring up our child, I wanted her people to be as similar to us as possible; to be college educated and Catholic. My child should be given the best chance at a substitute family. Even at my young age, I knew temperament, appearance, and intelligence are in a child's DNA. Mrs. Chau and I reviewed these requirements many times. I hoped she understood, but I couldn't be sure.

It was during the last weeks that I walked outside in the backyard on a day when the sky was the solid gray of winter, and rain had melted most of the snow. On my walk, I felt desolate and despondent. Everything about me felt wrong. I deserved to be shut away. There was no changing what I'd done.

My baby was a real person to me by then, moving most of the time. That day outside, in my aloneness, the name *MaryLynn* broke through, almost hauntingly. I don't know where it came from or why. I didn't choose it. Something about the name Mary-Lynn felt beloved, intimate, precious. Yes, I thought, MaryLynn. *She is MaryLynn.*

That was as close as I could come to thinking of the baby as my child.

12

Roselia's lounge was a place to pass the interminable two months—a room for relaxing, learning, creating, socializing. A window stretched nearly the length of one wall. Plain draperies covered the window to keep out the cold air, obscuring the view of a courtyard through which a sidewalk led to a distant parking lot. It had easy chairs and a couch with floor lamp, console radio. Close to the doorway, there was a cream-colored, tiled countertop with sink and running water, a hot plate and stacked ceramic cups. At one end, there were a few card tables with folding chairs and a larger game table for puzzles and crafts. Knitting needles, crochet hooks, and pattern books filled storage cubbies in a shelving unit. On the top tier sat a Yahtzee cup and score pads, mostly filled with my own writing.

It was midmorning in the lounge and quiet as a library. On the radio, popular music played on low. At the bridge table were a girl, who looked middle school aged, and three ladies, in their last weeks of pregnancy; they murmured and stared at cards they held. A small woman, from whom I'd learned the game of bridge and canasta, crouched next to a near-term brunette. The woman gestured to a card and suggested the next play. From the radio, "Next we have this year's top of the chart, 'I Heard It through the Grapevine' by the one and only Marvin Gaye!"

Drippy, just-washed hair dampened the blousy top that stretched over my enormous front. I stirred Nestle's hot chocolate in a Steeler's mug.

A large-bellied, blonde girl paced, waiting for her turn at the bridge table. She had a stormy look and said too loudly, "I can't stand this dark room anymore. I have to do something. And I don't care if it gets cold as an ice box in here." She jerked the curtains apart dramatically, with the flair of a theatrical performance. Newly fallen snow covered the yard, pure and breathtaking as only untouched snow can be.

Rosie waited for me in our usual place at the puzzle table. Seventeen, she could have been a little sister of mine, doll-like with shiny chestnut hair in a long ponytail, a pixie face, and ski-jump nose.

Rosie may not have been her real name. On admission, we were each assigned an alias. Mine was "Jane." But right away, I told everyone I was Cathy. I figured we're all in the same boat here, so who cares? Somehow, changing a first name seemed irrelevant. But we did talk about due dates and ages. One poor girl was thirteen—something whispered to me and never discussed. It was too much to think about.

I headed toward the puzzle table, awkward and unbalanced. Rosie cupped her chin in one hand and leaned on the table, a thousand-piece jigsaw puzzle before her. She laughed at a comment from the bridge players.

I said, "I see you're still here."

Rosie looked up, sat back, and pulled the chair out for me. She said, "I see *you're* still here."

"How many days over now?"

"Seven," Rosie said.

Back when I first entered Roselia, isolating in my room was discouraged. I'd taken every class. Bridge, knitting, flower arranging, home décor, choir. But now, as the "senior" member, I could stay in my room if I wanted, no questions asked. I was the "last one standing"; everyone I'd met in November had delivered.

Holding the puzzle table with both hands, feet wide apart, I dropped onto the seat. Rosie leaned closer to the box and studied the puzzle's picture of a snow-covered mountain with forests along the tree line.

"Hey," she said, "did you hear about Sally?"

Sally had delivered a few days earlier in the week. I hadn't spent time with her but knew who she was. I reached for my drink and shook my head. My hair fell in my eyes. It'd been eight months since a haircut.

"No, what about her?"

Rosie looked from the mountain picture to the myriad of identically colored pieces. "She's keeping her baby."

My hand lowered the mug. "No way. Whoa." I sat up straight, pushing my hair behind my ears. "That's crazy. What happened?"

Rosie's face fell as she said, "I heard she couldn't let go of the baby afterward. Then she kept going to the nursery window."

"I thought we weren't allowed to do that." I hadn't thought of breaking this rule.

"I guess you can do whatever you want," Rosie said as a simple matter of fact.

"I don't get it." For me, the path ahead was set in stone. No equivocation. The decision was done. I was giving up my baby. I thought all of us were.

"She nursed her baby," Rosie said.

Incredulous, shocked, I said, "Nursed? I thought you got medicine for that. You know, to stop it. The milk."

"Yeah, so did I. But I heard she refused it."

"Are you sure? I mean, who'd you hear this from?"

"Tonya. She said that Sally snuck over here to see her. You know, to talk about it."

Once a girl "graduated," she stayed on the other side in postpartum. We never saw her again. A revolving door, friends disappeared, and new ones took their place.

"Is she okay?"

"Yeah, I guess so. Tonya said she's going to make sure she doesn't do what Sally did. You know, see her baby and hold her."

What is this? Some sort of spell? Get too close, and you're done for? What'll I do if that happens?

I said, "That's crazy. To go through everything here and end up with her baby. I never heard of that before."

"Me neither, but everyone's talking about it. I guess if you want to give the baby up, you can't see it. And definitely, definitely can't hold it. Did you know Paula went last night?" Rosie asked.

"She's not due for two weeks."

"I guess she came a little early."

I blew on the hot liquid. Marvin Gaye's song on the radio ended. Rustling in the hallway, clicking footsteps, then a red-haired girl carrying a suitcase and coat passed the door. Her head swiveled toward me. Pretty, pale faced, slack mouthed, eyes large. Scared shitless. I understood her frightened expression, because I felt the same way when I came in. A natural thing, this fear of the unknown. She hadn't yet settled in shoulder-to-shoulder with her peers. Same as me, same as all of us. I recall the feeling of utter powerlessness; we were prisoners without a crime.

"I don't think I'll ever have this baby," I groaned. "Shit, my date was two weeks ago."

"Jeez'o'man," Rosie said, "I'll die if I have to go another week. I mean, I was ready a month ago." She held a puzzle piece under the light, compared it to the picture, tried the fit, and put it back in the pile.

I said, "The doctor keeps telling me, there's nothing to do except sit tight and wait. Easy for them to say. I can't even sleep anymore."

The bridge table girls howled and pounded fists. Plastic red, white, and blue chips bounced on the linoleum. One of them rolled toward us. Rosie leaned down and caught the chip, and at the same time discovered a puzzle piece on the floor, snatched it up, and pushed it into the empty space—a perfect fit.

"Yes. There's the missing piece. I've been lookin' for you, you sweet little thing." She rested back on the chair and turned to the window, blank faced.

"Hey, Rosie. Did you ever think about jogging?" I asked.

"What?"

"Jogging."

"Jogging? You're kidding, right? Jogging? For what, to lose weight? Ha, ha, right. You're so funny." She tilted her head back, face screwed sideways.

"No. I'm serious. Listen, I read one time that if you jog when you're pregnant, it can start labor." I leaned closer to the window.

Rosie pawed through the jigsaw pieces. "S'that right. Well, a magazine *I* read said running's 'contraindicated,'" she said, bending two fingers in the air.

"Yeah, and guess why. Premature labor. Well, that's not something I am worried about. I'll do anything. I'm serious."

Rosie said, "I doubt that I could run two steps. I mean, I can hardly walk. You know?" She arched her back and twisted shoulders side to side.

The bridge players scooped up the cards. The girls laughed and agreed to try again the next day. One said, "I'll never learn this game." The room emptied.

"Well. They're kind of loud," I said, haughty like I owned the place.

Rosie said, "Give 'em a few weeks. They'll get quiet."

"So, what do you think? Tomorrow?"

"I hope I won't be here tomorrow," Rosie said.

"Me too. But if we are, will you do it with me? We can go out in the courtyard. Run on the sidewalk."

"Think we'll get in trouble?"

"Pfft, Rosie, who cares? If they make us come in, we'll come in."

"Okay. Maybe. If I'm still here. Tomorrow afternoon. Come find me."

Many times, my belly tightened till it became as hard as stone. "Braxton Hicks," the nurse said. "Practicing for the big day." I thought about labor starting and worried about how long and painful labor would be, but what I really wanted was to be done. Each day I woke up disappointed. My belly grew until I thought surely the skin would split open. More and more stretch marks, silver snaky-looking streaks, covered my abdomen. Stomach acid escaped into my throat leaving a bad taste. My sleep was fretful, and finally I propped myself on three pillows so that I could breathe. My low back pain was a constant distraction. The days dragged on.

The next afternoon, under a gunmetal sky, Rosie and I cringed in the bitter air without gloves and wearing coats that no longer fit. A thin layer of snow covered the grass. Pebble-sized salt crystals scattered on the snowy sidewalk, each one surrounded by a halo of bare concrete.

Already my knuckles hurt in the wind, gripping both edges of my navy wool coat.

"Are you cold?" I asked.

Rosie's red and white striped maternity top stuck out between the edges of her coat. "No, are you?" she said.

"I should be, but I'm not. I'm always too hot," I said. "But my hands. Gaaaa, that wind."

"You go first, since it's your idea."

"Right. Right. Okay, I'll go. Oh, sweet Jesus. On three. One, two . . ." My feet stayed as if glued to the ground. "I'm scared, Rosie."

"Go on, Cathy. You can do it. You want to deliver, right?"

We both laughed. *Preposterous, desperate.*

I started out, schlumping along the sidewalk, hands under my belly, a bushel basket with a floating watermelon. My back, my belly, my pelvis, every part of me moaned. At around twenty-five feet, I stopped for a moment, turned, and in slow-motion, ran back toward the beginning.

Rosie lumbered past me. I started once more and stopped, watching her make it to the far end and back.

"I can't . . . I can't do it," I said, huffing, leaning over, hands still around my belly-basket.

"You giving up?" she asked.

"I can't do it. It's too hard."

"I'm going to try a few more laps," Rosie said, laboring every breath. She slow-ran down the pavement.

I waddled toward the door, one hand buried in a coat pocket; with the other, L shaped next to my mouth, I yelled, "Don't hurt yourself."

I trudged back to the empty lounge and dropped onto the couch, facing the window. Out in the courtyard, in the dusky light of day's end, a weird silent movie played: of a ponytailed girl with a huge front plodding back and forth on the sidewalk.

The following morning, the bridge-playing brunette perched in Rosie's seat at the puzzle table. I stood next to her, wishing Rosie the best, but feeling forlorn.

The brunette smiled up at me, "I hear Rosie had a boy last night."

During daily pelvic exams, the doctor wagged his head and said he didn't know why I was taking so long. Four days later, a taxi drove me to the hospital.

☙ 13 ❧

Dark now, I startled awake and knew it was after five. I'd been in labor for twenty-four hours, in the hospital room with a night-stand, white metal bed, and crucifix over the door. In the corner sat an empty brown vinyl cushioned chair. I drifted in and out of sleep between pains. The head of my bed had been raised slightly, side rails up so that I couldn't fall out (or get out). The door remained closed, a Roselia policy. Even staff visits were limited. One nurse per shift, sometimes a second one for breaks.

A quick tap on the door. The hallway light blinded me and Mom entered my bedroom, her figure a silhouette against the brightness. I grabbed the kidney-shaped basin next to me and threw up.

It wasn't Mom but an overweight nurse who padded in, her gray hair braided and wound into flat saucers, pinned over each ear. They reminded me of cinnamon buns.

"I'm Mrs. Peterson," she said, her voice low and kind. "Here, let me take that for you," she said and took the basin away. "I'm going to check your IV and time the pains." She dug into a big patch pocket on her uniform dress and produced a pen light, clicked it, lifted my wrist, and studied my ID band. She compared it to her notes. *Roselia, #3324, age 19. Admit 1-21-69.*

"What is your ID number?" Mrs. Peterson asked.

"Uh. Uh. I think it's 2433 or 3234 or 3324."

"Close enough. You want to tell me your first name?"

"Cathy."

"Well, Cathy, how are you doing tonight?" Mrs. Peterson asked, eyes on the notes.

I groaned. "How much longer do you think I'll be?"

"You've been here since this morning. I imagine you'll go sometime tonight. You're three minutes apart. Your baby will come when it's ready and when your body is ready to let him or her go . . ."

Mrs. Peterson thrust the notes in her pocket then wrapped the BP cuff around my upper arm. The stethoscope's cold disk uncomfortable against my skin. She leaned close, fffff, fffff, fffff, the bulb forced air, inflated the cuff. Her scent, light and floral. *I know that fragrance. My Sin.* I closed my eyes and remembered.

Gavin and I posing for the camera. The Christmas semi-formal, my hair parted down the middle, teased at the crown, flipped at the shoulders. The sleeveless white brocade dress with empire waist defined by a black velvet ribbon whose ends streamed down the back. Gavin, in white tux jacket and black pants. Pulling open the white box, inside a wrist corsage of red rosebuds. The scent of roses and My Sin. I still loved the memories and tried to pretend this was a bad dream, that none of this was real.

The next day, I heard rustling outside my door, then a hesitant rap; two knocks, and the door opened. I saw the nurse first and then the man behind her. The nurse said, "I'll leave you two alone."

Edward stopped a few feet away from the side rail, grim-faced and holding a prayer book. I remember him as a blur dressed in black, looking official. His forehead wrinkled and mouth set in a line, lips tight. He tilted his head and said, "How are you? Your mother sent me. She wants me to check on you. She's wondering what's taking so long."

"I'm wondering, too. Sorry. I'm so tired. At least I'm still alive."

"I'll give you a blessing." He murmured a prayer and made the sign of the cross with his hand in the air. "I'll let your mother know that you're making progress and you're okay."

His visit was over in less than five minutes. It only intensified my misery, resentment, that he was the one to break through Roselia's stronghold. A priest, it seemed, easily passed through barriers. His visit was to check on me, not to sit with me, care for me, or keep me company. It was okay with me. The worse I was treated, the better. Anger burrowed down, adding to the rest that had made a place for itself in me. Animosity grew inward; instead of seething over Mom and Gavin, I turned against myself, and the hostility became self-hatred.

My hair clumped in thick strands, stuck to my neck. I'd grabbed the side rail earlier which had dislodged the needle in my wrist; the IV fluid flooded the tissue in my hand, and made it puff up to tennis ball size.

Lynn, a nurse from the night before, now at my side, was an apparition next to my bed. She said, "Dear God. You're still here. And look at that hand."

"I didn't hear you come in," I said, my voice feeble and small. Lynn brought freshness with her, the scent of Dove soap and newly pressed scrubs. I figured she was in her early twenties, not much older than me. I loved her as a friend, a familiar face, someone I had a history with even though we'd met only twenty-four hours ago. My first night of labor, Lynn and I had talked. She asked about school. I revealed that I'd been in nursing school and dropped out for the year. "Just think," she'd said, it could be me laying there, "and you could be taking care of me. I feel so bad for you."

Lynn put in a new IV needle and restarted the fluid. She touched my hand, hers cool and thin. She wiped her eyes and stood without moving for a minute. "Has anyone been in to see you?"

"Only my priest-cousin. He came to give me a blessing."

Another contraction, my abdomen hard as a board, my breathing rapid, my face screwed tight, my head bent forward. Lynn held my shoulders from behind until it passed.

"Isn't there anyone I can call for you?"

"No. No one."

"It's tearing me up, watching you go through this alone. I'd stay with you myself if I didn't have to work. Honestly, I can't believe you're still here." She checked my blood pressure, then lifted my gown and exposed my enormous belly. Lynn put the stethoscope to my abdomen between contractions.

"What's wrong? Is the baby okay?"

"The heartbeat goes down with contractions but comes back strong afterward. The baby's doing better than you are." She laid a cool hand on my forearm. "Let me get you a fresh gown and pillowcase."

"Do you think I'll ever deliver?"

"No one's ever pregnant forever. It can't be too much longer now. Doctor said if you don't go within twenty-four hours, they might have to do a Cesarean because of fetal distress. You're already going on forty hours."

Her words were as gentle as reassuring arms around me.

🖎 *14* 🖎

My eyes opened to blinding light and the blip, blip, blip from a cardiac monitor. Loud talking, echoes of metal basins banging against metal. An operating room light, in the shape of a flying saucer, above me. A pile of bloody green towels lay on the table next to my feet. I drifted under again.

A woman's authoritative words, "Time to go back to your room." I heard her but couldn't respond. Her voice now close to my face, yelling, "Wake up. It's time to go back to your room."

Ether left a chemical taste and smell that irritated my dry throat. My lips cracked and tongue thick, words came out slurred and garbled.

"The baby?"

"Don't worry about that now. Everything's fine."

"But where is the baby? I can't hear any crying."

"Can you move over onto this cart for me?" Still shouting, loud enough to be heard throughout the delivery suite, or hospital.

"The baby? Where?"

"The babies are always taken to another room to be checked and cleaned up. You didn't want to see her, or . . . did you?"

"A girl? I had a girl?"

"Yes, a healthy girl. Do you want to see her?"

The warnings: *Don't look at your baby, don't hold your baby, don't feed your baby. Don't change your baby. You'll never be able to give her away. Or if you do give her away, you'll never be able to move on with your life.*

"No. I guess not." Weak and groggy, I struggled onto my sore elbows, raw from days on sandpaper sheets. My head fell back onto the delivery table. The voices talked over me.

"Let's move her. She's too weak. Christ, how could they let her go so long?"

That first night, I slept with the exhaustion of a triathlon finalist run over by a truck. The next morning, a high-backed wooden wheelchair carried me into the hospital's bustling kitchen through which Roselia girls were discharged. Gleaming stainless cabinets and countertops, high ceiling with big white ceramic pendant lights, bare windows, and the smell of cooked bacon. Water ran, and metal pots clanked. The chair's oversized wheels bumped over the tiles, ushering me through a staff of women in white dresses and aprons—loud and joyful, calling out to one another.

"Hey there, Miss Jackie. You going to the church tonight for choir practice?"

"Well, I sure do hope to do just that. Depends on what—"

The chatter quieted when they saw me. The women kept about their business, one of them a slim young lady, wiping her hands on a towel. A second worker, heavyset and wearing a white hair net, stopped and turned with her hand poised to open the oven. The oddity of a patient in the kitchen, Roselia girls, discharged in secret. I wondered what those women thought. Did they feel ashamed for me?

The old wheelchair kerplunked through the Receiving Department behind the main hospital, then outside. Fresh cold air and open sky. *Ahhh*, I breathed deep, and my shoulders relaxed. Ice melted along the alleyway. Mounds of snow caught sunlight, sparkling diamond chips through vapor rising from the warmed pavement. There was relief in the air, as if I'd finished a marathon, exhausted. But more than wrung out, I felt sad. But I was done. And that felt good.

A yellow cab parked near the curb, its door open and motor running. The wheelchair stopped six feet or so away from the taxi. The nurse flipped a lever over each wheel. Painful, weak, I pushed up with the nurse's arm holding me and stood. Thank you, goodbye, goodbye. She unlocked the chair, spun it around, and hurried back to the building.

I struggled into the taxi's back seat and reached for the door handle, pulling it closed. Suddenly from the hospital came frantic shrieking, "Wait, wait, don't leave yet." The sun was in my eyes. I squinted toward the voice, twisting my hand to block out the light.

A nurse in green scrubs and no outer wrap ran toward me. "The baby. You have to take your baby."

The old nurse, her mouth turned down in an expression of determination, leaned to me, holding out a pink bundle. I raised my palms at her, as if she offered a burning log, "No, no. I can't hold her. I can't hold her."

"What in the world is the matter with you? Why can't you take your baby?"

"They said never to hold your baby. I can't."

The nurse stepped closer. "Who said that?" she asked, exasperated. Her shoulders hunched in the freezing air.

"Everyone says so. At Roselia. They said if you hold your baby you won't be able to give her up. I can't see her. And I can't hold her."

The cab driver hummed to a tune only he could hear, thrumming wide fingers on the dash. A delivery man waited for us to move, leaning against crates labeled "Chiquita Bananas."

The nurse said, "I don't know why they told you that over there. How's the baby supposed to get back to Roselia?"

"Well, I don't know." I paused, trying to think. "Can't you bring her?"

"No. Look, this is the way it is. We always do it this way. Let's get this baby out of the cold. Let's go, get a move on. I'm freezing out here."

She lowered the pink cocoon to my arms and pushed the car door shut. The cab pulled away with sunlight shining over my priceless cargo.

This wasn't supposed to happen. But here we are, together. The two of us with no one frowning or turning away. No "you must" or "you must not," no "why did you" or "why don't you." No questions. No demands. No lies.

I held my child, hours ago a moving bulge inside me. Now corporeal, irrefutable, real and for me, legitimate. A triangle of the blanket still covered her face. Words haunted me, "Don't hold your baby; don't look at your baby." From the bundle came a barely audible sound, her tongue clicking on the roof of her mouth. An utterly wild urge overcame me. Not one of curiosity, but with the instinct of a mama bear driven by nature's chemicals to protect and care for her cub.

The cab turned a corner. Out the window, we passed bare trees and dirty cars, a hunk of snow hanging from beneath a back bumper. Her warm body lay in my arms. I thought of Sally again and how she could not stay away from her baby. But this was me. And this was my child. I lifted the blanket's corner, a little at a time, as if a genie might escape and throw an invisible net over us so that we could never be apart.

My daughter.

Dark hair and flushed bubble cheeks, tiny rosebud lips. My fingers lighted on her satin skin. My sweet, beautiful baby. I soaked up every molecule of her angel face, forging her image into my memory, wishing for a picture of her so that I'd have her with me.

The cab stopped at a traffic light; the driver tuned the radio to local news. He turned toward me, his dark hairy arm across the back of the front seat.

"Hey, you care if I smoke?"

"Well, if you don't mind, I'd prefer you didn't. The baby. You know."

"Uh, sure, I get it."

The taxi had a manual shift on the column. The light changed, and the cab jerked with each gear.

My hand tightened to protect her. At the next stoplight, I caressed her little plum cheek. One side of her mouth turned up in a half smile. I pictured us walking on separate paths, never knowing each other. *Where will you go, and who will go with you? I'll always love you, little one. I'll never forget you. I wish you all the blessings that the world can offer. A happy life and good people around you to love and protect you. I have to trust in God.*

The cab traveled on, shortening the distance to Roselia, while the distance between my daughter and I grew. Those moments in the cab, less than the time it takes to brew a pot of coffee, were our entire lifetime together.

Her forehead was velvet under my fingertips. *I'm sorry it has to be this way. I hope someday you can forgive me.* She slept on, with the peacefulness of a newborn.

Cinders ticked the car's underside. The cab rolled onto Roselia's driveway, then rounded the corner of the building toward the rear entrance.

"Where are you going? I need to be dropped off here," I said.

The driver turned toward me, his arm outstretched, finger pointing to the back of the building. His head dipped, and eyebrows up, he said, "Well, miss, see them there? Way over there by the door? Supposably they stand by waiting, irregardless. They know you're coming, and they're waiting for you. See? Look there."

New mothers and babies were delivered out of sight from the rest of the world. Anonymity was everything. The cab drifted toward the door and stopped next to the curb near the small, covered entryway, where two women waited. The driver braked hard, and the car lurched. He shifted into park and turned the ignition off. The engine thunked to silence.

A flash of white took the shape of a nurse, her arms folded across her front and shoulders up to her ears, as she wore no coat or scarf.

"Man, it's getting cold," the taxi driver said. He reached to the passenger seat and brought up a pilled stocking cap, yanked it over his ears, exposing a hole where the loops of yarn had separated, their ends broken and loose. The man turned to me again and, in a fatherly way, said, "You be careful now, ya hear? It's real slippy today."

I didn't open the door. Instead, I leaned down to my sleeping baby and pressed my lips to her forehead. Two people in Pittsburgh at that very moment planned and prayed for a child. Their lips, their arms, their hands waiting empty, hoping. MaryLynn's name would be changed, and that couple would call her their little girl. She would be kissed countless times but only once by her mother. It wouldn't be my voice reading to her at night, or my hands plaiting her hair, working out the knotty nest little girls sometimes have in the morning. Someone else would teach her to ride a bike and to print her name, take her to the park and to the pool.

The taxi driver waited with his arm still on the seat back.

I told myself, *stop it*, and kept on going over what I'd been told, that *adoption was best. Her life will be better than mine.* I knew she would be special, not extra, not one of too many kids. My little girl would be truly welcome in someone's life, bringing with her not only the romance of a growing child with the accompanying joy and laughter, but the work, noise, expense, and worry, too. Things about raising a child that my own parents suffered. *My little girl will grow up knowing that she was chosen, wanted, and treasured.*

The nurse emerged and held her hands forward as if to push back the wind or some greater force that kept her from us. She moved quickly, even as her dress was flattened against her form by the gusts. I pulled the blanket's corner over my baby's face. The burly cab driver said, "Good luck, Miss. Now you get going before you freeze to death."

Good luck, a tender thing to say. The taxi driver must have delivered many young women to that back entrance. Girls like me, holding their newborn child for the one and only time. He must have wondered how their lives went from there. His kindness was a gift.

Outside, the nurse pulled the door handle; it clicked and then opened. The hinges whined. Snowflakes swirled in, cold sharp air over my arms. I tugged the blanket tighter around MaryLynn.

"I'll take the baby," she said and reached in. I saw only her hands slipping under my baby's back and cradling her head, with the expertise of one who had picked up a thousand infants. Out of my arms, up and away. The nurse held my newborn against her shoulder, fingers spread, palm flat against the tiny body, then she spun around and hurried to the door.

❧   ❧

The postpartum unit was lifeless as a morgue, with lower-than-normal ceilings, dim fluorescent lighting, covered windows, dark hallways. Solemn nurses moved in and out of the medicine room and from behind the charge desk without a sound. The nursery was located one floor down, and we were told not to visit.

Our children might as well have been stillborn. There were no signs of babies anywhere.

A grandma-looking nurse stood next to my bed holding a brown plastic tray. She said, "Go ahead and turn over now. I have a shot for you."

I must have looked startled and did not turn over.

She said, "It's for the milk. You know, the milk comes in, and we don't want that."

I wandered alone through the halls, dragging my slippered feet, taking painful steps, blinking as if the light were too bright. There were no other girls around, only a nurse here and there. I was sad, worn out, too tired to think. I found myself on the same floor as the newborns and walked by the nursery window, not stopping or looking, but watching the water fountain at the end of the hall. I made it to the fountain, turned the faucet, and leaned over, slurping. Then, wiping my wet chin, I turned back the way I came. This time, I glanced toward the bassinettes that filled the small room. I stopped right there, in front of the window, fully facing the infants. Boldly, despite consistent warnings not to, I watched them. Babies swaddled in white blankets, the tops of their little heads toward the hallway. I searched for MaryLynn, unable to see names. Then at the window's far end, I strained at different angles, trying to catch a glimpse of her.

My chest thumped as if hit by a fist when the nurse looked up at me. Her head tilted and eyebrows raised. I turned up my wrist, showing the ID band. She peered close, nodded, found the matching ID, and turned the bassinette toward the window. My daughter slept, her face peaceful. Framed by curly dark hair, she was swaddled in the baby blanket, so close with only the glass between us. I felt real pain in my chest. After a few moments, I nodded to the nurse and turned toward the elevator.

The next day, I went back to the window one more time and stood alone, watching the sleeping infants. I couldn't figure out which one was MaryLynn. This time, I didn't tap the glass. *It was a mistake to look for her. I'd been warned to stay away.*

I turned away and retraced my steps to my room, laid down, and wept.

I returned to my parents' home not as the hopeful girl I'd been months before, but as a demoralized, inexorably damaged young woman.

Home felt as crooked and painful as my body. Only five months since I'd left for Lexington, where the furniture was mismatched and worn out, and cigarette smoke and foul litter boxes made the air rank. At Roselia, the air was clean and filtered, sterile as institutions are.

Strangely, the rooms seemed smaller, the old mahogany furniture crowded together—and the house was strong with the smells of unwashed hair, musty paperback books, and dampish wool. The TV turned on to a variety of daytime shows: *Search for Tomorrow, The Guiding Light, Mike Douglas.* Evenings it was *Walter Cronkite,* Steelers' football.

Home was not a happy place, but it was familiar. Like the time when Corrine and I were left in Pittsburgh while my parents and brothers flew to Florida. Mom made arrangements for my sister and me to stay with Aunt Kathryn, my grandfather's sister. She and Uncle Jack lived in a "rich place," as Corrine and I had named it. High ceilings and spacious rooms decorated with powder blue furniture and white woodwork. Best of all was a built-in swimming pool. Corrine and I shared a double bed in our own room with a television. Aunt Kathryn let us take a box of vanilla wafers to bed and munch away while watching TV. We giggled about being royalty and pretended to ring a call-bell for the maid.

But, after three days, the rich house lost its magic. I had trouble sleeping and missed my mother. Corrine, too, wanted to go home. And so, we were sent to Mom's sister's, Aunt Nancy's, where we had stayed many times. Aunt Nancy was harsh with her four kids. I'd seen her yank my cousin by her hair and pull her out of the room. *No worse than my own mother.* Nancy's was more like home, and that's where I felt comfortable.

I knew it was up to me to take care of myself. I was determined to recover quickly and get my life back on track, to live happily ever after. Everything will be fine, I told myself. *Buck up. Let's get on with it.*

There was in me a sense of having survived a deadly medical treatment. I could barely walk or lift my weight on steps because of hip and back pain; getting into a sitting position was excruciating, and once down, my bottom complained. Labor and delivery injuries plagued my sleep. My hips seemed to have been disconnected and reattached off center. My pain intensity was unrelenting for the first several days, no matter what I did or what position I tried. I had no prescription pain medicine. Mom said I would be okay. It was a matter of time. It was two months before the bleeding stopped.

Dad was quiet as always and helped when he could. He offered his arm when I struggled to stand and told me he was glad I was home. Mom said nothing about the baby or Roselia. She wanted only to look forward and ignore the previous nine months. I spent the first week mostly in bed. Nine-year-old Jeannie and fourteen-year-old Roger were oblivious to my absence. I told them I'd gotten really sick and had to come home. They had their own worlds and had little regard for my problems.

The calendar turned to February. The days lengthened, although the heavy cloud cover masked sunlight. Kaufmann's Department Store held Valentine's Day specials on jewelry. Heart-shaped gift boxes filled drugstore shelves.

On a weekday, midmorning, with the washer humming in the basement, I shuffled into the living room, still wearing my nightclothes as I had since coming home a week ago. Frowning, concentrating on each step, painful as it was to twist, I moved till my back faced the couch and, grabbing a pillow, eased myself down. Every movement was a chore. Mom scuttled around the house, her hair clean and styled, voice light and happy, exuding uncharacteristic energy.

I knew Mom, knew what she was doing, trying to make up. For not visiting at Roselia. For not staying with me during my labor. For the shame she inflicted on me when she could have been loving; even so, she did not embrace me or reassure me of my worth, my lovability. She did not tell me she was proud of me.

As if on a mission to get me back on my feet, Mom was as perky as a cheerleader, as vigorous as a high school coach. "French toast and bacon? We can have brunch."

"Uh, sure, Mom. That sounds good. Isn't brunch a word for a party or something?"

Mom tittered. "Maybe. Well, we'll have a party then, won't we?"

"How can I help?" I asked, knowing I'd be expected to do my part.

"You take it easy. I'll call you when it's ready. Do you need anything?"

I needed more than French toast. I needed a mature, caring mother to sit down with me and talk about the last four months. Listen and listen. Hug me and let me cry.

"Well, no, I'm fine then, I guess."

Gingerly, I rested back on the pillows, then forward again. Hands under one thigh at a time, I lifted my legs and rested my feet on the ottoman. My eyes closed.

Somewhere, my baby lay against a shoulder and felt a hand pat her on the back. Maybe she heard a song and slipped into the peaceful slumber of her new life.

Dishes and frying pan clanked. Mom showed up again.

"Do you want the TV on or anything?" She sat next to me on the couch. In her discount store house dress and gray sweater, she looked smaller than I'd remembered.

"The toast is going." She fussed with the sweater, pulling a loose thread from the hem.

Out the back window, a pair of cardinals, one bright red with a black mask, the other fawn color with a hint of red over her wings. Fluttering together, resting on a dark branch, brilliant against the snow. Cardinals are courting, I thought. *Spring is coming.*

"Mom?"

Eyebrows raised, she said, "Hmmm?"

I closed my eyes and said, "I'm still so painful. It hurts so bad." The house was quiet and as cold as an empty refrigerator.

"I don't think I can stand it," I said.

"You'll get better."

"Mom, it was so awful. I thought it would never end." My eyes closed. I rubbed my forehead and said, "It was torture."

"I realize that. It was a tough time. But you're past it now. Keep your mind forward. Leave it behind. You need to focus on getting better."

Outside, a car spun on the icy hill, its engine revving. Silence. Then an intermittent high-pitched whine of tires as the driver tried again and again to find purchase.

I shifted on the pillow, and with both hands on the cushions, I pushed up, held myself off the pillow, then eased down again.

"You ought to get in the shower after we eat."

"I don't think so, Mom. I can't take a shower."

"Why *couldn't* you get in the shower? What are you worried about, the water?"

Our plumbing design wasn't the greatest. The washing machine filled and took the hot water, scalding or freezing the unfortunate bather on the second floor. I never knew what to expect. A shower was hot, cold, hot.

"Oh, no. I wasn't even thinking about that. I was thinking . . ." I looked away.

"Well?" Mom folded her sweater cuffs back.

"I'm still so sore. I don't know if I can step into the tub or not. I can't lift up my leg."

"I can stand there with you. Or hold your hand when you get in."

What Mom didn't know was that I couldn't stand seeing my body. The ugliness slammed against my heart.

"I don't want you to see me."

"Oh, for heaven's sake," she said, impatient. She stood up and walked out of the room, "I have to check the French toast."

I thought about what she said. I knew of nothing I could do to change things. It's time to move on, I decided. *Keep on going.*

Mom sat next to me again.

"It's almost done. So, what about me helping you to the shower?" Mom said with exaggerated perkiness.

"Okay." Exhaling, I said, "I'll keep a towel around me until I'm in."

"I won't look at you. And if I did, so what? I'm your mother."

The warm water ran over my hair, covering my shoulders and swollen breasts. I closed my eyes and held my face under the spray for moments longer than usual. The golden yellow, Breck shampoo I rubbed over my scalp did not lather with the first go-round; as oily as a frying pan, I rinsed and soaped my scalp three times before it cut through the grease. *Man, this feels good.* I stayed in the shower until the water ran cold, and I finally had to turn it off.

The shower drained my energy, but I made it to the living room and lowered myself to the sofa. I'd settled in with a *Ladies Home Journal* when the phone rang. Mom answered with her usual perky "Yello?"

"Pssst," Mom stretched the cord into the living room and made a face as if she had swallowed spoiled milk. She whispered, "I think it's Gavin's mother." Her expression reminded me of the mantra she preached last summer: *He's no good. His family's no good. You're lucky you didn't marry him.*

I took the phone. "Hello?"

"Hi. This is Irene," she said. "Irene Makis."

"Hi," I said, flat, expressionless. Irene and I had not spoken since the "telling" seven months past.

A hand-etched, antique mirror hung on the wall in front of me—in the family for over a century. I looked at my reflection.

"How are you doing?" Irene asked.

Our exchange was a slow drum beat with long pauses between. For those few minutes, I traveled into the treasured mirror.

"I'm okay." I pushed my hair away from my face and let it fall. *I look older.*

A beveled groove defined a frame around the mirror's border. A single daisy etched on the bottom center with two blades of grass.

"A girl," Irene said.

"How did you know?"

"I called Roselia and talked to Sister Maria, the one in charge." Irene's voice had a low, musical tone but, regardless of the subject, she always sounded sarcastic. Irene never wasted words. She spoke with purpose, never chatty. Like Gavin.

The intricate mirror patterns had framed my image from the time I was finally tall enough to see my reflection, an eleven-year-old girl with goofy teeth. Now I was a hollow-eyed woman, at least, I was on the outside. *A surreal conversation, this. Gavin's mom, my baby's grandmother. The one who suggested abortion. The woman who insisted her son graduate from Notre Dame, whatever the cost.*

"Big baby," Irene said.

Holding my hair in a ponytail, I turned my head side to side.

At the corner, a stem curved out from under the clover. Two tiny, petaled flowers each with a single round center. My stomach turned.

"What was the weight again?"

Above the miter, a round glass. *Is that a screw covered with glass?*

"Nine and a half pounds." I pulled my shoulders back and looked at my upper half from the side. *Still extra-large.*

"How long?"

Each side was the same pattern, I realized. Throughout the years I looked at the delicate etchings, I never noticed the repetition.

"Twenty-one inches."

At the top of the mirror, a cord whose center was a medallion-like flower hid the nail hanger.

"Oh, a fat one then," she chuckled at her frank comment. As if we'd come across each other in the grocery store, gayly sharing details of a friend's newborn. She laughed again.

"Yeah, she had great big cheeks and dark hair," I said.

I felt my protective shield soften. I pictured my baby. It felt so good, talking about her, a real human being. Not something to "move on" from. Not an "experience" to cast aside and not think about.

"Gavin and my other ones were around eight pounds. Were you a big baby?" she asked.

"No, I was seven something."

This was the most Irene and I ever talked. And the most I'd talked about my baby.

"Tough labor?"

"Forty-eight hours."

The words "tough labor" brought back the long painful hours.

The mirror's cord stretched from the hanger to each side and disappeared behind it.

"What are you going to do?" Irene asked.

"Do? About what?"

I needed water.

"Have you made a decision?"

Where have you been? Have I made a decision? You can't be serious. My head began to pound.

"Decision? That was done a long time ago," I said, growing more annoyed by the minute.

"Adoption?" Irene asked.

"Yes."

"Are you sure? Don't I have any say in this?"

Say? You had your say last summer. I remembered her suggestions of ways to manage the pregnancy. None of them included an offer to raise the child or help with childcare.

"No, I guess you don't. Not now, anyway."

"This is my grandchild, you know." It was the first time, and the last, that anyone said the words "my grandchild." With that short phrase, Irene put a tiny touch of reality and relationship between herself and the baby.

"Yes, she is." The silence between us, suddenly heavy with hostility. I reached up to brush a cobweb from above the mirror.

Irene said, "Well, I just wanted to see how things were going."

"Everything is fine," I said, monotone.

Margaret, my old classmate, called. She wanted to get together and catch up. She sounded warm and genuinely glad to connect. I thought it'd be fun to see her and the other girls again, hear about their term.

My birth injuries had quieted, and I moved around normally. They'll never guess, I thought. Of course, my figure was wider but in the baggy sweater and jeans, who can tell? As Mom kept saying, leave it behind, and now I could pretend none of it ever happened. I wanted to forget the embarrassment and shame. Girls I knew got married if they were "in trouble." There was shame in that, too, a shotgun wedding; but it only meant snickers behind your back. In 1969, in other parts of the country, women's lib was picking up steam: *Burn the Bra* signs amongst women marching for women's rights. But that was only on TV, not in my world.

My secret was safe, and now, I could get back in step with my life, connect with my girlfriends who'd been next to me in class and clinicals. Together, we'd gone from high school seniors to student nurses. During those first few weeks of school in clinical lab, Margaret had given me a bed bath, and I gave her one. We practiced vital signs, body mechanics, and patient transfers on each other. We looked forward to our capping ceremony in the fall. But in the fall, I'd been far away, hiding.

৵   ৵

I took the elevator up to the dorm lounge. Drapes hung over tall windows from the high ceiling to the floor. The parlor's cherry wood paneling and old cityscape pictures looked the same. Overstuffed furniture with magazines scattered on a coffee table. My former classmates gathered in the dorm's living room.

I stomped, knocking off the remnants of melting snow, pulled my boots off, and set them by the entryway. One of the girls draped her coat near a steam radiator. I walked to the sofa in socked feet and parked myself on the couch's soft cushion; my still tender bottom welcomed the easy landing. Holly approached carrying a stainless-steel bowl full of Chex party mix. In her robe and slippers, hair in rollers and the signature pink net stretched over her head, Holly reminded me of Ethel Mertz from *I Love Lucy*.

She called out, "Cathy, you're here. I couldn't wait to see you." Holly waited while Margaret cleared a spot on the coffee table in front of the stone fireplace. Margaret was as cute as ever, with high cheekbones and full shiny black hair in a new short style. And Holly, who smiled easily and entertained those who knew her, set the bowl down. Everyone greeted me with hugs and smiles as if I were an important person. They chattered at once, making a happy din, a camaraderie that I'd missed since leaving nine months before.

Margaret sat cross-legged on the floor near me. She smiled, eyebrows up, arching her back and bobbed side to side, searching beyond the furniture to the doorway.

"I guess everyone's here." Margaret stood easily without touching her hands to the floor, as only strong thin people can. I could do that once, too, I thought. Soft spoken, she called out, "Okay, everyone, let me start," as if this were a committee meeting. Margaret said, "Isn't this so great, having us together again? Cathy, I'm so glad to see you."

Suddenly, I sensed the odd quiet in the room.

Margaret sighed and took my hand. "You know, Cathy, when you left, you didn't say goodbye."

My toes curled inside my damp socks. My heart sped up while Margaret's big, almond-shaped eyes fixed on mine.

Oh God.

Margaret lifted her hand away and moved to the floor, resting her back against the table. "Last summer, we came back from break, and you didn't. At first, we thought maybe you were on a trip or got sick or something."

Holly, the happy-go-lucky head of the class, interrupted, "Yeah, I couldn't believe it. Your name was missing from the roster. We asked Miss Bornamin about you. No one in administration told us anything except you quit. Just like that. None of us ever guessed you'd drop out."

"Well," I began, "I really feel bad about quitting. I wanted to catch up with you once I had a plan for . . ."

"Listen, Cathy. We know."

I froze. About to take a drink, my hand sank to my lap. *What do they know? Maybe they discovered I've transferred to another nursing school. Maybe someone from there told them, and they're pissed because I took off without telling them.*

Holly said, "We were sitting around the lounge, and this guy walks in. A priest. None of us knew who he was. Said his name was Father Ed. He asked if we knew you. Said he wanted to make sure he had the right class. I remember sitting up, thinking he was about to say you'd been hit by a car or something awful. But then he said, 'It's finally over. She had a tough time, but Cathy had the baby at last. She's okay, and the baby's fine.'"

My head rang. My heart raced. No one, not Mom or Edward, said anything about this. *Wouldn't he have called Mom and let her know what happened?* He knew this was my secret. I'd told him explicitly at that meeting in the summer. *Didn't he know he'd blasted me to the world?*

"I don't know what you're talking about."

Holly said, "It's okay. You don't have to pretend anymore."

Margaret continued, "We told him we knew nothing about it. He said he was surprised. He thought we were close friends and I told him we *were* close friends. Or at least I thought we were."

Someone said, "We were shocked. Speechless actually."

They were speechless? I was dumbfounded. I wasn't ready. For the last nine months, my routine was to lie and deny. The room turned into a chamber of silence for what could have been a quarter of an hour, but it must have been more like a quarter of a minute. Everyone's mouths turned down, eyes to a chipped nail or toward the floor.

I felt betrayed, angry. *A respected Catholic priest.* I didn't understand. Was this Edward's way of finding support for me? Or did he think my friends wouldn't contact me, or that it didn't matter who knew, or that it wasn't worth worrying about? What, then, was the point of my going away?

"Listen, no one knew. Gavin didn't want to get married, so the best thing to do was to give the baby up for adoption. I went away and kept it quiet."

I kept up the façade of a strong woman, hiding the disaster I was inside. My trust reserves, if there is such a thing, were completely dried up leaving only wariness and fear of rejection.

"I'm transferring to Shadyside Hospital to finish out my training. I dreaded seeing my class graduate ahead of me."

They reacted with pity and crooned their sympathy. There was nothing else to say on the subject. I turned the topic away and asked about their classes, kept them talking, then came up with an excuse to leave. With a look of sincerity on my face, I said goodbye at the door. They said to keep in touch, and I laughed a lighthearted happy farewell.

I couldn't wait to get out of there. I never went back.

At home that night, I waited until the others went to bed. Mom and I were the only ones up. We sat at opposite ends of the couch. The TV was on, but neither of us watched. She asked me how the get-together went; was everyone glad to see me?

"Mom. Did you know that Edward told the girls from my class? He went into the dorm and announced it." I stood and paced.

"Be quiet, you'll wake everyone up. What happened?"

"What happened? What happened? I'll tell you what happened." I told her the whole thing, explaining every detail about the afternoon as I spun around the room, arms flailing. When I finished my retelling, I sat down again and leaned my head in my hands. "Mom, how could this happen?"

"I guess he thought he was helping. He must have figured your friends would want to know."

"Oh, really? What about going to Roselia for the strict privacy and going to Ohio and keeping it a secret? He knew about that."

"I'm sure he meant well. He probably thought they would support you or whatever."

"That's a bunch of shit, Mom," I said, as my eyes began to sting.

Her mouth dropped. She sat straight up. "Watch your language. Edward wouldn't do anything to hurt anyone. It was simply a misunderstanding."

My teeth clenched like a locked vise; arms straight, I let out a growl and shook my head. The way Mom brushed it off infuriated me as much as Edward's announcement. But my outburst with the word "shit" was further over the line than I'd ever allowed myself. I felt like I'd thrown a bottle of ink on an ugly rug—ashamed and proud.

❧ 17 ❧

The last snow dump disappeared, but ice covered the trees and roads. The temperature headed toward single digits.

I didn't date during the months before starting back to school, but after talking to his mother, I called Gavin. His voice was flat, but when I asked if we could get together, he agreed.

When Mom learned I was going out with Gavin, her only comment was, "You know, Cathy. Once is an accident. Twice is a tramp. If this happens again, you're on your own. Don't expect me to stand by you." The comment utterly floored me. Wasn't I on my own the first time?

"Okay," I said, "I understand. Don't worry, it won't happen again."

Gavin stayed in the car, two short taps on the horn to let me know he'd arrived at the curb. The baby blue Cadillac had more miles on it, otherwise it was the same as when I last rode in it. We stopped at one of our old favorite places to park, high up, overlooking the city lights. Gavin kept the engine running for warmth and the radio off. The heater purred. I leaned against the passenger door, and he stayed behind the wheel seemingly a football field away. A year ago, we were like two polyester shirts coming out of the dryer, stuck to each other, sparks flying. Our new situation felt so awkward, as if we'd been making a film that now turned into a movie set with fake meaningless props. Even so, I pressed on, wishing us into our past lives of teasing and laughing—and touching.

I couldn't wait to tell him everything, as if he had no hand in the odyssey I'd survived. I talked about how sick I was, how awful it was in Lexington where the cigarette smoke made me ill, and how their attacking cats had terrorized me—jumping onto my shoulder from behind the couch. About how I watched my belly grow beyond where my skin could stretch, until it nearly split. About the labor, when my hips felt broken. As if I could make him feel what I felt by describing gory details and torture of labor.

"Seriously, Gavin. Three weeks past my due date. Three weeks. That's unheard of. No one goes that long. Honest to God. I thought I'd never go into labor. Then once I did, I thought it'd never be over. Laying there for two days and nights in agony. Can you imagine? I was so scared. So alone. It was horrible."

"Huh." Gavin faced me, leaning against the door. He didn't touch me, not even my hand or shoulder. I leaned for my purse and dug out lip gloss, uncapped it, and pressed it to my lips, not using the mirror. Back in the day, when I'd turned the rearview mirror down to apply lipstick, he had said, "You can drive a guy wild doing that."

But that evening, he wasn't going wild. He was detached, as if he'd looked up from a book, distracted by an urgent TV news report, a bleeding unconscious woman dragged from a burning car, and said, "Huh."

"You cannot believe how scarred my belly is. Want to see?"

"Uh, not really."

"Yes, you do. I want you to see it. Its horrid."

I opened the glove compartment for light, slid down a little on the seat, and pulled down the top of my pants, exposing the hanging skin with vertical silver stripes of wrinkled snakeskin.

He made a sound like on the *I Love Lucy Show* when Lucy realizes the catastrophe she created.

"That's bad, Cath. Repulsive actually."

"They wouldn't do a C-section on a Roselia girl, secrecy and all, you know, it would leave a scar they said, and in the future someone would see it and know. Bullshit. As if anyone wouldn't know by these stretch marks." I pulled up the pants, suddenly embarrassed, disappointed by his reaction. I wanted to share the misery, to garner sympathy, to squeeze a drop of remorse, to hear him say the things I wished for—that he was sorry and loved me and that he never should have allowed me to go through the birth alone; that we should have gotten married and that he regretted what happened.

When he wouldn't engage about the pregnancy, I switched topics and brought up school, asking how it was going for him and about how my plans to start at a different hospital program were working out. I asked questions. He gave disinterested answers, like he was fulfilling a duty by going out with me.

I felt as if I had an old pack of matches, striking one after another, none of them catching, in spite of scratching harder and faster.

Later, Gavin pulled up at the curb near my house and did not shut off the engine, or ask me why I was sitting so far away, or get out to open my door.

"It was nice seeing you. I'll let myself out; you don't have to. Take care," I said.

He turned only his head toward me, his hand still on the wheel. "Bye, Cathy."

"'Night."

I hadn't broken through Gavin's cool attitude, but there was something in me that wouldn't let go. I needed his love.

I had no idea of myself, my power, my very selfhood, my importance as a human being, my own majesty as a young woman. Gavin had given it to me. And he'd taken it away.

A few weeks later, rain came down on the car as loud as ball bearings. The water hid the potholes from winter's freeze-melt cycles. My sister treated me to dinner out, just the two of us. Her hair lightened and long now, she exuded a working woman's confidence. Corrine thought I had been in Ohio, working for a dentist since the summer. At Christmas, she insisted to Mom that I should be home for the holiday. Mom put her off, saying the bus didn't run from there during the holiday week. Corrine threatened to drive out to Lexington for me and bring me back. Then Mom said I didn't have any time off and that I couldn't come to Pittsburgh.

Corrine looked small behind the huge steering wheel of the old black Ford sedan with the gearshift on the column. The showers covered the windshield momentarily before the large wipers swooshed over the glass. The view cleared briefly, then again smeared out of focus. The darkness that night covered so many things besides the deep holes in the road. The duplicity weighed on me. *If Corrine knew, what would she think? Would she be ashamed like Mom? Upset like my school friends for keeping it a secret? Disgusted like Gavin? Would she put me down for feeling sorry for myself?*

A water-filled pothole caught the wheel. The car banged and jerked, and I gritted my teeth, holding onto the car door. But when Corrine asked what I wanted to do, I said, "Let's keep driving. I don't want to go home yet. You know, dinner was so much fun. It sure feels good to be out. You and me. Why haven't we ever done this before?" I smoothed my skirt and pulled my slicker across my lap.

During dinner, we'd laughed and reminisced like old ladies catching up on life. Corrine asked in several ways about my time in Lexington, but I managed to deflect that conversation with vague answers, casually as if the whole subject bored me.

Soft and never harsh, her voice was lively. "You were at nurse's training, then on this crazy, hare-brained idea about Ohio. It seemed like forever, but who cares? We're here now."

The rain pelted, and the wipers swung at high speed. The front wheel thunked again against the uneven road. She braked hard, easing the back wheel through it. The car dropped, recovered.

Corrine said, "Shit, I hate those things. And I can't see when they're coming. So, what do you think? Ready to head home?"

"No, not yet. I know it's miserable out here. But can we keep going for a while?" Wet, dark, and cold. But I loved being with her. The radio played Ben E. King's "Stand by Me." Corrine turned to the left onto a side street.

"This rain. What's the saying? April showers bring May flowers? Well, it's not April yet and imagine what this would be if it were snow," she said. The rain sheared sideways across the glass. The heater blasted, and the windows fogged. Corrine said, "Dammit. The defroster doesn't work. Roll down your window, will you?"

I cranked the old window winder. Water blew in covering my shoulder. "Listen, Corrine?" Tense, tentative. I could barely see. My eyes blurred as I tried to focus straight ahead.

There had been enough of the lying and keeping secrets. Her questions about my job in Lexington, when I supposedly worked for a dentist, became more specific, so that I had to seriously make up stuff. What did the dentist look like? What was my job exactly? What kind of house did I stay in? Telling her lie after lie made me feel small and fake.

"I want to tell you something."

"Okay . . . should I stop the car?" she asked.

I cranked the window handle, bringing it almost closed.

Corrine loosened her neck scarf.

"Actually, if it's okay with you, I'd rather keep going," I said.

Having her buy me dinner, having *her* invite *me*, laughing together, giving me space and showing real interest, loving me when no one else would. Corrine drove on. The wipers thumped.

How do I say it?

Corrine glanced at me in the light from streetlamps. "Are you crying? What's wrong? What's going on?"

My chest and throat throbbed and felt thick. I pulled a tissue from my coat pocket.

"Ah, Cathy. Don't cry. Whatever it is, I'll help you. I love you, whatever it is, it'll be okay." She kept driving. Finally, she said, "What's wrong? Please tell me."

I looked out the side window, calming the spasm in my throat. Corrine reached for my hand, touched it gently, then took it away to manage the shifter again. Rain poured from awnings and downspouts. It flowed from drainpipes into gutters along culverts.

I held my head in my hand. The silence between us magnified as rain battered the car. Finally, I looked up.

"I was in Ohio, that part's true. But I wasn't working. I was hiding."

The turn signal, tick tick tick. The car went silent, lurched as Corrine braked on a hill. She turned the ignition and popped the clutch; we lurched forward. Behind us a honk.

"Oh, take a pill, jag-off!" Corrine said to the honker. I started laughing and crying at the same time.

"Gavin and I broke up because I got pregnant." I said it looking straight ahead, in the dark.

Corrine sucked in a quick breath.

"What?" Her voice puzzled; head tilted. "Say that again?"

"I was pregnant. Gavin didn't want to get married. He said he had to finish school."

"Oh, Cathy. Does Mom know?"

"Yes, it was awful."

"Did you have an abortion? How? Where? That must've been horrible."

"No."

Silence.

"I had the baby. A little girl. I gave her up for adoption."

"Oh, my God. You're serious. You had a baby girl? Oh, Cathy."

My words came faster, about going to Lexington, and coming back to stay at Roselia for the final two months, about the labor and delivery, about all of it. The details gushed out of me in a flood of tears.

It needed to be out, and telling it brought it rushing back. The night before delivery with Lynn. Purging. Telling. Unashamed. I'd been full to the breaking point, but I didn't know it until I opened my mouth and talked. Corrine let me go on. She listened and felt it with me. Corrine pulled to the curb, put on the parking brake, turned the ignition off. She reached over for me and wrapped me in her arms as I cried. It poured out of me and her, too.

The rain slowed to a soft patter.

"Oh, Cathy. If only you could have told me. I would've been right there with you. I'm so sorry. I'm so sorry."

"Don't be sorry, Corrine. It was my own fault. I'm the one who made the mistake. It was supposed to be secret, and I tried to keep it that way. But I *had* to tell you. I couldn't lie to you anymore."

I never knew how much I loved Corrine till that night. As kids, we'd rubbed our fingers together with a drop of blood so we'd be blood sisters, something we'd seen on a TV show. We spent hours at night giggling and talking, days fighting and complaining about one another. When she married at eighteen, our lives went in different directions. She worked for a utility company. I went to school. I had Gavin, and she had a husband—too busy with life to spend time on the phone. But the night she comforted me was a gift that bonded us like no other.

❧ *18* ❦

Several months passed between the birth and the beginning of my new nursing program. I took a job canvassing for a census, knocking on doors, asking generic questions, earning under a dollar an hour. It was a way to pass the time until school started. A way to keep busy until June, when I'd appear in court to sign papers for the baby.

Finally, the court date arrived. Cars jammed the streets, delivery trucks honked at streetcars, pedestrians—working people mostly in high heels or coat and tie—walked briskly as if on a mission, whatever that was, with their mouths set tight.

A scraggly bearded man sat on the sidewalk on a piece of cardboard. He held up a dented metal cup.

"Can you spare some change?" he asked.

Mom used to chide, "Don't look at bums; keep walking." And so, with eyes straight ahead, I passed him as if I heard and saw nothing. I hurt for the man. *We are all human.* But Mom taught me to be callous. "Don't be so soft-hearted. People will take advantage of you if you keep that up."

The stone courthouse was close to a hundred years old, situated in downtown Pittsburgh. I reached for the door handle. My reflection looked back at me in the glass door: a somber-faced woman wearing a blousy, sailor-style top and navy skirt. It was my first time in the courthouse. High ceilings, massive hallways. I checked the notification letter for the room number and headed in the direction of my appointment.

The area was an echo chamber with its elegant stone walls and floors, cold and unforgiving. My shoes clicked over the stone floor through hallways of marble walls, past arched doorways and wide stairways until I came to the assigned room, whose door was closed. Next to it, folding chairs lined the wall, where I sat, but soon got up again and paced in the corridor. A group of several nice-looking men in business suits approached, engaged in a serious discussion. I searched their faces, wondering if they were important people, attorneys or judges.

My leg jittered. Even though I didn't want to miss my call, I had to move and walked away from my seat, looking back again and again. An old-fashioned water fountain appeared as I rounded a corner and headed for it. The liquid ran down my chin and dribbled onto my navy skirt. I slow-walked back in the direction of my appointed courtroom. The door remained closed.

I can do this, I can do this, I can.

A long-forgotten memory came up. One day as a child, I mustered my courage to climb the tallest slide at a public pool. I knew that once I decided to go, there was no turning back since the ladder was solid with a line of kids. I put one foot on a metal rung, hands on the wet vertical bars, and followed a girl bigger than me. The pool was crowded, and noisy with shrieks, splashing, and the diving board's reverberating boing. The lifeguard's whistle intermittently caught swimmers' attention. An odor of chlorine surrounded me. I kept looking up, waiting for the girl ahead of me to move. More frightened with each rung, I questioned myself, what if I can't do it? In spite of this, I was determined to be like one of the big kids and prove to myself that I was brave enough. Finally, at the top, the silver slide's sharp drop below with its curve at the bottom tested my decision. My throat squeezed. My chest stiffened. I leaned down, gripping the curved braces on each side of the platform, unable to move. It's my turn, I thought. Stiff legged, I sat and grasped the slide's low edges. The kid behind me shouted, "Hey, what's the hold up? Get going."

☙ ❧

The frosted glass door opened. It was my turn. A musty odor met me as I stepped into the ornately paneled courtroom. Only a few lights were on, like church when I used to arrive before anyone else. A black-robed judge sat behind a high bench, like I'd seen on the Perry Mason TV show. There was a witness stand, but I was instructed to sit on a chair in front of it. Without warning, my mouth opened, hungry for air. I took in a wide yawn and covered my mouth, embarrassed that I might look bored.

"Raise your right hand," a grim-faced woman said.

I sat straight and lifted my forearm, thinking again of Perry Mason.

"Repeat after me, I solemnly swear—"

My tongue turned dry as toast. I stuttered and struggled with the words. When asked if I understood the agreement of relinquishment, I nodded.

The judge admonished me, "Please state out loud that you understand."

"I understand," I said.

"Records are sealed for ninety-nine years. Do you understand?"

Nodding, eyes closed for that moment, I replied, "Yes."

"Speak up, please. Do you understand, and do you agree?"

With my eyes straight ahead, looking past the court recorder and the two or three others in the room, I said, "Yes, I agree."

"A new birth certificate will be created without your name. Do you understand?"

"Yes, I understand."

"Write your full name, please. Sign here."

The woman gave me a pen. My hand trembled. I wrote my first, middle, and last name on the bottom line of a legal-sized paper covered in tiny print.

It was over in less than ten minutes.

Outside the courthouse, I looked up to the blue sky beyond the building's shadow and felt the pleasing relief of facing my fear. I'd let go of the sides, splashed into the water, down under where sounds went muffled. I resurfaced to life's hooting and hollering. I'd be Mom's daughter again.

I don't know how many young women passed through court that day. But in that decade, hundreds of thousands of young women across America went through the same process and buried their child's existence. Many keep their secret even today.

Part II

❧ *19* ❦

1969

The transition into my new nursing program was smooth, and my classmates did not challenge my reason for leaving St. Joe's after I told them I'd taken time out to be sure I wanted to be a nurse. Now in my new dorm, rummaging through the closet for a party getup, I thought of the remark made by Dr. Z, a big-deal heart surgeon. Still in OR scrubs, he followed me on the hospital stairway and said, "You ought to have your legs insured for two million dollars."

I smiled at the memory when my hand landed on a pleated miniskirt. *This will do.* Over the skirt, a figure-hugging, rib-knit sweater, and a low-slung, wide belt, accentuated my curvy figure. A blue paisley scarf wrapped around my head, knotted on the side with the silk brushing my cheek, and chunky strapped shoes, finished the look.

❧   ❦

My friend, Celeste—top in our class, good natured and funny—drove her father's old boat of a car, creeping through a neighborhood with ancient oaks and maples while I searched for the party-house address. Her plump figure, receding chin, and hooked nose conflicted with her popularity and confidence. She didn't date and didn't care. Her attitude was, "I don't need a boyfriend. I have to get through school."

Good for her, I thought, but that's not me. Who am I without a boyfriend?

As a teenager, like many girls back then, I locked on to the romantic movies: *Dr. Zhivago, West Side Story,* and *Gone with the Wind.* I was the girl in the arms of her lover. Back then, Gavin's attention gave me the starch my self-esteem needed.

"So, what should we do about—" I asked.

"Do? About what? Oh, here's the address," Celeste said.

"You going to drink?"

"Of course, I am." Celeste gathered her purse and keys.

"I want to be sure one of us can drive home. And it sort of . . . well, it has to be you. I mean . . ." I stopped, looking out the side window. "Well, I don't have a driver's license."

She turned to face me. "No way. Seriously?"

"My dad wouldn't allow me to learn on his car." My voice was steady, covering my embarrassment.

"Someday you'll get it. Don't worry, I'll drive us home." Celeste's hand on the door, she asked, "Wait. Are you . . . planning to get plastered?"

"Not exactly. But you never know," I said, a lilt in my voice.

"I don't usually have more than one beer; it's not my favorite thing to drink anyway. If they have pop, I'll take that."

We climbed a dark, creaky stairway. Vibrations thumped against my already pounding chest. *Gimme Gimme Good Lovin'* blared from an apartment where the door stood wide open. The scent of cigarettes, cologne, and body odor grew stronger. I slipped one hand in my jacket pocket, gripped a lipstick tube, snapped it open and closed.

Nearly every week I partied with college kids and drank beer to the music of Hendrix and the Doors. I wasn't into Peter, Paul, and Mary or Joan Baez with their political messages. I had too much angst and unrealized anger, even though I thought I was being cool.

The guys looked clean cut—not hippies or druggies, not city boys, but boys from beyond Pittsburgh, out in the country. Students at the local technical training school. Their dads worked oil and gas lines, pulled wire for utility companies, or "ran dozer." They were an unusual bunch, different from college boys who always had something smart to say or were stoned or aggressive. They weren't college material, and neither was I. Nursing school was hospital based, as were most nursing programs, and with that education came a diploma, not university credits. The men at this party were down to earth, not fancy. Refreshingly so. In an easy chair by the window, a handsome Glen Campbell lookalike with French doll lips, high cheekbones, and almond-shaped eyes sat in an easy chair holding a can of Pabst Blue Ribbon and a cigarette. A half hour later, he was still there, sitting with the can of beer. Not brooding, but not rocking to the beat. Simply sitting.

From the stereo, the Rolling Stones shouted, "Can't get no satisfaction."

I sat down next to him. "Hey, how are you?" I asked, feeling confident in my fringed suede jacket. As if he were Jim Morrison in the flesh, I turned on the charm, smiling, looking him in the eye.

"I'm Cathy. What's your name?" I shouted close to his ear. He smelled of cigarettes and beer.

"Jimmy," he shouted into my ear.

"Jimmy what?"

"Seng," he shouted.

"Seng? That sounds Chinese."

"Do I look Chinese?" he said with an edge.

"Uh, no."

Irritated, he shouted over the music, "I hear that all the time." The music stopped.

"Oh. I'm sorry. Don't be hurt. I was being silly."

"French. It's French. It used to be D'Seng but they dropped the d," he said.

The music changed. I'd finished my beer and so had he. Feeling jumpy, I needed to move. He wouldn't dance or talk about himself, so I told him about school and where my parents lived and the street my dorm was on. *In-a-Gadda-Da Vida* the seventeen-minute head trip music blared. I closed my eyes, lost in inebriation, the beat of organ and drum.

Beer after beer, we were getting sloppy drunk, laughing, then kissing. I had to let Celeste know, Jimmy would be taking me back to the dorm. I found her, stone sober, talking to a bearded guy in the apartment's tiny kitchen. My body weaved; I touched her arm. She turned around, holding a bottle of Hire's Root Beer.

"Oh, hi, how're you?" Her voice sweet and innocent, peppy. Happy. I wanted to be her, but didn't know how.

"Great, I'm great. Listen, I wanted to let you know. I've got a ride back. You don't have to wait for me."

"You sure? Sure you're okay? I can wait if you're not ready yet."

"I'm sure. Thanks." I turned back to the party and bumped into the door frame.

Jimmy's keen appetite for beer was in character with his buddies from "back home." He'd never used pot or illicit drugs, didn't grow his hair long or have a tattoo even though he'd spent two years in the army. He was a good ol' country boy, from a blue-collar family who lived in rural PA, completely new to me. A novelty, this handsome young veteran from the woods.

It was late, close to eleven. With the Temptations blasting, *I can't get next to you,* I walked, well-lit from alcohol, into the room and sat on Jimmy's lap. "So, can you give me a ride back to the dorm?" I shouted into his ear. "You have wheels, right?"

His cigarette ash grew and lit red as he took a drag.

I said, "My ride's about to leave, but if you can give me a lift, I'd rather go with you. Besides, I want to see that hot car you've been telling me about."

We leaned in for a kiss. My head swimming, the music blaring, I was kissing a good-looking man.

He called a few days later and asked me if I wanted to get something to eat.

⤖   ⤖

Jimmy and I dated, mostly drinking beer with friends and spending weekends at his parents' trailer in the woods. I learned what he was about: deer hunting, playing softball, watching football and baseball, drinking beer and falling asleep in the chair after dinner. A real gentleman, he held the door for me. I never had to say "stop" or "don't" when we were making out. He wasn't sarcastic. He treated me with respect, unlike Gavin who'd called me Chippie, Chip for short.

Sex came sooner than with Gavin and without guilt, as I had nothing to preserve. My worth lived in my sexuality; a lesson well learned from years with Gavin. Jimmy used protection without any prodding.

Before we made love the first time, I said, "Hold on. I need to tell you something. I had a baby. And I wasn't married."

He didn't react but said, "You did?"

"Yeah. I had to put her up for adoption."

"You ever see her?"

"No. I don't know where she is. It's not anything to you. But I thought you should know."

"Okay."

We never spoke of it again. I wondered if he told anyone but guessed he didn't. It's not something to be proud of; I was used goods.

Jimmy wore a brown canvas jacket and blue jeans one evening when he picked me up after school. The Road Runner engine's deep rumble reminded me of an Indie race car. I climbed in and closed the car door. We were on our way to his parents' place for the weekend; it was two weeks until Christmas. I didn't know what to get for Jimmy. He couldn't care less about clothes. I'd never seen him wear anything besides blue jeans and button-down shirts unless it was camouflaged hunting gear. The advantage for me was I could wear jeans, too, and sweatshirts. I'd figure out the gift later.

"You have one more week till you're done. Graduation," I said, whooping.

"Yep," Jimmy said.

"Have you heard anything yet from those job applications you put in?"

"I got a call from an outfit in Columbus, Ohio," he said and down shifted, then shot onto the highway.

"Columbus? Wow."

"Yep," he said. "I'll probably take it."

"Think we ought to get married?" I asked. "I mean, if you're way out there, and I'm here . . ." I waited for him to pick up the conversation. I wanted to be married more than anything. More than money, security, even love, I wanted to be a wife. Just the designation of "Mrs." before my name would give me status, announce that someone wanted me, and allow me the right to have a legitimate child. I was only twenty-one years old, but it felt like time was running out. Ending up an old maid, like Miss Meredith, a friend of Mom's, was a fate worse than death. Mom always spoke of Miss Meredith with sadness: "Poor Miss Meredith, never married, never had a family."

"You want to get married?" Jimmy sounded surprised. The subject hadn't come up before, although we'd spent plenty of weekends at his parents' place in northwestern Pennsylvania.

"I'll graduate in April. I need to know where to apply for a job. And I'm not moving to Columbus unless we're getting married," I said. It was a deal breaker for me. If he didn't want to get married, our relationship wouldn't survive. Beer and sex wouldn't work over the phone, plus Columbus, Ohio, had no draw for me.

"Well, I guess we should get married then," he said.

"No kidding? You want to? Are you sure?" I needed him to want me, but as soon as he said 'married,' I wanted to rewind the tape and wait for him to propose.

"Sure. I guess. I mean, if *you* do."

That weekend, Jimmy and I walked along a dirt road used for utility vehicles that came to pump gas wells. The road wound through the woods and stopped at a huge cylindrical metal storage tank that Jimmy's dad leased to the utility company. We kept walking, holding gloved hands, watching through the trees for deer. The landscape was brown and white, a colorless canvas of bare forest, peaceful soundlessness where imperfections disappeared under bright glittering snow. I was happy in the beauty. I wanted to be happy. A fresh start. Leaving last season's dirt beneath. Look at the here and now. Splendor. Hope.

"Do you want to talk about the engagement ring?" I asked. Jimmy froze in his tracks, holding onto my hand, pulling me still.

"Shhh. Look there. See? See that bark rubbed off there?"

"Yeah," I whispered.

Jimmy did not move, only his head turned in slow motion. We stood for many minutes until he decided it was okay to start again. Eventually, we spied movement in the distance with dozens of trees between us. Jimmy whispered, "There, there! See that? And look, look, it's a buck. See the rack?"

"Wow," I said in awe.

"He'll be mine tomorrow."

The opening day of buck season.

As a child, I saw a deer hanging by its back legs from a tree branch, right in front of my neighbor's house, a startling gruesome sight. It hung there for well over a month. I couldn't stand the sight of it and turned my head when passing by. I'd seen deer cross the road at night, beautiful magical creatures that came out of nowhere and gracefully jumped road barriers, then disappeared in the dark. Hunting made little sense to me. But I tried to appreciate Jimmy's passion for it. I wanted to understand him. I wanted to be in love.

"I think they're beautiful," I said.

"Yeah, so do I," Jimmy said.

"Then why do you want to shoot them?"

"'Cause that's what we do. That's called a trophy, you know?"

"Then will you eat it?"

"Uh huh, I'll take it to the butcher and have it cut up and wrapped for the freezer. That's good eats."

Our walk continued in silence. If I didn't talk, no one did. I thought of the ring again but said nothing. I didn't want to annoy Jimmy. I wanted to be exactly who he wanted. If that meant the happy wife of a hunter, so be it.

I nudged Jimmy toward marriage, still wishing to be someone's princess. I wanted the diamond-studded crown that, in my mind, married women had. There was no status in being a single woman. If I had a ring, I'd be one of the privileged girls who planned their wedding without a shotgun. I'd be *wanted*.

๛ 20 ๖

It was 1971, when a postage stamp went for eight cents and a lady's two-piece knit suit cost nine dollars, ninety-eight cents. Walt Disney World opened its Florida theme park. The first video-taped sitcom, *All in the Family,* aired on television. The voting age was lowered to eighteen. We listened to George Harrison's "My Sweet Lord," sad and beautiful to me. Two years had passed since Mary-Lynn's birth. Two years that felt like ten.

On New Year's Eve Jimmy and I stood alone on a snowy deck at a holiday party.

"I got it," he said and pulled a box from his pocket, handing it to me like a pack of cigarettes.

"Don't give it to me like that," I said. He looked confused.

"Huh?" he asked.

"Oh, never mind. Let's see it," I said. "Can you open the box?"

He opened the box, and I removed the white gold ring with a small solitaire oval diamond. I put it on my finger and said, "Oh, Jimmy. It's a perfect fit. Aren't you going to ask me to marry you?"

Incredulous, he said, "I figured you knew that already."

A few days after New Year's Eve, I waited under the awning outside of the nurses' dorm. Dad's car rolled up to the sidewalk right on time as always. I hurried to the car and jumped in.

"Pshew, what a mess out there," I said.

Dad's gloved hands wrapped around the steering wheel, his figure bulkier in the dark wool overcoat. I held his fedora on my lap.

"Glad the snow stopped. But how ugly everything looks now," I said. Streetlights glowed over the empty sidewalk as cars crawled by, caught in the Friday evening rush to start the weekend.

"Mmmm huh," Dad said. I knew by the tone, even of that brief reply, that Dad's mood was okay. He was a good driver, unless mad about something; then riding with him was terrifying. He'd cut someone off, gun it and slam on the brakes, play chicken. It didn't happen often. I never knew when to expect it, but that evening I sensed no tension. If I had, I would have kept silent.

"Thanks for picking me up," I said after we got on the main road.

Radio voices took the place of our own. I wore my engagement ring but said nothing to Dad about it. Indirect communication through Mom was best.

⮞   ⮜

"Oh good, you're home." Mom stood at the stove, apron tied around her neck and waist, smiling. Steam rattled the lid of the boiling spaghetti noodles. The mouthwatering delectable aroma of cooking onions, garlic, and tomatoes filled the room. She greeted me, then gave Dad a peck on the mouth. Dad walked to the hallway coat closet. I waited in case he came back, but he went upstairs to change.

"Mmmm, that smells delicious." I set my bag on a dining room chair. I anticipated, dreamed about, and envied others for the news I wanted to share with Mom. *Finally, I'd be a grown-up. A wife.* It was real, and I had a ring to prove it.

I raised my left hand near her face and wiggled my ring finger.

"Oh?" Mom's head ticked back; her mouth flattened. "What's this?"

"Jimmy and I are engaged."

"Oh? When?"

She turned to the stove, flicked the burner off, grabbed worn-out potholders, and dumped the boiling water and spaghetti into a colander. "When did he ask you, and when do you plan to get married?" She stirred the sauce, put bread in the toaster, pulled the parmesan cheese from the refrigerator.

"New Year's Eve," I said. Her frosty reaction was not how I thought this would go. *Wasn't this what we wanted?* "We're planning for a week after my graduation in April."

She lifted a stack of dinner plates from the cabinet and onto the countertop.

"Uh. To tell the truth, I'm surprised you're getting married so soon after you finish school. Why can't you wait?"

"Wait? Wait for what?"

"To be on your own, get an apartment. Work and have your own money. Give yourself time."

I didn't want time. I'd fallen off a cliff, and now I was flailing for anything to grab onto to anchor myself back on solid ground. Couldn't she see that I wanted to be a wife? There was no "me" without a husband.

"Jimmy's going to Columbus to work. And we thought since I'll be graduating in April, it makes sense to get married and for me to get a job there instead of Pittsburgh. I don't see any point in me working here and him working three hours away. Why not just be there together? I can get a job anywhere. But this was the only one he could get this close to home. Even though it's not exactly close."

Mom did not offer congratulations, and her damp reaction pissed me off. She was not taking part in my performance, and her cool response dragged over my self-doubt, roughing it up.

But I would not let it get to me. I would not let go.

⤚   ⤚

I woke in my parents' house to ice covering the metal window frames beside my bed, a pool of water on the marble windowsill. I turned away from the window and looked at my little oval diamond sparkling in the sunlight. I was *engaged*. I'd be *a wife*. *Happy*. I didn't care what Mom said.

I found Mom in the kitchen putting groceries away. Lazily, still in my robe, I reached for the cereal and a bowl.

Mom said, "Let's talk about this wedding."

The hair on my neck tingled as I poured myself a bowl of cereal.

She pushed the refrigerator door shut, put one hand on her hip, and faced me. "Dad and I want you to wait. It's too soon after you finish school."

"Mom, I already told you why I want to get married in April. I don't know why you're not excited for me." Then came the ultimate defense, a hard punch in the gut. "You and Dad don't want me to be happy." My spoon clattered against the sink; I stomped out of the room leaving my cereal untouched.

After that, no further objections came.

My spirit hovered behind and around me, shaking her head, knowing there was no hope, as my body went through the motions of planning for my future. No chance to grieve my baby. Never mind that I cried when I was alone, and that a voice inside ordered me to shut up.

But something wasn't right. I knew it from the constant stomach pain. The feigned jubilance; the disappointment around the marriage proposal and my parents' unenthusiastic response; excessive energy around planning the wedding, but little toward my groom. As if he were a prop, rather than the love of my life, I whirled around him, caught up in my own status as a bride-to-be. Jimmy didn't seem to mind; in fact, I felt like he didn't care one way or the other about getting married. His detachment made my act easier, but in hindsight, I wish he would have noticed our incompatibility and cancelled the wedding. I was a runaway train, and my groom was along for the ride.

21

We were married that April as planned after I graduated from my nursing program and got my diploma. We married in the Catholic church with my cousin Edward officiating.

My wedding gown had the popular Juliet style with empire waist and high collar. There was a light blue ribbon around the seam between the bodice and skirt. Mom offered to switch it out for white, but I told her that the light blue was okay. Secretly, I considered it a mark of my impurity, that I was no longer fit for all white.

Jimmy and I rented a one-bedroom apartment on the second floor in Columbus and went about buying furniture, one piece at a time. My jitters calmed. My work at Children's Hospital in the recovery room was challenging and fast paced. Jimmy worked for the Ohio Bell as a technician. We drove four hours to Jimmy's parents' home every chance we had. Living in the woods was Jimmy's dream. His mother cooked delicious comfort food every time we were there and always had homemade dessert. Pork roast, beef stew, baked ham, home-canned peaches, apple pie and ice cream were typical. While Jimmy went hunting, I stayed inside reading or watching TV.

As a wife, I had every right to want a baby, but I waited two months before bringing it up.

"What do you think about starting a family?" I asked on one of our long trips to Pennsylvania.

Jimmy kept his eyes on the road. "I don't want kids yet. It's too soon."

The furrowed fields passed; electric poles whizzed by. I chewed at my lip. "When do you think you'll be ready?"

"I don't know. We should get some money put away first. And even then, I don't know."

"I thought you wanted kids. What's the big deal?" My voice tightened.

"I just don't think it's time." He reached for the radio dial and turned it up.

We were far from a radio tower, and the reception went fuzzy. I leaned over and snapped the knob to off. For the next hour, we rode in silence.

Five months after our wedding, I threw up in the morning. I'd missed a period one time and knew the signs. Jimmy hardly reacted when I told him I might be pregnant and needed to get tested. But when the doctor later congratulated me to confirm the results, I hopped off the table, dressed, and hurried out to meet Jimmy in the waiting room.

"Well, guess what?" I said, a bit faster than normal. I tried to hide my urge to dance and twirl.

"No," Jimmy said, and his lips pursed, then widened into a smile.

"Yes," I said. "You are going to be a daddy."

"I hope it's a boy." He stood and walked beside me to the elevator.

This time, there was no acting. I laughed at droll jokes, moved with a sway, swung my arms high when walking. For the first time in years, my brain and heart agreed. The spirit around me smiled, too.

The pregnancy went quickly. There were baby showers and congratulations as normal as any couple beginning a family. Like a bird feathering the nest, I had the baby's crib set up and decorated in pink, blue, and yellow, not knowing whether it would be a boy or a girl.

It was finally my turn. No one would take this baby away. Nothing touched my bubbly mood. Secrets and lies, living with strangers, laboring alone, separation at holidays, shame, shame, shame—forever in the past.

Natural childbirth had become the "in" thing, allowing the new mama to fully participate in the birth without drugs. It was on a Tuesday at five-fifteen in the morning, right on the due date, in the delivery room, after six hours of labor. Jimmy sat next to my head, the sheet draped between the doctor and us.

"Let's have one more *good* push. There you go, that's the way," the doctor said, "and . . . we have a beautiful baby girl." The nurses yay-ed, as my head flopped back against the pillow.

Jimmy said, "Oh. That's okay, honey; next time it'll be a boy."

The comment shocked me. How could he say that, at such a time? But it rolled off, water on Teflon. I had my baby girl.

"Congratulations to you both," my doctor said. "The nurses will clean up your little girl, and we'll give you a rest. When you get back to your room and settle in, we'll bring in the baby. By the way, she weighs seven pounds, three ounces." I thought of the difference in the two pregnancies: of the three weeks overdue birth; of the forty-eight-hour labor with MaryLynn. This time, everything was as it was supposed to be.

Worn out, weak from labor, I moved with help from the gurney to the bed. Voices in the hall, tapping metal on metal, meal trays delivered to rooms nearby. The fragrant smell of hot coffee confirmed that it was indeed breakfast time. The hospital bed had been set up for me with the head raised, sheets folded in a welcoming arrangement. Pink and yellow roses with hyacinths sweetened the air. A gift card from Nana and Papa poked out from the bouquet, *Congratulations on your first baby.* The nurse pulled the covers over me. The sun shined across my bed, still low in the sky. I felt as if I'd accomplished a trip to outer space and arrived home safely.

Jimmy leaned in to kiss me on the forehead and said, "I'm going home for a while to rest. You take it easy here."

I kissed him goodbye and thought I'd take a nap. After he left, I relaxed and thought how lucky I was. *Things turned out okay.* The door opened, and a smiling nurse padded in with a bundle of pink blankets tucked in the crook of her arm.

"Here you are, Mrs. Seng. Your little girl wants to say hello. She's a beauty."

My baby girl. Bertie's little birdlike legs, fine hair soft as a duckling's feathers, baby doll fingers, nails as tiny as dots on a ladybug.

I had known "happy" in my life. Mom's layer cake with tiny rosebuds around my birthday candles. Drawing my name with sparklers in the dark. Christmas mornings with wrapped presents and my parents' pleased faces. Summer evenings with robins' chuker sounds. Fresh sheets taken from the clothesline. The first bite of Mom's warm cream puffs.

But now the word *happy* didn't fit. This was so much bigger; it was joy that couldn't be told. It was air into drowning lungs. It was my body floating above the mattress. As if the endorphins from three years ago had been stored up, they flooded my insides like water from a broken dam.

MaryLynn was never mentioned. Mom, Corrine, Dad, Jimmy—no one, including me, brought up the fact that I'd borne a child two years before. *Why make everyone uncomfortable? It's all in the past.* Bertie was born two months after our first wedding anniversary—*nice and legitimate*, like the world wanted.

22

I was fully immersed in the world of mothering and relished my role, determined to be the mother I wished I'd had. Bertie was two years old, and our other daughter Opal had joined us a few weeks prior.

Before Opal's birth, we had moved from our one-bedroom flat into a three-bedroom townhouse with an open floor plan and large windows that made the house bright. It felt like a home to me.

On a warm October Saturday in Columbus, Ohio, a few weeks after Opal's birth, my parents were on their way to visit us. It would be the first time they would meet Opal. Before they came, I gave Opal a bath in the sink, working warm water and baby oil over her stubborn newborn hair. It wouldn't lay flat; one side stood up and leaned to the right while the left side pointed in the other direction. After her bath I dressed her and placed her in her baby swing. She soon fell asleep.

I then started to get Bertie ready to see her grandparents. Bertie stood statue-still allowing the gentle brush strokes through her long fine hair, looking up at me under straight-cut bangs that emphasized her cornflower-blue eyes and dark lashes. She had grown so much. She was four months past her second birthday and had been using the potty regularly without accidents for weeks. She was a smiling girl who laughed and took suggestions easily. I ran my fingers through her hair to free any errant strands from her collar and hugged her close. "I love you so much, my little Pookie," I told her.

She hugged me back. "I wuv you, too, Mommy," she said and skipped away.

I was happy.

My weight had already returned to normal, since I gained very little during pregnancy. My long hair had been permed and the volume came out full and curly after using hot rollers. The carpets had been swept, rooms dusted, bathroom scrubbed. I'd put together chicken pot pie for dinner and whipped up sour cream dip, laid out chips, stocked up on soda. Out the back window, I saw my parents' Ford pull into a visitor parking space, five minutes ahead of schedule. I felt grown-up, now the lady of the house. They were on my territory with my pride and joy to show off.

We hugged short hellos, not the extended warm "I missed you"-type hugs. But then we weren't that kind. I was too happy to be nervous and thought nothing of it.

I called upstairs to Jimmy and Bertie, "They're here." Then, "Come on, let's sit in the living room."

Dad kept his jacket on and stood at the window looking out at the parking lot, hands in pockets as if waiting for a bus. Mom sat on the couch, smiling at the room. Opal slept in my arms, swaddled in a blanket. Trying not to wake Opal, I sat down in slow motion next to Mom.

"Well," I said, delighted to show off my baby, "here she is. Meet our Opal." Tilting her toward Mom, I said, "I don't want her to wake up. You can hold her after a while, okay?"

Bertie stood next to my knee, two fingers in her mouth, looking down.

Mom scanned the room. "I like your shaggy rug. What color do you call this?"

Opal began to cry, whimpering at first.

Bertie pushed back her silky hair. She tapped my leg, "Mommy, can we go to the swings?"

I shook my head and patted her hand, whispering, "Not now, sweetie. Play with your blocks. We'll go later."

She said nothing but plopped on the floor and kicked a wooden block away.

"The rug? Oh, it's a short shag, called celery green. But it's lighter than that, don't you think?"

Opal's soft sound revved into full wail.

Dad said, "I think I'll take a walk and check out the area." He stood up and walked to the door. Bertie stood, too, and asked to go with him to the swings. Beyond our building was the playground with swing set, sliding board, and sand box.

"No, I'm not going to the playground; out back, that's it." And out he went.

Bertie's mouth turned down—her eyes, so large that she looked like a greeting card character. "Mommy, I want to go out, too. Why can't I go out?"

"No, no, sweetheart, don't cry. Maybe Grandma will go out with you."

Mom raised her eyebrows, fixed her mouth in a line, and said, "Oh, all right, let's go. You'll have to show me where it is."

Bertie jumped clear off the floor and clapped her hands.

I wanted to say, "Oh, Mom, aren't these two the most beautiful kids you've ever seen?" But that's not how we were with each other, so instead, I said, "I'm going to feed Opal. Maybe she'll quiet down. I know you don't like the noise."

I looked up as the screen door closed behind her.

⤳   ⤳

After Opal and Bertie had both been fed, the adults sat in the main room with a football game on TV, snacking on cheese and crackers. I went into the kitchen for more soda and Bertie came in behind me. She stood in front of the refrigerator, looked up and without a word, she made a puddle on the floor.

I shrieked at her, "How could you? Right in front of me! Why didn't you tell me you had to go potty?" And then I did what Mom had done to my sister Jeannie as a three-year-old. I pulled down Bertie's pants and yelled, "Now that is a bare bottom spanking for you, young lady!" And I smacked her pale tender skin three times, held her by one arm and marched her upstairs for clean clothes.

There was something in me that wanted to show my parents what a good mother I was and that I knew how to discipline my children. That evening I couldn't stop thinking of Bertie's face as she peed in front of me. I thought she was being defiant, trying to get attention, unhappy about visitors. But she wasn't a defiant child, and even if she was, spanking wasn't the answer. I despised myself for it. *I am better than this. I will not be like my mother.*

Mom and Dad left early that evening, light and breezy, thanking Jimmy and me for a good visit, asking when we would come to Pittsburgh next. I watched their car pull away, feeling grateful for my family and glad for a good day. Jimmy and I cleaned up the paper plates and washed glasses while I thought about how things went. He saw nothing unusual about the visit. But at that moment, it occurred to me that Mom and Dad didn't like kids. For people who had five children, they were awkward, intolerant, and uncomfortable around little ones.

It was days after my parents' visit, and life had returned to normal. Bertie called from the bathtub for me to help her finish up and I hurried upstairs, stopping at Opal's door and peering through the crack to check on her. She lay still and asleep, the vaporizer purring in the corner.

In the steamy bathroom, Bertie splashed behind the shower curtain. She was built like a baby bird with fine bones and no baby fat. A neighbor had once said that she was a little girl who was all hair and eyes.

"There you are," I said as if I'd been searching for her.

Bertie said, "I don't want you to do my hair."

"It will be okay, don't worry. I'll be very careful, and you can hold the washcloth over your eyes if you want."

She took the folded cloth and held it over her eyes while I added warm water to the tub. She laid back in my arm. An oversized cup held the water that I poured over her hair, then No More Tears baby shampoo. I held her again, laying her back into the water to rinse.

Memories came up of Mom holding my head under the tub faucet, burning my scalp before she realized and turned on the cold. The soap stung my eyes. I squeezed my eyelids tight, tried to breathe through a waterfall washing over my face, trying not to cry. I sat up when she finished and with my eyes shut tight, banged my forehead against the water's metal spout. I began to cry. "Shut up," she'd say, "you'll wake your baby brother."

"Shut up and stay out of the way," words that I heard constantly as a child. They were like threads woven into the fabric of who I would become.

After her bath, Bertie sat on the shag rug, banging a wooden piece into the wrong space of her new puzzle, her full cheeks partially hidden by her straight, shiny locks. I held Opal at my breast, stroking her downy hair that still refused to lay flat. Snowy light filtered through the front windows in the living room, where I sat with the TV volume low. The house felt like a safe, warm envelope. My girls were more precious to me than any possession could ever be. I had everything I ever wanted in these two children: acceptance, trust, innocence, promise, attachment, pride.

I held Opal close and sang to her, enjoying her softness against me. Opal watched my eyes and began cooing along with my song. It was the best feeling I'd ever known.

Bertie had three blocks stacked up and held her hands out, "See Mommy? See what I did?"

She added another block, and the tower toppled over.

I laughed, "Try again, sweetie."

Suddenly, for the first time since MaryLynn's birth, the reality of what I'd done five years earlier startled me as if a flashbulb went off. I had another child somewhere, one that was one hundred percent mine, same as the two in front of me. Somehow,

I had succeeded in placing MaryLynn in another dimension where she was someone else's baby. But MaryLynn was my baby, the same as Bertie and Opal, regardless of who her father was.

Time folded and wrinkled so that it was no longer 1974 but 1969 again. MaryLynn's warm body was in my arms; I lifted the blanket and saw her sweet face. The nurse hurried away from the taxi. I'd fooled myself into believing MaryLynn belonged to someone else. Not to me. The truth covered my face and chest so that I couldn't breathe. *What have I done? MaryLynn is my baby, the same as the girls in front of me. Not someone else's child. My own child, every bit as much mine as these two.*

Opal squeaked a loud chirp; Bertie's tower tumbled again. I breathed deeply, and as I did, the wrinkle over which I'd traveled began to open and smooth. In those brief moments, I left MaryLynn behind one more time.

I can't think of MaryLynn, not ever again. If I do, I'll go crazy. I'll lose my mind.

My resolve was powerful and solid, a matter of self-preservation. I closed off the path to that part of my life. Five years before, I'd signed legal papers in court. It was absolutely final. I vowed to think only of Bertie and Opal and be the best mother possible.

≈ ≪

During the following years, I kept my promise. I thanked God every night for my blessings, for my children and husband and for my good life. But my prayers always turned into petition. It seemed that no matter how much I wanted to be free of the guilt I carried, it stayed with me. Father in Heaven, have mercy on me, forgive me for my sins. Lord have mercy. The words came automatically, like they had as a child when I lay awake in the dark with rosary beads in my hands.

❧ 23 ❧

1977

The girls were five and two years old that year. We drove three hours from Columbus to Pittsburgh to visit Mom and Dad for a long weekend. Mom and I sat up late on Saturday after everyone had turned in for the night. It was our chance to catch up. We chatted about our sewing projects, Bertie and Opal, the challenges of mothering small children, my work in the recovery room at Children's Hospital, gossip, weight, hair, and the lump under her jaw.

The almond-sized bump was most likely a swollen gland due to a bad tooth, and I suggested she see a dentist the following week. The dentist sent her directly to a surgeon. It turned out to be thyroid cancer related to radiation treatments for acne she'd had as a teenager. The diagnosis was grim. The disease had already advanced to the final stages. Her life expectancy was six months. I was devastated. Mom was fifty-four, and I was twenty-eight. How could I live the rest of my life without my mother? But at the same time, I accepted her fate. There would be no miracles and I never asked God to heal the cancer. As a nurse, I knew she would not live long. Instead, I prayed that she would not suffer.

I began searching immediately for a place to live closer to Pittsburgh. Within two months we relocated to New Waterford, a northeast Ohio village near the Pennsylvania border, about an hour from Mom. Jimmy kept his job with the utility company, and they accepted his transfer. I took a part-time job as charge nurse on the evening shift at the community hospital twenty miles away. I visited Mom every chance I had. Ironically, the radiation treatment ravaged her throat and vocal cords but extended her time on earth.

During a respite from therapy, she and Dad traveled to Hawaii. After she returned from the trip, Mom stood in my kitchen and beamed. She said, "I've never been so happy in my life." Women who raised kids in the fifties and sixties put their heads down and plowed ahead, dealing with whatever came their way the best they could. But at that point in her life, when she could at last find her footing, her world crumbled beneath her. The day she proclaimed her joy, I did not question it or want to undo that moment when she smiled and had a freedom about her, like a newlywed. But the juxtaposition of deadly cancer and her sparkling eyes gave me pause. *Did it take a death sentence to make her embrace life? Or was it truly the small window of freedom she so enjoyed?*

ᔆ   ᔆ

On a hot August morning, Mom lay on the sofa-bed in her living room, a few days from death. She could no longer eat and had difficulty swallowing and speaking. Weakness prevented her from sitting up. Beside the couch, perched on an end table, was a suction machine for clearing her airway crowded next to tissues, deodorizer, and a cup of pink moistening sponges on a stick.

Mom's head, freshened by dry shampoo, rested in my hand. I combed her thinning hair and gazed at the sunken pale woman she'd become. Her eyes remained closed. I positioned her onto her side, pulling a flattened pillow between her bony knees. She was always cold. A clean cotton blanket lay nearby. I unfolded it, straightened the sheet, and gently pulled it up, covering her. I stepped back watching her, and thought of how unfair life was, how much I loved her—and of Dad trying to survive without her.

I turned the box fan toward the hallway, away from the room to draw out unpleasant odors. Mom's clean hair and linens lent a feeling of peacefulness. Her relaxed expression helped me feel secretly proud to have done my job. I felt lucky to be the one who knew how to take care of her. She murmured in a gravelly whisper, startling me since she rarely spoke by that stage. I doubted I'd heard right. I spun around and asked her to repeat. She did, but again I could not understand. I turned off the fan and leaned my ear to her.

"Did you say, am I okay with everything?" I asked. She moved her head in a microscopic nod.

"*Everything?* Do you mean *that time?*" I used the phrase "that time" instead of "my pregnancy" or "my baby I gave up" or "when I went away." We communicated in this sort of code that avoided naming what it was we thought about.

She nodded again.

Mom had never mentioned my baby, and now it was too late. There could be no conversation, no back and forth. The question caught me by surprise, so unexpected. What could I say? *What should I say?* She opened her eyes and looked up.

Shaken by this sudden entry into my heartbreak that came in the form of a whisper, so far past that time, and with life's door about to close between us, I said, "Mom, I regret that it happened. I feel sorry for everyone involved." I paused. "It was a very hard time. That's all I can say."

She nodded ever so slightly. "Good," she said and closed her eyes.

There was so much that should have been said years before but wasn't. I would have liked to say *It was an awful way to treat a daughter you loved*, or *I wish we could have discussed the possibilities with candor and love.*

And afterward, *I wish I had had a chance to grieve, to have some outlet for my heartbreak, some sympathy.*

I wish I knew how it was for her. At the time, I had no perspective on how this affected her. It seemed to me, that she was mortified by my out of wedlock pregnancy and ashamed of me. But she must have wrestled with her reaction and handling of the situation.

1979, the year I turned thirty, Mom passed away.

My dad had a terrible time after losing my mother. He'd visit me in Ohio every Wednesday for lunch, tennis or scrabble, and dinner. We talked about philosophy and news, but never my past. He lived to be ninety-six. He never remarried or even dated. He kept no pets, had no social life, except for people he said hello to every morning when he walked at the mall for exercise.

The girls grew up, entertaining as kids are. Our docile black kitty, Midnight, added to our fun, perching outside on the window ledge by the kitchen table meowing to be let in, sometimes losing his balance and disappearing, then just as quick showing up again, watching us at the table. Opal would dress Midnight in baby doll clothes and bonnet, strap him in her doll stroller and zoom around the house while he sat still, seeming to enjoy the attention.

We had camping trips to Kentucky, Cook's Forest, Ohiopyle State Park, and Ligonier. One year, we saved up and flew to Disney World when the girls were six and eight. When Opal got off the plane in Orlando, she thought the airport was the same as Pittsburgh and said, "I knew you were tricking us. We aren't in Florida. All we did was fly around and landed back at the same place." But when she walked outside and caught sight of the swaying palm trees, she knew it wasn't Pittsburgh.

Bertie was quiet and loved reading. Opal loved riding horses and playing the piano.

MaryLynn never entered my thoughts.

It was 1987 and that year, Mary Beth Whitehead broke a ten-thousand-dollar surrogacy agreement and fled the state with her newborn. The evening news covered the story, and the country became riveted on the question of surrogacy, parental rights, and adoption.

I was thirty-seven and outwardly the happy wife to Jimmy and mother of Bertie and Opal. By then, I'd worked in pediatrics for fifteen years, part-time in the evenings so the girls wouldn't be too long with a babysitter.

It was that year when I discovered, through a painful and somewhat frightening series of events, that my insides were riddled with endometriosis, a disorder in which bits of uterine-type tissue grow outside of the womb and bleed with menses.

In the emergency room where I landed with acute abdominal pain, my doctor said, "Treatment is fairly straightforward; remove the ovaries. We'll have to wait a bit till this inflammation recedes. Make an appointment for an office visit, and we'll get you set up for surgery."

Two weeks later, I sat on the paper-covered exam table, wearing a drape over my lap covering me from waist down.

Dr. O'Hare, a handsome man with graying dark hair, examined me and said, "Oophorectomy. Small operation. No large incision." Dr. O'Hare and I had worked together at the hospital for a decade, and I had confidence in his expertise.

"Just the ovaries? Not the uterus? I mean, what good is the uterus? I'm not having any more kids. If the ovaries have to come out, why not take everything? Then I wouldn't have to worry about uterine or cervical cancer." Mom's death put cancer up front in my fears.

Dr. O'Hare put the chart down on his desk. He stood for a moment looking down, hands in his pockets. The sleeves of his pristine lab coat had been laundered and pressed, making a sharp crease from shoulder to wrist. He faced me, eyebrows raised.

"Well, I don't know," he cocked his head, "Some women feel it's an important part of who they are."

"Nah," I leaned on my elbow and said matter-of-factly, "when you're in there, take all of it."

"You're sure? It means a bigger incision and, you know, a longer recovery time."

"Yeah, I'm sure."

"If that's what you want, and you have no questions about it, that's what we'll do."

I was an expert in separating emotions from my body, or so I thought. As a pediatric nurse, I was as detached as a scientist. Caring for burned children, kids in body casts, fevered screaming babies in isolation, I steeled myself and compartmentalized the suffering. I thought, I'm doing a job here. I refuse to let it get to me. And I separated myself from my parts. They were useless organs. Who cared?

The surgery was completed within the month. Afterward, Dr. O'Hare told me, "It was bad in there. Healthy ovaries have a tough fibrous capsule around them. But when I took yours out, they literally fell apart in my hand."

Ovaries are more than flesh and blood, I later discovered. They can be a container for deep emotions, holding what the conscious mind cannot.

～　～

I'd fully recovered from the hysterectomy. To the rest of the world, I was doing great. I'd been elected president of the garden club and I soon became skilled at designing and building stained glass lamps and windows. Over the years I made many pieces, but the first piece, my pink flowered shade, would remain my favorite. Renovating our 1940s house and working part-time at the hospital kept me busy. But on the inside, I denied the loss of what "*some women feel is an important part of who they are.*"

Sudden hormonal changes of surgical menopause are jarring. Instead of diminishing my estrogen over the course of years, it happened in hours. Estrogen therapy diminished the usual fatigue, hot flashes, lower metabolism, weight gain that comes with menopause. But an estrogen pill did not alter the impact of losing my womanhood: a loss that was compounded by my history.

～　～

I poured my energy into the house—renovating, decorating, beautifying—as if a beautiful home, if made exactly right, would make my life right. The newly remodeled kitchen had been a successful improvement. An alcove with an arched ceiling cozied around a built-in table and bench next to a window. One of my creations, an umbrella-shaped, stained-glass lamp, hung over the table. I'd chosen each piece of glass in large sheets. Using patterns, I cut the glass, wrapped each one with copper foil, and soldered them together. I took pride in the house renovations and enjoyed showing them off to my family and friends.

Late one afternoon when the girls were in their rooms after school, I covered quartered potatoes in a pot with salted water, placed the pot on the stove, and turned the burner to high. In the oven, roasting pork chops hissed and let off the herbal fragrance of rosemary, thyme, and parsley. Jimmy would be home soon, tired and stinky; his lunch pail would clank on the counter, and I'd throw out the gross banana peel and wrappings. I was a clone of my mother, waiting on my husband at day's end.

The second-floor reconstruction had been my most recent project. I had the stairway opened, raised the ceiling, installed a full bathroom, enlarged the bedrooms. The girls had chosen paint and wallpaper for their rooms. I wanted to invite them to take part in decorating their personal space in order to show respect and foster self-confidence.

From above me came a loud beat, then Robert Palmer's voice, the song "Simply Irresistible." A click, then slams and vibration with a door closing. Knocking, laughing. Robert and the whiplash sound reverberated down the stairway. Bang, laughing. Bang, louder laughter.

"Hey!" I yelled from the foot of the steps. The music changed to Bon Jovi, drums, guitars, "Your Love is Like Bad Medicine." Bang.

"Hey!" I roared and walked back to the kitchen. I turned down the flame under the potatoes, tilted the lid to keep it from bubbling over. Another bang, laughter.

At the top of the stairs, I found Bertie, perched on the bathroom door, one foot on the inside knob, the other on the outside knob—and holding onto the top of the door. Fourteen-years-old, narrow as a stick, blonde hair curled behind the ears, Bertie's foot pushed against the jam, propelling the door open and closed. Opal, too, was standing with socked feet on her bedroom doorknobs. Curly hair via "permanent wave" by Dolly the town hairdresser, eleven-year-old Opal held on tight, the pink shirt collar turned up around her neck. She'd pushed hard on the doorjamb. The fast-moving door slammed against the baseboard's springy wall protector. Her light hair flew back as she held on to the top of the swinging door, one socked foot on each doorknob.

"What on earth?" I shrieked. Inside, I seethed. The high-pitched Bon Jovi voice and guitar solo set my teeth tight. Over the racket, I yelled, "Turn down that music. You're shaking the windows."

I was standing right there, but they ignored me, as if I didn't exist.

Opal yelled out to Bertie, "Help! I don't know how to get down." Their faces red from laughing, the music booming, impenetrable joy, oblivious to me.

Bertie said, "Jump."

Down she went, landing on two feet, giggling.

I spun around and stomped down the steps.

Their raucous fun made me feel like a kid on the playground no one wanted. Life had become them and me, instead of us. Mom used to say, "A parent can't be a friend to their children. A parent is a parent, and the line should stay firm. Otherwise, you lose your authority." I didn't want to repeat my mother's parenting, but how to be a mom and still be a friend? Inside I still felt seventeen years old.

Bertie and Opal were separating from me. I was no longer number one in their eyes and felt as though I was disappearing. I knew it was healthy for them to become their own unique selves. But since their birth, I'd built my identity on being their mother. My other roles—wife, nurse, friend and sister—were cellophane compared to "mother of Bertie and Opal." My children completed me. They filled the empty space inside.

Other things were changing, too. Cracks had formed in my solid religious beliefs as the Vatican made proclamations. Women's head coverings in church were no longer required. Priests had been exclusively permitted to touch the Holy Eucharist, but that changed, too. Communion was no longer laid on the tongue but in the palm of the hand. Abstinence from meat on Fridays, fasting before taking communion, were changed, too. These used to be sins but were suddenly allowed. The Church taught me that dying with a sin on your soul meant suffering in Purgatory where you burned until your sins were cleansed.

But human beings were changing the rules, not God. I felt as though I'd been tricked. I ruminated on God and what I believed in the context of these changes. A friend who was many decades older than me and not Catholic, listened while I ranted about my shaken faith. I wanted someone to prove to me, with solid finality, that God is real. Her answer was simple: No one can do that.

The exodus from the Catholic Church began slowly but went only in one direction—forward. I kept attending Mass regardless of my dwindling devotion to the ritual. After a lifetime of instilling the Church's teachings into my children, I couldn't abandon what had been so important to me. I hoped they would develop a strong belief in God as a loving father, a protector, without the Catholic teachings around original sin and guilt. I found myself making subtle remarks about God's love; the Church's rules change over years, but God does not.

In the kitchen, the pork chops were nearly done; the knife sank easily into the boiling potatoes and religion was not on my mind. Placemats, napkins, cutlery, plates, butter, water, milk, canned green beans—on the table out on the screened porch, an enclosed space overlooking the flowers. My impatiens were twenty-nine inches tall (according to the tape measure), and so lush that the garden had no weeds. Every summer, after Memorial Day, I'd put in seedlings. By June's end, we had a fairytale collection of dainty pink, white, red, and violet flowers on thick greenery that lasted all summer till the first frost when they'd resemble a pile of cooked spinach.

At six o'clock by my watch Jimmy's truck pulled up to the house and turned into the garage. He'd taken off early that day to stop at the firing range.

It had been a year or two since Jimmy bought the gun. He had carried it through the doorway, a silver box with a handle like a big make-up case, holding it on the side away from me as he walked through the living room. His face said, "Don't pay any attention. I have something to hide."

Of course, I asked, "What do you have there?"

"Oh, it's something I got a good deal on." I pressed for an answer, and he confessed: it was a gun.

"What do you want that for?" I said in a snippy voice. "You already have a deer rifle."

"Target practice. There's a shooting range I found. You could come if you want."

"No, thank you. I don't like guns, remember? Mom would never allow a gun in the house growing up. I think it's because of Dad's temper. Guns are dangerous."

"Only if you don't know how to use them. I want to go rabbit hunting, and you can't shoot rabbits with a rifle. I'll keep it in the back of my closet. You'll never have to do anything with it."

"Well, I'm telling you right now. Don't expect me to cook a rabbit. That's disgusting."

"Fine with me."

At dinner, Jimmy and I faced each other from opposite ends, while Bertie and Opal sat side by side along the table's length, their faces still pink from laughter. Opal had beads of perspiration along her hairline. She made no sound, but her mirth radiated, nonetheless. Bertie, the less passionate of the two, reached for her milk, looking straight ahead through the screened window.

"How was your day?" I asked Jimmy. His blue, plaid, button-down shirt allowed a triangle of white tee shirt to show at the top. Jimmy "climbed ladder" (his expression) and sometimes went into crawl spaces to pull wire at his job. On warm days, he came in smelling of hours in the sun and an un-air-conditioned work van.

"Fine." He took a bite.

Jimmy was a handsome man: high-cheekbones, light blue eyes, thick light brown hair combed to one side. But I'd have given up his good looks for interesting conversation.

Jimmy and I filled our marriage with the girls. Even though I wanted a close friendship with him, we couldn't make it to the honesty and openness that best friends have. His interests were in activities and work, not in talking about feelings or life's mysteries, or hopes and dreams.

He turned to the girls. "Opal, honey?" *Honey* came out high pitched, his northwestern Pennsylvania accent strong, "How was *your* day?"

Bertie said, "I'm not eating the green beans."

I said, "Bertie, honestly, you're getting too old for this. Eat at least a few."

"What's a few?" Bertie challenged.

"I don't know. Three." This pork's tough, I thought. *What am I doing wrong?*

Opal answered Jimmy, "What are you asking *me* for? Why not Bertie?"

Bertie said, "*Laverne.* Don't be a dweeb."

Laverne was Bertie's nickname for Opal, pulled from a TV show, to aggravate Opal.

Opal said, "I'm *not* a dweeb. You're the dweeb." She elbowed Bertie in the ribs. Bertie poked her in the shoulder.

"Stop it, girls. No fighting at the table," I said. "You're in enough trouble as it is. Jimmy, I couldn't believe what they were doing. Swinging on the doorknobs."

Jimmy frowned, "What do you mean? How?"

I explained.

Jimmy laughed, saying to Opal, "Opie. How'd you get up there? Now, you two know that's not safe. You'll bust your noggin doing that." He wiped his plate with a slice of buttered bread. "Well. Back to work. The boss gave me an order when I was walking out. Overtime, you know. Can't turn down that time and a half."

The girls stood and picked up the dinner plates. I sat alone, elbow on the table, chin resting on palm.

"Go ahead," I said to them. "I'll clean up. You need to get your homework done. Leave the music off, will you?"

≫   ≪

I felt in-between my loved ones, not part of them. Out the kitchen window I watched my daughters play on the swings that hung by long ropes from the old tree, pushing off the trunk and making wide circles, laughing wildly.

Daytime routine for me was praying, exercise, housekeeping, yard work, baking, canning peaches, and freezing strawberries. I helped myself to the homemade zucchini bread, snickerdoodles, and apple pies I made for Jimmy and the girls.

In the evenings, if he wasn't working, Jimmy and I sat in front of the TV—usually tuned to sports, his favorite (anything but soccer). Soon his head laid back and his mouth slackened. After a while, I'd walk across the room and turn the dial, advance through the stations, each one making a click. Often, he'd wake up and protest with, "Hey, I was watching that."

Some nights I busied myself with a needle project. My pattern book lay at my side, guiding each stitch according to a grid.

I'd customized the picture to match our house, with tiny flowers at the entrance and a circle-top door. Over the home was a traditional prayer BLESS THIS HOUSE. My intention was to have it matted and framed for the wall over the fireplace. When I was on the final 'e' of "house," snoozing Jimmy startled with a knocking snort so fierce that my needle jumped out of the pinhole.

My mood sagged if I had idle time alone. Increasingly, I felt sad and tearful. I despised myself for the extra pounds I'd gained, for being an ingrate. I knew that I should have been happy. What was wrong with me? It seemed as if life was draining from me, and I could not understand why.

❧ 25 ❧

End-of-summer warmth surrounded our northeast Ohio village. Post-harvest fruit orchards and plowed fields lined the country roads with lopsided farmhouses in the distance. The community focused on attending high school football games with parents, grandparents, aunts, uncles, teachers, and kids pouring into the stands. Jimmy and I sat among the townspeople and watched the line of majorettes; Bertie was in the middle twirling, throwing and catching her baton. Long legs extending from the short skirt disappeared inside white tasseled boots. I envied her looks, her innocence, her youth.

The evening air was beginning to chill, bringing with it the feeling of another time in my life when, at sixteen, I watched my high school band and envied the majorettes. I missed out on the normal growing pains that most kids experience in high school. Those years with Gavin, when I excluded friends and school functions, I had learned my value was in my breasts, long legs, soft skin, and other parts of my body. My development had been stunted and, in a way, deformed, so that I became a woman physically, but remained a girl inside, frozen in time and confused.

Jimmy leaned forward, shouting at the opposite team. The metal bleachers were cold, and I shifted to tuck my coat under me. A friend sat on my other side, with her hands on her lap, intent on the football game. I noticed her flawless skin, red lacquered nails, and smooth cuticles. Mine were torn and my nails chipped. I slid them under my thighs.

Opal marched in the band. Sometimes off key, the kids flushed in their white uniforms and brimmed policeman-style hats with a straight-up feather above the brim, blasting "Louie, Louie." We searched the brass section and found our daughter where she marched among band members, blonde curls flopping below the rim of her hat. She held the massive trombone, twisting it side to side in sync with the rest of the band.

Simple life in Midwest America. This beautiful scene so full of smiling young faces and sounds in this safe place. As happened to me more and more lately, I felt grateful, but at the same time, oddly out of place. *How did I get here? How did this happen, this man next to me who was called my husband, and these girls and this place?* As if I'd somehow ridden on a time travel express from way-back-when to the present with very little in between.

I felt hollow inside, disconnected as if I had no place here. I began wishing I could disintegrate, as if I'd never existed. No sadness or funeral, or wondering *what happened?* Bertie and Opal would have a different woman as their mother. They would never have known me, and all would be well.

∾   ∾

There had not yet been a hard frost, and flowers remained although with yellowed leaves and sparse blooms. It was a September day when the kids were at school and Jimmy at work. Dandelions dotted the lawn beyond where I sat under the old shade tree in our backyard, the wide wooden swing under me. I dug my toes in the dirt, staring blankly at the row of swaying pines in the distance. My hands splayed on the seat. I dug in again, and the swing rose higher. Behind the trees, dry corn stalks clicked in the breeze, adding to the solitude I felt, along with the wind and the sound of the swing's chains clanking. My feet gouged the earth again and again, pushing the swing higher each time until it lurched at the highest arc and nearly tipped me off.

Anger scratched at my insides, wearing away whatever I had left. But instead of knowing it as anger, I felt only a maddening desire to *be gone*. Not away from the girls, but from myself. From life.

Later that afternoon in the empty silent house, I pulled the last hot roller from my hair and combed out the long waves. I brushed Maybelline onto my lashes, wishing I had larger eyes. Some people complimented me on their beautiful blue. But to me, my eyes were beady like Dad's.

I stepped into my uniform for the evening shift at the hospital, fixed my graduate nurse pin on the left side above my name tag, pushed the sharp point into the thin fabric, and pricked my skin. A tiny drop of blood seeped from my chest. I pressed a tissue to the nick, but the little dot showed up again. I mashed more toilet paper over the spot and wadded the rest in a ball.

When I lobbed the tissue toward the trash, a mere two feet away, it bounced on the rim and landed on the floor. *Of course.* I couldn't even make a basket. The mark dried and left only a red dot on the white uniform.

A train's whistle echoed from across the valley, one long blast, two short and one long again: *warning, warning*. Behind the house, came the chug chug of a harvester starting up, and its roar drowning out the train whistle. Brittle stalks of dried dent maize were caught by the harvester, leaving the damaged stalks scattered with dust floating behind the big machine. The scene was utterly familiar, yet I felt oddly separate. Something in me caved in.

There was no plan, but the urge ran over me, pulled me in like those corn stalks to the harvester. It was a natural next step. I turned back toward Jimmy's closet where that morning I'd hung his clean laundry.

The bi-fold doors banged and shimmied when I pulled. I felt in some way hypnotized and moved in slow motion, knelt and reached in, groped side to side, then leaned in further, past Jimmy's hunting boots. My knuckle banged against metal. I grabbed the steel handle and pulled. *How could it be so heavy?* Muscles straining, I lifted the silver case over boots.

I laid the box on the carpet and opened the latch. Beneath a thin gray pad, a pistol rested in its foam cradle. I sat back on the floor, mesmerized by the deadly design: mesh-patterned grip and comma-shaped trigger. I slipped my fingers under the gun and lifted. *Out of here, let me disappear.* I sat cross-legged on the floor, closed my eyes, elbows on knees and hands tented around my face. I let my breath out.

A long-forgotten memory surfaced from my student days in the emergency room. Thundering in the hallway. Commotion, shouting. A metal gurney bumped through the doorway. A woman, her head bloodied, dying gasps and gurgling deep in her throat, frantic nurses lifting the dusty cloud of hair. Someone yelled, "I found it." They pawed through the mess, searching the other side of her skull. A nurse's voice, "Where's the exit, where's the exit?"

I found that odd, them looking for an exit hole.

The field harvester went silent.

I opened my eyes. The silver gun struck me as modern art, strange and out of place in my lap. My spirit and body had split, but now in an instant those parts of me merged and cracked open. *Me on that gurney in the emergency room—in my white uniform covered with my insides—nurses shouting, "Where's the exit?"*

The nagging thoughts had become concrete.

I'm going crazy, like that poor woman.

Oh, Bertie and Opal, my sweet girls. There was no way out. No way to disappear, to disintegrate without hurting so many. I covered my face and sobbed. Maple leaves outside the bedroom window fretted with the wind, whispering *ssshhh.*

The gray cushion that had held the gun in its box expanded during the few minutes that I held the pistol. Funny how that happens. When something's gone, the world goes on, filling in the space.

I shoved the pistol back into the spongy cutout, but it didn't fit. I pressed hard, working the gun into its resting place, closed the lid, and dropped the case in its spot behind the hunting gear. I backed out from under the clothes, lifted the toppled boots, and lined them up, soldiers standing at attention: *shape up.*

Eye make-up smudged and red nosed, I dabbed my face clean. At the sink, I filled a glass with water and drank it down, then filled it again, trying to calm myself. On the long drive to the hospital, I resolved once more, as I had so many times, to stop my self-pity. I vowed to be happy, to be grateful for my good fortune of husband and children. I was ashamed of myself, a dramatic fool holding a gun.

That day when my footing went out from under me, I slid down a steep grade to the lowest point of my life. My parents' commands still spoke in my mind: *Stop that crying. You must have rocks in your head. What is the matter with you?*

❧ 26 ❧

1990

Things had to change if I were to survive. In the morning newspaper, there was an ad for "NONTRADITONAL STUDENTS." Youngstown State University invited applicants past the usual college age to consider returning. My nursing education had been through a diploma program, three years of nursing-related courses. I'd never been to a college session. It was a big step for me—cost-wise, time-wise and most importantly, smarts-wise. The next week, I mustered the nerve to call the admissions office.

I enrolled in one class; only one, in case I didn't like it.

❧   ❧

In the university's tiered auditorium a rotund, fiftyish man, who reminded me of the jolly singer Burl Ives, waited on the stage until the students settled, then he delicately placed the needle to a 33rpm record. Woodwinds, horns, and strings filled the hall as Beethoven's *Eroica* played. The professor stroked his beard, smiled up at us, and lifted the arm from the record. He introduced himself and the course, then reviewed the requirements and schedule.

It was my inaugural college class, art-music history, and I was beyond elated, envying everyone in the room for their bored-casual demeanor. I tried to stop looking around, to sit still and keep a somber expression. Kids in pairs or alone were scattered throughout. I wore my new outfit of pastel cotton pants and short hemmed T-shirt, hoping to blend in on my first day of school.

College held a mystique, a high place in my mind, and the fact that I had no degree was embarrassing. Each class was an event that I looked forward to. I devoured the homework, reading assignments and lectures. Impassioned, energized, alive. In time, my attraction to school morphed into a crush on the fat bearded gentleman in his brown three-piece suit standing on the stage. *The absurdity of it.* I was that enthralled.

❧   ❧

After the first quarter, I enrolled in several courses, one of which was anthropology, the study of human societies and their cultural development. I learned that primitive groups may have developed religion as a way to encourage social cohesion among groups. Humans gave natural events like drought or flood an explanation, that something outside of their control was at work. My Catholic upbringing and the tenets that I accepted as fact seemed narrow and story-like. The Vatican's wealth, the subjugation of women in the Church, and the Catholic way of teaching guilt were points I'd ignored and now stood out as proof of the flawed religion that I'd based my life on.

Anthropology class was the flip side of catechism and Catholic dogma. The evolution of life is scientific and rational. Australopithecus and homo sapiens. Not Adam and Eve. No original sin, no heaven or hell or purgatory.

I began reading about world religions. I tried the Universalist church but felt uncomfortable with the secular environment, as if it was a town meeting instead of a spiritual service. The contrast from where I'd spent my life was too great. I read about Buddhism and decided it made the most sense with peace and love as its core belief. I'd been taught that religion doesn't have to be logical. That's why we say that faith is a gift. I began thinking Christianity was made up, like a political platform, to control the populace.

After accumulating enough credits, I needed to declare a major. College tuition was getting expensive, so I took the credits offered for nurses' training and finished up with a bachelor's in nursing.

Jimmy questioned what I was after. "What's the point? You going to do something different? Be a supervisor or something? Seems like a waste of time to me." I didn't expect Jimmy to understand.

College became a new passion of mine, one more thing that Jimmy and I didn't have in common and couldn't talk about. I made the decision for us to start marriage counseling; maybe we could save what was left of our marriage. Jimmy and I sat in a small office, lit with table lamps. In the far corner, Jimmy slouched in a chair. The marriage counselor, named Aaron, moved about constantly, placing hands on the chair arms and adjusting himself in his seat, as if he suffered from hemorrhoids.

In a nasal but sincere voice, he said, "What brings you here tonight?"

I turned toward my husband, but he sat silent in the corner, like a background decoration, an office plant.

"Well, we don't have much to talk about, and we never do anything together. I mean, I make suggestions, but he doesn't want to," I said.

Aaron said, "That right, Jimmy? What do you say?"

Jimmy shrugged and *hmph-ed* dismissively. "I'm always at work. You know. How am I supposed to do anything else?"

"You don't have to work so much, Jimmy," I said. "We're able to make ends meet." I paid the bills, filed taxes, kept the budget, and told Jimmy whether or not we could afford a big purchase.

"I can't turn down the overtime," he said, still leaning back in his chair, in semi-darkness.

"Can you think of something you'd both enjoy and commit to it?"

"Okay, I guess I could do that," I said.

"Jimmy?" Aaron asked.

"Yeah."

"Jimmy, you seem to be out of this conversation. Would you like to sit closer?"

"Nah, I'm okay over here."

"You need to participate if anything is going to change."

The hour was strained with Aaron doing his utmost to get us working together in the same direction.

That evening on the drive home, I suggested we go to a movie, or on the weekend take a bike ride without the girls. He agreed, and we followed through. But in the end, we were still two very different people with mismatched interests. Without the kids, we had little to say.

Jimmy and I lived separate lives under the same roof. True to our beginnings, his interests were hunting, sports, and work. Mine had evolved from childcare to decorating to college. I had let go of the idea that we would ever be close. Our future seemed like it would be empty without the girls at home. I began thinking of life on my own.

One evening, after Bertie had been away at college for months, Opal and I sat together watching *Cheers* on TV. She curled up on the sofa under the afghan. I sat in the rocker nearby with a counted cross-stitch pattern book and a close weave material through which I slipped a needle and thread. On the sitcom, Sam and Diane sparred, laughed, and kissed. When the commercial came on, Opal turned toward me.

"Mom. I want to know, why don't you and Dad do anything together anymore?"

"Anything like what? We go to the football games."

"I'm talking about something like a date. You never do anything unless it's for Bertie or me. You hardly ever talk. Do you even like each other? It seems like you don't."

I put the cross stitch down. I'd thought of my future. I had no concrete plans and no idea of what my long-term goal was after college, but I felt alive again, invigorated by thought-provoking discussions with thought-provoking individuals. It was as if I had landed in a place where I should have been twenty years before. I assumed that Jimmy and I would divorce after Opal left home. Even so, Opal's question surprised me; every day I was cleaning and shopping, fixing meals, running the household, doing my job as mother and wife. But sixteen-year-old Opal noticed the missing something. I should have known.

Opal sat up and said, "Well? Say something, Mom. Why don't you and Dad go ahead and get divorced?"

"Oh, Opal. I can't do that. I have you, and we have a home here. I can't up and leave," I responded, aware that I'd skipped over protesting that Jimmy and I loved and enjoyed each other.

"Mom, if you stay here just for me, I will never forgive you."

"Opal, I won't leave as long as you are here."

"Mom, I'll come with you."

The following morning, after breakfast, I asked Jimmy to sit down at the kitchen table so we could talk. Jimmy and I never chatted. It was April and the sun had broken through for the first time in days. Opal was gone for the morning, to the mall with girlfriends. The refrigerator kicked on and hummed.

He said, "I have things to do. Whatever it is, go ahead and talk."

"Okay then, have it your way. You know how unhappy we are."

Jimmy started to speak, but I held up a hand, "Wait, let me talk. I've decided to find a place. I'm going to start looking today."

He said, "You think that's going to make you happy? What's wrong with *this* place?"

I crossed my arms and breathed a deep sigh. "We never do anything together. You are always unhappy and hardly ever home. I'm sick of trying to please you and trying to have a decent life here."

"I'm not unhappy," he said with arms flung out. "I was just *acting* that way."

"You weren't onboard with marriage counseling. Opal is noticing. I think it's best for every one of us if we live separately."

"You're nuts. I'm going up on the hill with the dogs." He turned and walked outside where his two beagles barked at the sight of him; he unlatched the gate to the dog pen and let them run free as he strode behind, the same as any ordinary Saturday morning.

And that was that. We did not talk more about it. He didn't try to stop me. Over the years, I'd found his passivity maddening. But no more. His dispassion made it easy for me to leave.

∽   ∽

Opal and I moved into a furnished apartment a few weeks into April in the town where I worked. The place was the second floor of an old house, two bedrooms with a kitchenette and living room, tall windows and worn furniture. It was a temporary living space until I had a chance to plan my next move.

I took clothes and toiletries as well as a few of my special things—including my favorite stained-glass table lamp, the first one I ever made, my symbol of mastery.

Opal transferred to the high school near our apartment. She was a social butterfly, president of her class and friends with everyone. I had trouble understanding how she could so easily change schools. Yet she insisted the move was what she wanted.

Opal was rarely at the apartment, working after school or connecting with her pals from her old school. I wanted to go easy on her since it had to be harder for her than me. She wouldn't tell me how she was doing with the changes, instead saying that she was fine, and she was glad we moved.

About a month after I'd moved out, the doorbell rang. There had been no visitors and I wondered who it could possibly be. I crept down the wooden stairs and glanced out the screen door, wary of who rang. It was Jimmy. He stood like a tall statue placed on the other side of the screen. I opened the door, he stepped in, and I threw my arms around him and broke down. I cried for separating, for the humiliation I'd wrought on Jimmy, for our children, and for the loss of my happily ever after. He held me until I stopped.

Then he said, "Come on home now."

"Jimmy, I can't. You know we aren't happy. It's no good for us."

"You have somebody else," he said as if there could be only one explanation. As if the only reason a woman would leave her husband was for another man.

"No, there is no one else. I swear," I said. I couldn't look at him. "I just can't come home," I said.

Moving out of our house had been one of the hardest things I'd ever done, tearing apart the fabric that I'd worked so hard to weave. My reaction at seeing him must have been terribly confusing for Jimmy. But neither of us knew the load of mixed-up hurt, anger, resentment, and grief that stayed buried inside me.

"I'm sorry, Jimmy. I can't come home." I looked at him then and for the first time, saw tears in his eyes. He said nothing more but turned and walked outside, down the porch steps onto the sidewalk and away.

June arrived. School had ended and Opal took off to stay with her dad as usual for the weekend. The second-floor apartment lacked air conditioning; poor ventilation intensified the musty smell of used furniture and old carpet.

When I wasn't working or studying, my time was spent alone, walking the cracked sidewalks under old trees. There was no television. I read and studied for my course, sat at the small Formica table and stared mindlessly out the window, confused about what I wanted and what my next step would be.

I wondered about Opal's social life and how she would manage during the summer when her friends lived three towns away. She spent less and less time at the apartment with me.

The phone rang on Sunday evening late, long after sunset. It was Opal.

"Mom? I just called to tell you something."

"Okay," I said, holding my breath at this odd greeting.

"I'm moving back home, Mom. Only for the summer."

"But, I thought you wanted to live here. I mean, that was what you said, right?"

"Mom, I said I'd move with you. And I did. Now I'm going to stay here with Dad for the summer."

Certainly, I couldn't demand that she keep her promise to live with me. I couldn't blame her. I wanted to be home, too. But home without Jimmy. Now I was stuck in this small place while my husband and daughter lived without me, in the home I'd worked so hard to create. The whole plan to move out, to move Opal away from her school friends with whom she'd grown up, had been too impulsive. I'd given in to her pressure, likely because I wanted her, and me, to be happy. But it was a misguided fantasy. I should have stayed put until Opal graduated, as I'd planned.

Within two days, I met with an attorney, a dark-haired middle-aged man sitting behind a wide wooden desk with a tilt-back chair. The well-kept office, his demeanor, and the glowing recommendation I'd gotten from a friend buoyed my confidence.

"Here's the situation," I said and explained my separation, my intent to divorce, and my daughter's change of plans. "What can I do?"

He leaned forward and thumped his index finger on the desk. "Now you listen to me," he said, "you pack up your things, and get back home."

My breath stuck. I said, "What? Go back and live with Jimmy? I don't want to. Can't I make him leave somehow?"

"Right now, that isn't a consideration. He could file a restraining order on you. Since your daughter is home now with him, Jimmy can charge you with abandonment, keep you out of the house. You need to get back there. This afternoon. Not tomorrow. Now."

I felt like a chastised child who, two months before, had dragged my bedroom into the woods and now had to return to the house. At the apartment, I gathered up my belongings and drove the fifteen miles home, reversing the progress that took so long to reach. Once at the house, I struggled with the few cardboard boxes in the back seat, setting them on the ground. The stained-glass pull-chains clanked against the lightbulbs as I lifted the lamp from the back seat. This creation was a part of me, an old friend sharing my defeat. I set the lamp on the porch table and went back for a cardboard box, then through the French doors into the living room. Jimmy stood between me and the rest of the house with his arms at his sides. I walked past him.

"I'm not here for us. I'm here for Opal."

For me, the marriage was over. I had tried too hard for too long, and now I was ready to move on. I filed for divorce while we still lived together as a separated couple. We shared a bed and kept on as we had been, together for Opal's school functions. A pall settled over the house as if a dying person lay in a bedroom down the hall, with the death rattle that precedes the end.

The changes I wrought in the family and in myself led me to another decision: it was time to tell Bertie and Opal about their half-sister. The girls had become attractive young women with big, permed blonde hair that fell past their shoulders; both were slender and taller than me by several inches.

"Girls, would you come to the living room? I want to talk to you."

Bertie called out from the screened porch, "Now? Do I have to come right now? I want to finish this chapter."

"Yes, if you don't mind. This will take only a few minutes." I checked my face in the mirror, eyebrows up, smiling, then frowning deeply. Finally, I relaxed into a natural resting face.

Bertie walked in and sighed, looking away, her head at a tilt. Opal arrived sleepy-eyed and frowned. This reminded me of years before, when I'd called them together about a new plan for chores.

"Yeah, Mom," Bertie said with a blank expression.

"I'm here. What?" Opal said, clearly having been interrupted.

"What's going on?" Bertie said.

I pushed my hair behind my ears and straightened my T-shirt. "Sit down, will you?"

"Sit down? That's not good. Mom, is this bad news? What's wrong?" Bertie asked.

"Nothing's wrong. And there is no bad news. I need to tell you something. Bertie, would you mind sitting on the couch next to Opal?"

The telephone rang loud enough to be heard anywhere in the house. I startled, and Opal bounded for it.

"Don't answer it."

"Mom!" Opal said, "that might be Angie about tonight."

"She'll call back. This will only take a few minutes." Midnight jumped onto Opal's lap and rubbed against her arm.

"So," my voice quivered.

Bertie and Opal sat side by side, facing me, deadpan.

Since telling Corrine so many years ago, I'd confessed to counselors, to boyfriends, to best friends. And every time, whether it was a professional or someone else, the response was as matter of fact as if I were describing a long-ago sprained ankle. But these were my children. And my first child did not belong to their father. I braced myself for their reactions. I was changing, and little by little, they were seeing a new person, not their doting mother, but a woman with ambition, striving to succeed outside of the home, becoming independent, making big decisions without their father. And now this.

"This is hard. But I need to tell you. It's something about me that might feel shocking. When I was eighteen, before I met your dad, I got pregnant. And," I hesitated, took a deep breath, cleared my throat, "I didn't get married."

"What? You got *pregnant*?" Opal said.

"I was still in nursing school, and my boyfriend didn't want to get married." I stopped. No one spoke, but after a moment, I said, "I had the baby, a little girl. She was put up for adoption."

Midnight had settled on Opal's lap; now asleep, he began snoring, a sound that usually made us laugh.

They kept staring in silence. Finally, Bertie looked away, then back to me. Her puzzled, almost angry expression surprised me. I was back in my parents' living room. But no one jumped up or screamed. Bertie began jittering her leg, like preparing for a high jump. She frowned. "So, where is she now? And what about us?"

Opal said, "Yeah, Mom. Where is she?"

"I don't know where she is. I probably will never know. The adoption was secret, and the records are hidden for a very long time. But I wanted to tell you. You two will always be my daughters. Nothing changes between us."

"Does Dad know about this? What does he say?"

"Yes, he knows. I told him when we first met. It didn't make any difference to him. We never really talked about it."

Opal said, "So, we don't have to do anything?"

"No, nothing. I wanted to tell you."

Their faces reflected how I felt: sad, confused about how this news fit with us. My daughters acted disinterested—or maybe uncomfortable and too young to meet me on an adult level. Maybe it would have been better had I waited a year or two after I finally divorced Jimmy. Maybe there were too many changes.

☞ 27 ☜

1991

Work had always been a diversion from my anxiety at home and these days, it was the grounding I needed. At the community hospital, I worked part-time in the pediatric ward. I also took on extra day shifts in the adult wing where patients were admitted for surgery and returned for post-op care.

The two wards were so different: working in the adult wing felt like driving a semi-truck down the LA freeway; sitting with a sick child in the pediatric ward felt more like an easy trip on a back-country lane. But at the end of the day, I felt tired and glad that work gave me a break from my worries.

The day shift nurses were a tight-knit group and even though they occasionally invited me to go out after work, I never accepted. It wasn't as if we had nothing in common. Small talk came easy to me, but to go out, even for a burger and a beer, would have been to cross some imaginary line that even I didn't understand.

The surgical wing consisted of a long hallway of semi-private rooms with the nurses' station at one end. Sunlight streamed through east windows onto the gleaming floor as I padded past laundry bins and breakfast carts, my soft-soled shoes silent. A ruckus broke out from the nurses' station. *Dr. Fryman. He's at it again.*

I watched from down the hall as Dr. Fryman stood talking to a nursing assistant. He said, "What do you mean 'we forgot to write down the output?' *Dammit, this is important.* What kind of a place is this? I can't do surgery and have people willy-nilly throwing away the day's output. This is ridiculous."

The nursing assistant cowered. "I'm sorry, it wasn't me who dumped it; the night shift orderly forgot."

He lowered his voice, "Call the supervisor, will you please?" The ward secretary promptly placed a page. Dr. Fryman paced back and forth, arm over his head, then hand to his forehead, red faced. His rants didn't bother me. The pressured speech reminded me of my childhood, where I'd learned to stay out of Dad's way. Fryman expected quality care, and there was nothing wrong with that.

Paul Fryman had blue eyes and hair that curled at the collar, like a modified hippie. Sometimes he wore it slicked back, mostly when he had office hours and dressed up in a suit and tie, reminding me of a boy playing at being a grown-up. I noticed his mannerisms, the way he touched his moustache, sucked in his lip when deep in thought, the way he hurried through the desk area and down the hall with long strides. While the medical staff were mostly business-like, stiff and proper, keeping their eyes down, Fryman had a loose gracefulness like a dancer, and genuine connection with patients. I found Dr. Fryman attractive, and even though I was still married to Jimmy, our separation made it easy for me to take notice of other men.

Over the next weeks, I looked forward to Paul Fryman's morning rounds. I'd listen for the elevator doors and feel a little rush as he came around the desk.

One morning, as Dr. Fryman finished his notes at the nurses' station, I tried to squeeze behind his chair just as he stood and knocked into me.

"Oops, sorry," I said as I jumped out of the way.

"No, no," he said half smiling, "my fault. I'm sorry." He stood, stepped back, and motioned for me to go ahead.

"Hey, nice tie," I said. He wore well-made suits, probably bought in New York or on the West Coast. The necktie was a work of art with vibrant red flowers, like a summer garden. Other doctors dressed in white shirts and striped ties.

He looked down, as if surprised at what lay against his chest. "What? This?" He looked amused. "This old thing? Thanks."

"Did you get that around here? It looks like a designer."

He faced me then. "As a matter of fact, I did not. I bought this in San Francisco last time I visited my parents." His startling light blue eyes flashed behind wire-rim glasses; the slightest hint of aftershave drifted from him. Dr. Fryman glanced at his watch. "Oh, hey, I have to get going. Office hours started ten minutes ago. See ya."

The other nurses looked at each other. Mary Ellen, the charge nurse, cleared her throat and rolled her eyes. Heat flushed into my face, and with that, I escaped to the empty medicine room to prepare nine o'clock meds. Even though I was separated from Jimmy, in my heart I'd been a faithful, rule-following wife. This flirting was new for me—and unbelievably exciting.

One Saturday, after the doctors had visited their post-ops, I checked the clock: time for coffee break. It was a slow day, without scheduled admissions or surgeries. Mary Ellen looked up, dark circles under her eyes that gave her a raccoon-ish look. With a hint of sarcasm, she said, "Dr. Fryman was already in. Too bad you missed him."

"Right, lucky for me," I said, acting like one of the girls.

I figured everyone was talking. People knew each other's business at the community hospital. Sometimes I purposely avoided Dr. Fryman when he arrived on the floor, halfway convincing myself I didn't care about him, and hoping the gossip mongers would assume the flirting had ended.

One day as I rounded the corner to an empty hallway, my mind on a paper due for anthropology class, I saw Dr. Fryman leaning against the wall, pager in hand. White hair and mustache, tall, slender, dressed in his weekend blue denim shirt and low-riding, black jeans.

He looked up, grinned, and said, "Hi, Cathy. Hey, do you have a minute?"

"Sure," I said, expecting he wanted to add a verbal order for his patient.

He shifted from one foot to the other. "You've been rather friendly lately."

This caught me by surprise. I had no clever comeback; my mouth hung open.

"You know, I think you're really nice," he said like a schoolboy, not a ranting surgeon.

I blinked a few times, laughed and fidgeted with the notes in my pocket.

"I'd like to call you sometime. Would that be okay?"

It would be fine with me, I thought. *But maybe my husband wouldn't think so. Or my daughter still at home.*

"I suppose you could, but there's two problems." I glanced at the hall behind me, then took my shift notes from the uniform pocket and unfolded it. In case someone came by, I wanted it to look like I was only getting notes from Dr. Fryman.

"Okay, shoot." He clipped the pager onto his belt and folded his arms across his chest. We were about the same age, but suddenly, I was a teenager again.

Craig, who was the orderly on my unit, rounded the corner on his way to the elevator, his bulky frame leaning with his fast walk. His eyes flicked in my direction, I ticked up my chin and looked at my notes. Ordinarily we said hello, but he didn't that time, and neither did I. He rushed to the elevator, punched the button, then took the stairway instead. I waited until the door closed behind him.

"Well, I'm married," I said. "And I hear you are, too."

He held up an index finger, "Correction! I'm separated."

"That's interesting," I looked away again. "So am I."

"All right then. What's the next problem?"

"I'm taking university classes. I don't have much free time."

"You're going to school? That's wonderful," he said. "Listen, I can help you study."

Uncomfortable now, I shrugged. "I'm flattered but not sure if it's a good idea. People around here like to talk."

"So? Let them talk."

God, I wanted to give him my number. My heart raced. I twisted and looked behind me once more.

"So, what do you say?"

"Thanks, but honestly, I don't know. I'll think about it."

I used to believe my marriage vow, "till death do us part," was a true and solid promise. When Jimmy refused to continue with counseling, I went alone. The corner I'd backed myself into gave me only one choice: stay married, but separated emotionally, until I died. But the therapist disagreed. He convinced me that a marriage vow is not black and white, not "do or die." Through lengthy discussion, I realized I didn't need to die inside, or for real. A marriage vow, he told me, doesn't trump a life.

Then one day, Paul Fryman invited me to his place for dinner, and I accepted.

❧   ❧

The lane to his home was situated between two small, one-story houses on the main drag. I turned onto the dirt road like he told me, creeping over potholes and rocks until the main road disappeared behind me. Rain had been forecast for weeks but never showed up, and the unpaved lane of powdery dirt and rocks was imprinted by tire tread. A round house with a pointed roof appeared, a dusty gray Toyota pickup truck parked next to the rudimentary entryway. I straightened the folders and textbooks (my alibi for being *out*) but left them on the seat. The steering wheel was cool under my tapping fingers. I scratched my neck. The unusual and humble house baffled me. *This is his home?* Dr. Fryman was an unusual, unpretentious man, like his house. He was an outsider, a misfit, like me.

Weeds and an abandoned garden lay beyond. I unbuckled the seatbelt, as the screen door opened and Dr. Fryman stepped out. "You made it," he called from the doorway, beaming.

"That's some lane you have. My Honda could've disappeared in some of those holes," I said as I made my way to the door.

"I know. No one wants to drive over that mess. Back here, I don't even have to lock the doors. No one comes down that lane. I don't even have a mailbox."

He welcomed me in and said, "I'm glad you came. Do you like wine?"

"I do, but I don't drink it much. It gives me a headache."

"What kind do you drink?" he said, as the corkscrew wound in the bottle he held.

"Oh, I don't know. White zinfandel."

He chuckled. "That's because you drink shit-wine. I'll give you the good stuff. Drink enough water, and you won't get any headache. Trust me."

He worked the corkscrew like a professional, the bottle held against his side.

I crossed my arms, disbelieving where I was and what I was doing. I had to get past this part. Me, a married Catholic woman with two children, a rule follower.

A plate of brie, baguette, and a saucer of olive oil and balsamic vinegar sat on the bar next to a pair of crystal stemmed glasses. The cork came out with a loud pop. Paul slid a glass toward him, and the liquid glugged into it. He said, "Here you go. Try this and see what you think."

Paul grew up in New York, had lived in Switzerland and France. I grew up in Pittsburgh and fixed my family meatloaf and pork chops. Besides MD behind his name, Paul had a degree in restaurant management and was expert in culinary arts. That evening, he introduced me to the intricacies of vino. We hit it off right away: like two old friends we shared stories over dinner. He made me laugh, looked at me, listened to me, offered ideas, asked questions. Outside, a long-awaited rain came down, washing the powdery dirt from droopy leaves and dusty dry grass. The air freshened with the aroma of green and moist earth.

I left that evening and drove home where my husband still lived. But Paul and I kept on seeing each other, while the divorces processed.

Paul taught me to zest a lemon, eat an artichoke, suck raw oysters from the shell. I marveled at his cutting and chopping skills and said as much. He grinned, held up the knife, and said, "I'm a surgeon, what do you expect?" With Paul, I learned to appreciate fine wine, fine food, and classy restaurants. Wine should be room temperature; if chilled, the flavor is diminished. Never drink it out of a thick glass, as the taste will be dulled; let it breathe before pouring; leftover wine is wasted wine. If a bottle is open, it needs to be finished. The best isn't the most expensive; it's the one that is first drained while other open bottles wait. I learned to be a wine snob, favoring domestic Silver Oak cabernet and French Chateau Haut Brion.

Paul made every date special, cooking gourmet beef or lamb or pasta and tasty side dishes of fresh vegetables. I marveled at his artistic and expert approach to cooking. He looked more at ease in the kitchen than anywhere else. The knives were sharp as razors, and he never cut himself carving meat or very thin slices of peppers and onions.

Early in our relationship, after a dinner of pepper-crusted filet mignon and baby greens salad, crusty bread, a bottle of cabernet from his wine cellar with a second bottle open and half-full glasses on the counter, we danced to Chris Isaak's dreamy voice and the heady guitar of "Wicked Game."

Intoxicating. The rich food, fine French Cabernet, delight in working side by side in the kitchen, laughing and talking. He liked me. *Oh God.* Paul's gentle hands touching my hair softly, we held each other and moved as one in time to the music.

He stopped, lifted our glasses, took a sip, and passed the other to me. I rolled the liquid back over my tongue, sensing the years of waiting within an old oak barrel, the flavors changing over my taste buds, dense and smoky, hint of chocolate. I relaxed and melted into him.

He took my glass and set both down, then held me again, stepping side to side. Without forethought, I whispered, "Paul, I need to tell you something." I laid my head on his shoulder.

Our reflection in the sliding glass doors showed a couple embracing, moving in sync. His arms around me, his Lagerfeld scent, he nuzzled my neck.

"Hmmm?" he asked, "What is it? Wait. I bet I know." He stepped back, laughing, and laid his hands on my shoulders. "You and Jimmy are getting back together," he joked.

"No. Listen, this is important."

"Okay. I'm sorry. What is it? Jesus, you look so serious." He pulled me close, stopped laughing, then let go and studied my face. "What do you want to tell me?"

Suddenly it seemed stupid, the secret completely from left field. "No, never mind."

"What? You can't do that. Come on, tell me what you wanted to say."

"Okay. But don't look at me." He held me again, moved to the music. "Before I was married, I had a baby."

"Oh." He rocked back.

I said nothing more until he asked, "Then what happened?"

My words seemed flat, unimportant, and irrelevant. I looked up to the can light attached to a rafter above us. My eighteen-year-old self surfaced again, unaware that I sought forgiveness, acceptance, and empathy, but more than anything, a chance to grieve.

"I gave her up for adoption."

He pulled me to him again and laid my head on his shoulder, silent for a moment. "That's it?" he asked.

"What do you mean?" I wasn't sure if he wanted a more dramatic answer, like . . . *what?*

"That's what you wanted to tell me? That's all of it?" He reached for the wine glasses. "Why'd you tell me? Am I supposed to do something?"

"I wanted to tell you. So, you'd know all of me. My inside self."

The deep inside-self, my unseen hurt that shadowed me and colored my life with an off-black tone.

Paul held me tenderly, then said, "Let's open another bottle and do a taste test, see which one we like best."

As if nothing powerful had transpired between us, I left the subject alone, reached for the glass and sipped. "Mmm, this one is earthy," I said.

"You've got it! Goot'door," he said, "taste of the earth."

First Jimmy, now Paul. Both with similar reactions. I had no inkling as to what I wanted or needed or why the telling felt so important. After each time, the space between 'telling' in the present, and the 'knowing' of the past tense felt entirely impotent. I had no way of sharing the reel that ran in my head and the ache that never left my chest.

∾   ∽

We had been seeing one another for a few months, when Paul called with a proposal. "Listen, I have a medical conference coming up in San Francisco. I want you to come, too. It'll be great," he said, "We can drive up the coast. You can meet my parents."

"How cool," I said, "but I can't afford a trip like that."

"I know, but that's not a problem. I'll pay for everything."

"No way. I can't have you covering the whole trip."

"Why not?" he asked. "I have the money. You don't. What's money if not freedom to enjoy life? I want you with me. I want to pay so that you can go. So, why not?"

"I can't, Paul. It doesn't seem right."

"You need to get over that. There's nothing wrong with helping you out. You'll love the food in California. I'll have to be in the sessions, but we'll take extra time at the end. Come on; it'll be fun."

I told him I'd think about it. After we said goodbye, I mulled the invitation over, stewing about the imbalance in our relationship. Paul was not my husband or relative and had no obligation to me. I had done nothing to earn my way. *Wouldn't I be a free-loader? Didn't women do this all the time? Is that what it meant to be sophisticated?* He was insisting. I wanted to go. I didn't care about doing the right thing. I wanted to live. I called him back the next day and accepted. Plans were made. I told Jimmy I was going to a medical conference in California.

〜 〜

The generous, cushy seats were beyond comfortable from Ohio to San Francisco. Linen napkins. A flight attendant for us alone. Free this, free that. I hardly knew how to act. I'd moved from the cornfields to first-class.

In California, I learned about Alice Waters, owner of Chez Panisse, and the organic, locally-grown food movement, worlds away from canned vegetables I served in Ohio. In Monterey, Paul introduced me to his childhood friend. Matthew had the good looks of an Irish boy with black hair and blue eyes, a charming smile. At a large storage unit, Matthew rolled up the door, revealing an extensive wine collection, part of his high-end catering business. We agreed to meet Matthew and his date downtown the next evening at Union Square's Postrio, owned by the iconic chef, Wolfgang Puck.

I wore my little black dress and heels. Paul said, "Look at you," and took my hand, twirled me around. "Stunning," he said and kissed me. I felt beautiful for the first time since high school, when Gavin's face lit up as I walked down the stairs in my yellow chiffon prom gown.

The maître d' escorted the four of us to a curved art-deco stairway that overlooked the lavish restaurant. Original artwork graced the walls, and enormous, curvy, disc-type lights hung from the high ceiling; large urns filled with flowering plants graced the columns throughout the restaurant. I stood at the top of the stairs, enchanted, disbelieving. *Me, a part of this glamourous extravagant life.*

Matthew had delivered a case of reds that afternoon. The waiter set up glasses by the dozen and brought several bottles at a time, even though there were only four of us. Baskets of warm bread along with olive oil and balsamic vinegar waited. We each tasted the first two bottles, cleansing the palate before the next taste.

I couldn't make up my mind between two entrées, so Paul ordered both. We finished the first course with four open bottles at the table and a waiter standing by to keep our glasses full. Soon, I needed to use the restroom. I leaned forward, rose to my feet, and discovered my woozy head and loose muscles, nearly losing my balance. Immediately a handsome young man in a white shirt with rolled-up sleeves appeared at my side. He pulled my chair back, offered a hand, then his arm, and walked with me to the ladies' room. The waiter politely reassured me, "It's nothing. I often escort young ladies to the powder room. Please. Do not give it a second thought."

If I weren't so drunk, I would've died of embarrassment.

❧   ❦

I met his parents and siblings in California. They were calm and polite. His father was a chief executive of a big corporation and his mother an artist. They were well-to-do people with high expectations of their eldest son. Paul and I spent hours talking about his and my upbringing, about our demanding and disapproving fathers, our insecurities, successes, and failures. We had serious discussions about the meaning of our time on earth, what happens after death. He believed that death is the end of us, nothing occurs afterward. Religion is a myth; there is no higher power.

For the first time in my forty-some years, I skipped Mass, rationalizing that my varied shifts made it impossible. Little by little, I attended less often, until after a year, I stopped going altogether, becoming increasingly cynical. I agreed with Paul that religious congregations seemed like sheep blindly following a good salesman.

We skied the Rocky Mountains of Telluride, Colorado and skated on rollerblades beneath waving palms along the strand of Santa Barbara's coast. We shared a love for music and ran like teenagers to the outdoor arena in our tie-dye shirts to dance with the Grateful Dead. At the Indianapolis five hundred, I thrilled at the movie-like scene. Laughter filled our time, like kids without a care in the world.

Everything was an adventure. In Los Angeles, where he attended yet another medical conference, we had a free day. Up at first light, Paul made coffee while I lazed in bed, still disbelieving where I was. He appeared beside me in the hotel robe with two mugs of aromatic wake-up joe, set mine down next to me, and climbed under the covers.

"Hey, you want to go to Disneyland today?" he asked.

I laughed, knowing the park's immensity and very high entrance fee. Jimmy and I had saved for a year before we took Bertie and Opal to Florida's Disney World.

"Listen, you like roller coasters, right?"

I yawned and stretched, "Sure, I do. Loved them for my whole life."

"Okay then, get dressed. We're going to Disney," he chortled and hopped out of bed and into the shower.

At the entrance to the park, he bought tickets, grabbed my hand, and ran with me to the first roller coaster. We waited in line and finally made it to the platform about six people back. When the gate opened for the next group of riders, someone in front of us grabbed the first car. Paul held me back. "We'll wait. We want the first seat, right?"

As much as I thrilled on roller coasters, I never had the nerve or desire to ride up front. There was something about the middle, feeling safety in the cushion of humans around me. Paul held my hand firmly in his and rushed to the first car with nothing in front except the greasy track.

"Ohhh," I moaned. "I don't know about this."

"You'll be fine," he laughed, leaning over the front. "It'll be great."

The train lurched and rolled forward on the level track, picking up speed as it met the hill, jerking like an old lumber truck climbing a mountain. The sun shone hot in the California blue sky at the highest curve. The train hesitated above the world, away from the smell of grilled meat, crowded walkways, and Mickey Mouse. My heart choked in my throat. My arms braced straight ahead; bloodless knuckles gripped the bar as I stared at the hot oily rails a few feet away. I imagined the seatbelt ripping off, me flying forward onto the track.

The cars started down the next drop, picked up speed, combining gravitational pull and mechanical power; air pressed against my chest, my breath replaced by panic. Paul took hold of my wrist and pulled straight up, my hand off the bar for a second, then back down, Paul hollering, "Face your fear, sweet pea, face your fear."

That day was emblematic of my time with Paul. Wild and crazy, disorienting, and thrilling.

The fear I faced was living as a dead person, without joy or hope. I wanted to be a part of the wider world and understand life.

❧ 29 ❧

1993

My divorce finalized, then Paul's. We celebrated with a bottle of Silver Oak and appetizers at Ken Stewart's, the chichi restaurant back in Ohio. The waiter stood near, ready to refill our glasses.

Paul toasted to the next phase of life. "You know what this means, sweet pea?" he said.

"I do. And if you want to know the truth, it scares me to death," I said.

"Oh yeah? Why's that?" he asked.

"Last year, when I saw the marriage counselor, he warned me against a new romance. He said it's super common. People grab onto someone, some diversion or something. It gets them through a rough time. He called it a transitional relationship. They don't usually work out." I straightened my skirt and slipped out of my heels.

"Listen, Cathy. I'm not interested in getting married. I'm not good at commitment," Paul said, meeting my eyes as he sipped.

"No news there. You like to keep everything off-kilter," I said, "makes you feel in control." I took the last bite of beef tenderloin and white truffles.

Paul looked away. His hand still holding the fork, he faced me again, "I think you're exactly right. How did you know that?"

"We're not that different, Paul. We're both afraid."

Head tilted, he said with a huff, "Afraid? What are you talking about? Of what?"

"I don't know. Being hurt? We're two needy people, only it comes out in opposite ways. You can't get too close. I can't get close enough."

I was in love with Paul but could not imagine being married to him. I wanted things to remain the same but more relaxed.

Our lives settled into relative stability. At the house, on days off, we worked in the yard, filled the bird feeder, and enjoyed red birds, canaries, and robins.

Paul thrived on stimulation. There was a constant frenzy around him. Making love was no longer illicit, and with that freedom, it drifted into the realm of the familiar. He became occasionally unavailable, taking trips without me. More and more, his mood grew somber, sometimes irritable. I accused him of being afraid of real intimacy. He said, "Yeah, so?"

Two years into our relationship, at Christmastime, Paul left town on a ski trip without me, no apology or explanation. I simply was not invited. Wintertime desolate, cold inside and out, alone in my silent house, I struggled to fill my time that had been so full of Paul. I knew him well enough to understand that our closeness had become too much. I wanted a grown-up partner, but he was not able to tolerate the boredom that inevitably comes with normalcy. His ski trip wasn't the first time he had left me behind, only to reappear later without apology. The time had come to take care of myself, to let Paul go, yet I obsessed over what he was doing without me, until anger agitated me into action. He was out of town, and never locked his doors.

Untouched, two-day-old snow covered the lane ahead of me. I parked the car and sat for a moment, uncertain of what to do next. The solid gray sky, stillness, lack of footprints, and Paul's closed-up place matched the way I felt. I had come to the empty house many times in the past, delighted when Paul's pickup raced down the lane to the front yard. He'd bound up the steps, burst through the entryway, and wrap his arm around my waist, lean me back, kiss me, and say, "Sweet pea, I'm home," then change his clothes—and, back in the kitchen, he would pull out pans and give ideas for dinner, tick off orders, open the wine, tear up greens, blacken red peppers. We seldom discussed patient cases but shared our day's events, talked about the stock market or our next trip.

As usual, the unlocked door allowed easy entry. Silent inside and dark, lit only by the dreary winter light beyond the sliding doors. The tidy kitchen counters waited for Paul to come back and electrify the space. In the orderly living room, a stack of travel magazines fanned out on the coffee table included one featuring Bali, Indonesia: a trip we had kicked around for a future adventure. The empty bird feeder swayed listlessly as a cardinal flew off, searching for seed somewhere else.

I shed my coat and approached a door off the main room. Sometimes Paul locked it, but that day it was open. I padded downstairs to a temperature-controlled storage area lit by a bare bulb. The chain clicked as I pulled, and the light exposed racks lining the walls, filled with bottles. The Burgundy with sloped shoulders, Bordeaux with high shoulders, green bottles with chardonnay, pinot grigio.

Nervousness spurred me ahead as I darted from bottle to bottle until, at last, I found our favorite, the Chateau Haut Brion. I pulled it from the rack, turned off the light, and hustled up the steps, slipping into my coat and out the door to my car. I drove home with the bottle on the seat next to me. Instead of my usual guilty feeling, I felt something new. A sense of satisfied revenge.

Back to my own empty house, I set the bottle on the kitchen counter, planning to have it with my dinner. But after hanging up my coat and slipping into my house shoes, I opened the bottle, poured the aged, fermented juice into a stemmed glass, rolled it on my tongue, and swallowed. It had cooled in the car and lacked the burst of complexity it usually offered. I recalled Paul briefly heating cool wine in the microwave and I warmed it to room temperature. But its exquisite taste had disappeared along with the intoxicating affair. I lifted the bottle, tilted it to the kitchen sink, and poured it down the drain.

Paul called after he returned and apologized for taking off without explanation. We talked about our relationship. I confessed to stealing the Chateau Haut Brion.

He spoke quietly, "You shouldn't have done that. It doesn't belong to you. You have no right."

"I know. I'm sorry. I'll replace it."

"Forget it," he said. "You can't afford it."

I did replace the bottle, but it cost more than a day's wages.

We saw each other at work after that, and we had dinner together once. There was no doubt in my mind that our romance was over. Paul opened the world for me and sent me on my way. I was crazy about him, while at the same time, I guessed we wouldn't last. I felt below his standards, although he never said so. My heart was broken, but I couldn't blame him; I knew what I was getting into from the start.

☙ ❧

I finished my bachelor's degree. I graduated with high honors, but in my mind, it was a negligible accomplishment. I'd been a nurse for twenty years. *Of course, I should graduate summa cum laude,* and I did. Most importantly, I was a college graduate. I was certified through Cleveland Clinic as a wound-ostomy nurse. I sold the house, got a new job in my specialty, and rented an apartment two-hours from the little village where Bertie and Opal had grown up.

One evening after dinner in my second-floor apartment, I sat on my yellow beanbag chair, trying to read the daily newspaper and get used to my new normal. The words blurred and made no sense; tears came again as they often did, over nothing in particular. It had been a rough day at work. I flipped on the TV, looking for mindless entertainment.

The outside entry door buzzer blasted, giving me a start. No one visited except Opal, and she was away at Kent State. I went to the intercom, pressed the button, "Yes? Who is it?"

A quiet voice answered, but I couldn't understand. "Sorry. Who is it? Speak up."

"Paul. It's Paul."

I took a deep breath and buzzed the door open. I hadn't seen nor heard from Paul in well over a month. I had no energy to deal with him. I'd said what I needed to say, and he'd said everything I needed to hear. His footsteps grew closer. My sloppy, coffee-stained sweatshirt and unwashed hair didn't bother me. There was nothing to lose and nothing to gain.

At two soft raps, I unlocked the deadbolt and opened the door to a disheveled man in a worn-out sheepskin coat. Paul shifted from one foot to the other, his expression as tired as I felt.

"You don't look so good," I said. "Don't just stand there. Come in." He stepped in and closed the door. I did not ask him to sit down.

"What do you want?"

"I don't know. I guess I wanted to see your place."

I turned my hand out and swept my arm like a maître d'. "Okay. Here it is. There's a loft up there and one bedroom. As you can see, this is the kitchen." My place had little to show.

We faced each other, he by the door and me several feet away. I did not move toward him. "You like your new job?" he asked.

"Yeah, it's okay. Home health isn't a dream job, but it's work," I said and looked at the floor, arms folded.

"I guess I better get going," he said and turned to leave.

We said no more. I never saw Paul after that. He was a shooting star, blindingly brilliant in every way, hyperactive and thrilling. I missed him, the high he gave me, the way he looked at me, the things he taught me, the fun we had. With Paul, I was always off-kilter, never sure what would happen next.

I needed solid ground under me, unwilling to stand by at the ready according to his whim.

For me, the games were over.

∽   ∽

In 1999, I finished the Kent State University master's program as an advanced practice nurse, working in home health. That summer, I turned fifty. The number felt so ridiculously old, over the hill, and into life's latter half. I was living alone, drinking alone, hating myself, crying over what, I didn't know. That old familiar sadness sat like a weight on my chest; finally, I admitted that I was depressed and decided that it was genetic, something inherited from my dramatic parents. After all, I had nothing to cry about.

I needed a change. I decided to take back my maiden name, and at the same time, I changed the spelling of my first name from Catherine to Cathryn, taking the first half of my name and joining it with the last half of Mom's (Kathryn). I told my friends that I wanted to be called Cathryn. No more Cathy Vogeley. I had begun taking an antidepressant and resolved to stop drinking, stop crying over nothing.

Bertie had relocated to San Francisco and Opal became a hair stylist at a high-end salon in Charleston, South Carolina.

The home health industry was on the decline with new insurance and Medicare restrictions, resulting in the layoff of nursing specialists like me. A wound product development company in Portland, Oregon offered me a consulting position. My romance with the west, born from the years with Paul, had never left me.

Before accepting the job, I visited Portland. It was August, when every day was clear with pure fresh air and snow-covered Mount Hood and Mount Saint Helen as a backdrop. The natural beauty of the Columbia gorge with hiking trails above the river, spectacular Multnomah Falls, and the desert beyond the Cascades; the Oregon coast and its monoliths, air saturated with negative ions, fog hovering in the canyons. I'd never known anything like it. I packed up, hired a moving van, and by October, drove across the country to start anew.

This is it, I thought, my chance to be happy.

I arrived in Portland, as the rainy season began. Back east, fall was beautiful, and winters were often bright with sunlit snow. But in Portland, the shortened days and constant rain challenged my energy and dragged me down. I wondered how anywhere on earth could have rain every day. Yet, I never considered returning to Ohio. I fell back to drinking too much, hating myself, crying alone, angry at crying over nothing.

In time, I accepted a position in the clinic of a large hospital system, caring for my own list of patients and consulting for satellite clinics, writing treatment orders and prescriptions. Diabetics with nonhealing foot ulcers. Cancer patients who needed supportive care to control pain and odor. Amputees whose incisions hadn't healed. Many cases took months to heal, but we did not give up. I had a sense of purpose and felt dedicated to my patients who needed me.

Part III

Part III

ॐ *30* ॐ

Charlie and I met in 2007 over coffee at Denny's through a dating website. It was my first date since signing up on the site. Gone was the pretense of who I wanted to be and how I might convince a man that I was a confident, sexy, desirable woman. Charlie lost his wife to cancer and felt ready to begin again. We were both after the same thing: a long-term relationship.

He arrived at the restaurant early and I got there a few minutes late, not wanting to appear anxious. A few women sat at a table with empty sandwich plates and coffee in hands. Over by the window, a man relaxed in a booth, his swollen red face in startling contrast to the blue-purple Eddie Bauer jacket he wore. He made eye contact and smiled, eyebrows up. Crusty lesions moved with his grin.

"Charlie?" I said. I was accustomed to disfigurement, but not ready to be caretaking in a romantic relationship.

He'd been using a powerful cream for precancerous skin growths. He didn't think I'd mind, since I was a wound specialist. I found this exceedingly bold and wondered why he failed to warn me ahead of time. He said he didn't think it was important; then admitted it was sort of a test.

He wasn't the charismatic type I'd dated in the past. His demeanor seemed a bit flat. But I decided he was okay, not terribly enthusiastic, but he seemed quite intelligent and completely unconcerned with appearances, which appealed to me.

After coffee as I opened my car door to leave, he hollered from three parking spaces away, "Do you like stuffed peppers?" He invited me over to his place for a supper of stuffed peppers; I accepted. He lived in a 1902 house where he worked continuously at remodeling. There were a number of unfinished projects, like a dining room floor that appeared to be made from centuries-old planks through which the basement light shone. His two dogs, a golden retriever and an Irish setter, were his substitute for children he never had. I found him endearing, and my interest grew.

Charlie had retired from engineering two years before. He had a lot of time on his hands and offered to help me with a few household projects. A week after he hung my weighted pendulum wall clock, he offered to hang my bird feeder on the small patio's wooden fence, but evening traffic could be hours between his house and mine. I gave him a house key to save him from the highway gridlock. That evening after work, I threw my purse on the counter and opened the patio doors for fresh air, where I discovered a professionally crafted wooden hanger with rounded edges, sanded smooth, and lightly stained. Nothing else in the house had been altered. *A man who keeps his word, offers to help, and does so expertly.*

Back in the kitchen, I reached in the freezer for a TV dinner. Charlie had slipped a Reese's cup inside. It felt like a quiet hug, a gentle recognition of my favorite things. And he kept going that way, keeping track of what I liked and didn't. Years before, I would have considered Charlie's attentiveness as a sign of weakness. I'd preferred unavailable men most of my life and had twisted myself up trying to make them love me.

Charlie was tall and broad shouldered with a smile that made dimples in his cheeks. His mind was logical and astonishingly smart in problem-solving matters. He was nice looking, once his skin cleared up. We met often for dinner, both of us enjoyed wine, too much, but neither cared.

Over email he invited me to Maui where he'd made reservations even before we met. We had been seeing each other a short while and I wasn't having the familiar angst over whether or not he liked me. I'd never had a relationship that didn't start with sex. My feelings toward him were of curiosity and appreciation more than attraction. I hesitated to say yes and instead said I'd think about it.

The next day at work was so busy that I barely thought about Charlie's offer. But that evening, when again an email arrived, I knew I needed to give him an answer. Scuba diving was Charlie's favorite sport having served in the Navy for six years; he'd been all over the world and dove often. He wanted to show me what life is like underwater. I'd never been diving but loved the water and swimming. Maui was a huge draw. He insisted that we'd have separate bedrooms, that he was going and would rather not go alone.

I told him I was having cold feet. Being seen in a bathing suit in broad daylight made me cringe. He emailed back asking what my hesitation was about. The old me would never have admitted the real reason. But I was different now and wrote back explaining my embarrassment at the idea of people on a dive boat seeing me. The next day he sent an email with the suggestion that he would hire a boat just for us with a dive master. There was no belittling, only sensitivity, accommodation. I accepted his offer.

Charlie's old house was his life project which seemed like a part of him. The fenced property was about six acres with a view of the valley and Mount Hood. Beyond the living room bay window was a patch of emerald grass which, in certain light, took my breath away with its vibrant color, a product of winter's rain. White birch trees flanked a bubbler that drew goldfinches and scarlet tanagers.

It was on that lawn two years later that we married. A young violinist played classical music and a catering crew took over the kitchen. The guests were friends and close family, about thirty people total. An officiant, a woman who I found through friends, led the ceremony. My brothers walked me down the aisle between guests seated on white wooden folding chairs. Charlie was handsome in a traditional tux; me in a full-length gown with an elegant beaded bodice. Opal styled my hair swept up, tastefully adorned with fresh flowers. My wedding, exactly as I wanted, and without any pain in my stomach.

Charlie showed me what real love is between a man and a woman. He made no judgements, no comments one way or another about my appearance, and no demands. He was the first partner with whom I felt at ease and accepted for myself. Charlie knew about MaryLynn. He had no children, and while he understood that giving up a child was traumatic, to him it was in the distant past and wasn't relevant to our life together.

❧ *31* ❧

2013

By all accounts, I'd succeeded in life. As a wound specialist, my expertise was in demand. My work was satisfying, and I loved helping people. I published an article in a medical journal, lectured at national conferences.

The meetings were always out of town and meant a welcome break from the day-to-day routine. I felt proud of myself at the conferences, seeing my name up on a screen and answering questions with ease. But once they were over, clinic days began again, and my days resumed their usual routine.

Outwardly my life seemed to be at peace, but inside I felt overwhelmed with anxiety and agitated energy that were part of my everyday life. Simple decisions like what to wear or have for dinner took an hour of deliberation. I was snippy and short with Charlie. Every evening, after several glasses of wine, I dragged myself to bed. Then I lay awake for hours. I was more high-strung than ever, worrying about the most mundane things: getting lost, gaining a pound, whether I had enough money. I was starting to feel the weight of my past that I'd been running from.

One day, friends from work agreed to meet for dinner downtown. On my way to the restaurant, traffic was slower than usual. The guy ahead of me left three car lengths between the car in front, rudely blocking my way to the exit ramp. *If only he'd move up.* I got extremely irritated, honked, but he did not budge. I honked again and sped around him onto the shoulder and the exit. His horn blasted, and a voice shouted something obscene.

I finally arrived at the restaurant, stressed and angry. *Everyone's here but me.*

"Hey, how's everyone?" I hung my bag on the chair and took the only remaining seat out on the aisle. I was immediately bumped by a passerby. My anger flared again. *I need a drink. A menu. Water.*

My friends looked up from their menus; each greeted me with hellos and smiles. I didn't smile back. I huffed and said, "I hate this place. The wait staff is lazy. Where's my water?"

Soon the waiter reached around me and placed a glass of ice water next to my plate. I felt my shoulders relax and lifted the lemon water to my mouth. A hand touched my shoulder. Instantly, I jerked so hard the water splashed up in my face, dripped from my nose, and wet my blouse. "Oh, for Pete's sake," I shouted.

My friends laughed. "Jump much?"

"I am so touchy," I said. The linen napkin soaked up the puddle on my lap. "I'm always spilling and tripping. Shit. Let's not talk about it. What's for dinner?"

❧　　　❧

I began exploring stress reduction methods, including ways of building self-esteem. I joined a meditation group, where I tried to sit still for forty-five minutes, eyes closed, taking deep breaths. I peeked through slits in my eyelids, checking my watch, glancing at the others sitting still as stones, and wondered if I could ever be like them. The second try was more successful as I felt familiar, a little more relaxed.

Afterward, the group of a dozen or so men and women sipped warm tea and spoke quietly to one another. An older man with kind eyes said, "Hello, I'm Jack. Nice to see you. How are you feeling about the sessions?"

I smiled and said, "I'm beginning to relax. This is my second visit. I like it, I guess. Since I'm so antsy, it's really difficult for me to sit still and quiet my mind."

Jack put his hand on my shoulder, looked for a moment into my eyes. He said, "You are enough."

The words hit me like a laser, piercing right to my core. Tears welled up as I tried to catch my breath; embarrassed, I nodded and squeaked out, "Thank you."

I made my way to the door, taking my time to appear casual, and walked out. I never went back, but I never forgot his words to me, a total stranger. I still wonder how he knew my weakness, and I marvel at the chance he took by saying such an intimate thing.

I tried one remedy after another. I took yoga classes which helped to ease my muscle pain. I bought an expensive device that covered my eyes and emitted blue dots of light while a calming voice spoke of love and gentleness. Massage, acupuncture, aerobics, antidepressants, inspirational reading, adult coloring books. Some treatments worked better than others, but none of them stayed with me for longer than the treatment itself.

After months of remedies that didn't work, Charlie and I planned a two-week vacation to Bryce Canyon and Zion. I wanted to get away, and I was happy and eager to get on the road. The seventeen-foot, egg-shaped trailer was lightweight and perfect for the steep climbs up the mountains of Utah. The night before, we'd begun packing the truck, and now we moved food from the house into the camper. Inside, beige carpet covered the curved walls. Small white cabinets rimmed the upper area, a tiny stove and refrigerator for the kitchen, table with benches, and bathroom so small you had to back into it.

I kept the door shut to keep the bugs out while I stocked the trailer. Loaded cardboard boxes took up every bit of level surface. I grabbed a bag of almonds and a box of raisin bran, stuffing them in an open shelf. Dave's Killer Bread, peanut butter, donut holes, and canned goods squeezed and stacked in any open storage space. The trailer was hot and stuffy; I wiped my forearm against my brow. National Park tour books, maps, binoculars, sunscreen, and bug spray. I stuck them in a cubby hole between other nonfood items.

The boxes were finally empty, ready for the third and final round of tossing the empties on the driveway and picking up full ones. My left hand awkwardly held three boxes, and with the other, I pushed the flat, thumb-sized, plastic door latch to exit the trailer. But this time, the latch didn't budge. *Must've hit the lock.* I flipped the tiny lever under the catch. Again, the stubborn latch wouldn't give. I dropped the boxes behind me and tried again.

The air was close now and hotter with the sun overhead. I crouched, looking under the handle at the lock lever. No indicator for "locked" or "unlocked." I flipped it the other way, wondering if I'd locked it or unlocked it. I pulled the latch, down, up, in, out. The door did not release. The pile of empty boxes jabbed my bare legs. I tried again, pushing the door handle.

I felt trapped, suffocating, sweating, out of control.

I kicked and banged on the door, screaming, "Charlie, Charlie, I can't get out, help!" Hearing myself added to the panic.

Then, a click, and the door opened. Fresh air and light flooded in as I saw Charlie, head tilted to one side, mouth down, then smiling, eyebrows up.

"You okay?"

"The door was stuck, and I couldn't open it. I was trapped," I cried, throwing up my arms. It was completely out of character for me to panic. I remembered a few years ago at one of my conferences, I'd gotten trapped in an elevator with a fellow attendee. She grabbed onto the elevator's bumpers, wide eyed with panic. "I can't be in here like this," she said. "It's too small, I can't breathe," she continued between shallow inhales. "The cables might snap." She began crying.

"No, it's okay," I told her and rested a hand delicately on her shoulder. "These things happen. It's nothing. There are alarms to let people know about this. And loads of safety backup measures."

In truth, I'd never been in a stuck elevator before and found it exciting, knowing I'd have a good story to tell.

"Try taking a really deep breath," I said as I dug through my purse for a tissue packet. "Here you go," I handed her the packet as she inhaled a long breath. "That's it, keep going, nice and slow." She dabbed her eyes and nose.

About ten minutes later, after a loud thump the elevator moved and delivered us to our floor.

Now, one locked door had set me into near hysteria. Something was very wrong with me. I was falling apart at a time when I should have been more together than ever. My reaction brought up the voice, the angry adult voice from the old days, that questioned my behavior, demanded that I stop being so dramatic.

ଛ ✧

One afternoon, many months after that Zion trip, I sat in a room full of clinicians for a lecture on post-traumatic stress disorder, an important subject for my patient population at the Veterans Affairs Medical Center. A tall slender woman named Rebecca introduced herself as a social worker specializing in PTSD. I listened intently and suddenly realized that the symptoms listed on the screen next to Rebecca described *me:* easily startled, irritability, depression, hyper-vigilance, sleeplessness, and nightmares. I didn't know how or why I would fit the profile of post-traumatic stress. I'd never been in the armed forces, had never been shot at or held hostage or any of the horrendous events that resulted in PTSD. But there was something about that list that made me want to explore my own distress.

Rebecca made casual eye contact and smiled when I introduced myself. I explained how much the subject resonated with me and that I'd be interested in a referral.

She listened and answered thoughtfully, offering suggestions for how to find a counselor. She told me that she had a practice outside the Veterans Affairs Medical Center. Rebecca impressed me as articulate, compassionate, professional, knowledgeable. In those few moments, I knew she was the one to help me and asked if I might see her for therapy, even though we worked in the same health system. We had never met before that day, nor had I ever heard her name. Yet, I wondered if it would be unprofessional of me to see another clinician in the hospital where I worked. She agreed to take me on, saying it was up to me to decide, according to my comfort level.

❧   ❧

In Portland, unless the calendar shows July or August or September, most likely it's raining.

It was early spring, the day of my first appointment on the east side of the city where I seldom traveled, and the rain had slowed. The familiar pain knotted in my stomach and got worse when I realized I missed the building. I made an illegal U-turn and finally parked on a side street near the address. The clouds broke apart, and the sunlight bounced off the puddles. I stepped carefully around and over the water, trying to keep my brown silk trousers from dragging in it. I wanted to get to the appointment on time, anxious to begin. Recognizing the symptoms of PTSD, a possible diagnosis for my distress, gave me hope for treatment; probably managed in steps, possibly more work on self-acceptance or something like that, maybe special readings or meetings with other PTSD sufferers.

Rebecca's private practice was located in an old house on Portland's east side, where store fronts needed updating, sidewalks needed leveling, and store signs needed repair. A narrow stairway led up to a small hall with a kitchen to the right, and three tall doors to the left, each one closed. The floor creaked.

The only light in the hall came from a window in the kitchen where I heard running water and the sound of a dish on metal.

Rebecca greeted me and offered me a seat on the couch. The muscles in my neck cramped; my mouth went dry. I was embarrassed and uncomfortable. Rebecca and I worked in the same hospital system. I had a façade to protect. I wanted to bolt out of there, away from Rebecca with her large round eyes, away from her calm and intelligence, away from the blue couch where I sat facing the door. Who was I kidding? I'd never experienced war. Or faced a weapon. I didn't have PTSD. This was only me acting again, trying to get some attention.

Years before, in marriage counseling with Jimmy, I knew what I wanted. Jimmy and I were incompatible. I hoped for tools and guidance that might show us common ground and save the marriage. I don't recall any discomfort or embarrassment.

Rebecca said, "So, what can I do for you?"

I said, "I don't know what to talk about." I paused, waiting for her to speak. She didn't. I breathed deep and kept my eyes on the door. "I can't sleep. I walk from room to room searching for something, but I don't know what. I'm jumpy and always worried about the smallest things. I'm short with Charlie. God bless him, he's patient with me anyway."

She waited for me to continue. After a minute, she said in a breezy voice, "You can start wherever you want. Tell me about yourself."

I took a deep inhale. On the coffee table in front of me lay a half dozen smooth stones of different colors. I knew them as worry stones, meant to soothe anxiety.

"Let's see. I guess I should tell you that I had a baby when I was nineteen. I wasn't married, and you know, back then it was a big deal. But that's all over with. I don't need to talk about that."

"Okay," Rebecca said. Silence followed.

"My dad. And my mother. But mostly my dad . . ."

Now I was a parody of a patient in therapy where a woman sits on a couch blabbing on and on about her childhood. I imagined my parents rolling their eyes, shaking their heads, tsking.

"My parents were definitely good people. They didn't drink or run around. They were always there."

"Okay," Rebecca said, "sounds good so far."

"My father . . ." I started, then stopped, unsure. It seemed that any words I had would come out flat. I began again, and as I heard myself talk, I felt embarrassed, rather petty. Rebecca gave me her full attention without any facial reaction, only a barely noticeable nod. She waited while I looked around, adjusted my coat that lay at my side. I breathed in hard.

"There were too many of us. My parents shouldn't have had kids, but they had five and the first three of us were eighteen months apart. My sister was colicky. Corrine. She's eighteen months older than me. Mom said she screamed constantly and never slept. I can't imagine what it must have been like for her and Dad."

"What was it like for you?" Rebecca asked.

In my chest and throat there was an uncomfortable tightening.

"Oh, this is stupid." I'd begun crying, barely able to believe how I was acting. Mom would have told me what's past is past. Forget about it.

"Stupid is not a word I would have used," Rebecca said. "Go on."

"In the afternoons, before dinner, Corrine and I'd watch the *Lone Ranger*. We'd lay on our bellies next to each other. There'd be this vibration in the floor, and we'd know Dad was home and he was mad. Before I could shut off the TV, he'd be there and kick me hard in my side. He'd scream at us to get up and help Mom in the kitchen. But the kitchen was tiny, and Mom would throw a fit if we got in the way. When I cried, he yelled at me to shut up and do something useful. I remember trying to figure out what that meant. I knew it wasn't watching TV. And it wasn't playing outside. So, often, I snuck into my bedroom and pretended to do homework. The thing was, I never knew when or what would set him off. It was like I lived in a minefield, always sick at my stomach. I spent a lot of time in bed throwing up."

How can I sit here bashing my parents? They were good people.

"Our furniture was stuff from Dad's family, everything was too big for the rooms. We always ate dinner together in the dining room on a table covered with a cotton tablecloth. You had to squeeze between the furniture and slip sideways to sit down. They had a buffet cabinet, a mahogany table and chairs that seated eight, a china cabinet with glass doors, a sewing machine and a bird cage in that room. My chair was right up against the china cabinet with glass doors. If my chair touched the cabinet when I slid out sideways, the crystal stemware tinkled and Mom hollered at me.

"I was the clumsy one. If anyone knocked over milk, it was me and then it was like a bomb exploded. The main thing was to protect the table, which was always covered with thick felt pads. They were in two pieces that met in the middle of the table. The big deal was over whether or not milk had seeped between the pads and touched the table. Complete chaos and a lot of yelling. It's ironic, you know? After my parents passed away, the furniture was donated. That table. My god. The wood was pristine.

"Growing up, every single night we sat at the dining room table for an hour or more, most of it in fear of stepping on a raw nerve or knocking something over. What a price we paid for that perfect table."

The used tissues lay in a small pile on the table in front of me. I rested back and heaved-in a deep sigh. Rebecca had tilted her head and tightened her lips in an expression that said, "I'm sorry."

I went on. "I can still hear the sickening thud of Corrine's shoulder on the bathroom tile and when she hit the cast iron bathtub—the ring it made. The next day, Mom saw our bruises. She said, 'My goodness, what happened to you?'"

Rebecca said, "What did you tell her?"

"Oh, we didn't tell her the truth. But we were so scared, we told her we fell.

"Mom was always home when he raged but never did anything about it. I figured it was my own fault. I needed to keep quiet and hide when Dad came in from work. But then lots of time would go by, and nothing would happen. Dad would be calm, and I'd relax and it would happen again, kaboom, out of nowhere." I checked my watch, a few more minutes till the hour was up.

"He didn't talk to us kids except to yell at us for being stupid or in the way. He never laughed out loud. I never heard him, or Mom, say 'I love you.' I know this sounds whiney, and I'm sorry. I hate making you listen to this stuff."

"You have a right to be hurt and angry."

I squeezed my eyes and held my head with the heels of my hands. Words stopped in my throat and felt like a hand clenching my windpipe. A minute went by. I wiped my eyes and nose, moaning in frustration. "I hate this. I can't talk anymore. Can you talk now?"

"Sure. It sounds like you have a lot bottled up in there. I know it's hard to talk about. How do you feel about coming back? Do you want to?"

Rebecca waited.

I still had my head in my hands, unable to answer.

She added, "It's completely up to you. We can wait to schedule the next session, maybe go home and see how you feel." She bent forward, with elbows to her thighs.

I took a drink from my water bottle. She reminded me of a grasshopper in the weeds, listening.

The more Rebecca talked about postponing therapy, the more I wanted to return. Even though hearing myself tell private things about my parents was agonizing, and I felt wrung out.

I was a starving child who had been offered the first bite of food in decades. The idea of not continuing was like watching that food slowly move away.

"Do you feel like you want to come back?"

"Yes," I sniffed. "I think I need to."

I'd never felt good at being helped. It was my job to assess and order treatment. *I* didn't get assessed and treated. But there was something in the telling. My child-self spoke, and hearing my voice recount the terrors gave it perspective.

32

I waited at the computer in the wound clinic while Karen, my practical nurse assistant, brought Mr. G to the room. She broke out in a boisterous laugh at something our patient said. Karen's white-blonde hair and clear, rosy complexion matched her Scandinavian parentage. She positioned the wheelchair next to the oversized recliner, airily chatting as she went, and assisted Mr. G to the chair. On the last visit, Mr. G's wound that began as a large diabetic ulcer had been showing signs of healing.

My right foot splayed to one side, I balanced on the small, backless stool that easily rolled from computer to patient. Karen used bandage scissors to remove the ace wrap and leg dressings. Mr. G's leg wounds were gently cleansed with sterile saline. Karen used a disposable tape marked in millimeters and centimeters. The measurements were smaller than at the last visit. She aimed the wound camera close and clicked, the photograph to be loaded onto the clinical record. My notes included response to treatment, minor changes in the plan of care, and an order for his next appointment. I expected Mr. G's leg wounds to be fully healed in about a month and a half.

Mr. G questioned the rationale for his treatment. My response was something I'd explained so often that it rolled off my tongue without much thought. A student hovered inside the door and asked more questions about the wound healing process and why Mr. G's wound couldn't simply be stitched closed.

I answered, "Normal overlapping stages of wound healing occur naturally, and it's important to allow these stages. But healing can be stalled for a number of reasons, creating a chronic wound. If a chronic wound is sutured closed, it will fester and fall apart. An open wound must be allowed to grow tiny buds of flesh—moist, red, healthy, granulation tissue. From the wound edges, epithelial cells migrate over the granular surface and form a delicate scaffold for what will become multilayered skin." The student nodded as if taking in every word.

Mr. G said, "Go on, continue with what you were saying."

"Well, when the wound is protected, you know, protected with the right amount of moisture, oxygen, warmth, and cleanliness, the cells form skin. A scar develops. It's never as strong as the original flesh. But it's healed."

After Mr. G left, I completed my note in his electronic record. Karen refreshed the room, replenishing supplies and wiping down the exam chair.

I stared at the computer screen, fingers resting on the keyboard. Rebecca and I had been meeting for a few weeks by then, and I'd begun feeling impatient with my progress, hoping to move through treatment, get it over with as soon as possible.

The keys clicked in email. *Hi Rebecca, I'm wondering about my treatment. Can you give me an estimation of how long my therapy will take? Do you think six weeks is about right?*

I expected that she had developed a plan of care with a predictable outcome, including a time frame to healing. Rebecca replied that she didn't know how long it would take. There are no parameters by which healing can be predicted.

Unlike Mr. G's, mine was not a wound that would mend with six weeks of medicated topicals, behavior modification, or antibiotics.

Every time I drove to my therapy appointment, I'd think of what to say: *I can't sleep and when I do, the nightmares wake me up . . . I gained another pound . . . I can't stay away from chocolate.* But when the door closed, I ended up talking through the dark memories of my past and the quaking girl I'd been. Eventually, the well-sealed memories of my secret pregnancy bubbled to the surface. I still felt the shame and guilt from forty-five years ago.

After each session, I didn't feel lighter, or change my eating and drinking habits. I asked Rebecca, "What's supposed to happen? This is torture."

Rebecca told me, "You're letting the memories out a little at a time. In this safe space where you can tell it. And in time, you will heal. Try to be patient with yourself."

❧ ❧

For the next year, I sat on that blue couch. Mom's extreme moods, screaming tirades, how I was unplanned, unwanted, always in the way, the middle of five children, third kid in three years. How I wished I'd never been born. I talked about the Catholic Church, guilt, and fear. About trying to be good, about always feeling sick to my stomach. I described my depression in the eighties when I contemplated suicide and how I still thought about death frequently. That I welcomed the idea of driving off a bridge to get it over with. Each week, I talked and cried for the allotted hour, wrote a check, and made an appointment for the next visit.

Rebecca faced me across the room, sitting next to a tall window. Behind her on an expansive bookshelf was a white china vase, next to sprigs of lavender tied with a blue ribbon. I described the appointment at Edward's with Mom and Dad, and how uncomfortable I'd been.

"My cousin Edward, the priest who suggested I go to Roselia to have my baby, had my parents leave the room. I didn't know what to expect, but once the door closed and he sat down again, he said, "Cathy, did you want to get pregnant?"

Rebecca's mouth tightened.

"I wanted to scream, 'No.' It was insulting, as if I wanted to trap Gavin, force him into marriage. I've thought about that question a lot over the years. It's something that bothers me. I wonder, deep down, did I?"

"And, did you?" Rebecca asked.

"I didn't think so. But I remember a few times when Gavin drove his father's old, banged-up station wagon. I pretended we were poor and happy, making a life on our own. I can still see that car, white with red interior, split seats and a radio missing the knob. I loved thinking it was the future, and we were married. Gavin wouldn't talk about marriage. Always said it's too soon to think about it. We had to finish school. I should have seen it, that he wouldn't want to be married. I didn't want to be pregnant, that's for sure. But maybe deep down, I wouldn't have minded. I was programmed to marry, have children, decorate a home and take care of a family. Who knows, maybe it was a subconscious wish. He and I both knew what we were doing. I guess it's different for the guy."

"How so?" Rebecca asked.

"Guys can walk away. Girls can't."

"Some guys don't walk away."

"True. Most people get married. Something that still bothers me is what happened about two weeks after Gavin walked out. That whole time, Mom harped about Gavin and his family, how unworthy he was, and that he didn't love me. If he did, he never would have left that day. She said, 'and what about his parents? What kind of people they must be to have allowed this? He's ambitious. He doesn't care about you.'"

Rebecca tucked one leg under her. In the hallway, a door opened, and shuffling sounds were followed by the click of a door closing. Footsteps faded down the wooden stairway. "What happened after two weeks?"

I sipped the last of my water and set the bottle on the coffee table. "I was babysitting for a neighbor, and Gavin called. He sounded extra quiet, and I remember the conversation was pretty one-sided. After two weeks, my plans had been set in motion . . . going to Roselia. Anyway, Gavin said he figured out a way we could get married. He said he found a job on the railroad and could take classes at night."

Rebecca's eyebrows raised. She scooted down a little in the chair.

"By that time, Mom's badgering had been drummed into me so hard that I didn't want to marry him. I told Gavin, 'You didn't want to marry me two weeks ago, and I don't want to marry you now.' He didn't try to sell the idea. When I said no, he almost seemed glad, like he needed to make the offer, late as it was. He asked me what I was going to do. I said, 'I'm going to have the baby and put it up for adoption.' He said, 'Huh. Sounds like you've made up your mind.' We said goodbye, and he didn't call after that."

"Do you regret turning him down?"

"In some ways, I guess. I mean, I think we were too young to be raising a kid, whether or not we could afford it. There would have been resentment on both sides. But honestly, I wish I'd had the maturity to talk it over, give it time, and drop the drama. I blame Mom for that. But at the time, I thought I was being strong. It did give me a little sense of pride to say no."

With Rebecca's help, I gained perspective about Gavin. I understood his culpability was no greater or lesser than my own. He decided to leave but changed his mind and tried to do the right thing. I assumed responsibility for the pregnancy, including the possibility that, as Edward suggested, I wanted to be pregnant. But I realized I was not to blame, nor was I a victim.

At another session, I began, "It was before Christmas. I hadn't been outside since the first of November. Mom called one evening. She asked if I wanted to go out to see the lights with her and Dad."

"Did she call often?"

"No, and that's what surprised me. Not only the call, but the offer, too. I didn't want to go, worried about someone seeing me. Mom said it would be dark."

"Did you go?"

"I did, mostly to make her happy. Honestly, I was crying a lot, feeling so low that nothing could have made me feel better. But having my parents come over and take me out sounded nice. Home was a twenty-minute drive from Roselia. I waited inside for Mom and Dad. The station wagon pulled up to the curb. Dad was alone. Mom didn't want to see me, big and pregnant."

Outside the room were muffled voices, soft laughter, the kitchen tap squeaked on. I wondered if it was the massage therapist finishing with her client and wished I could have been that person, leaving refreshed and relaxed.

"How did that feel to you?"

"Surprised. Dad said she didn't want to come. I knew it was hard for her and felt bad that I'd been such an embarrassment. Mom was pretty much missing after I went to Lexington, Ohio between being home and going to Roselia. She wasn't happy about any of it."

"Did she call you during your stay in Ohio?"

"Back then, long distance calls were charged by the minute. I think she called a few times, but I didn't want to talk."

"Why didn't you?"

"I knew she'd be watching the clock, counting up the minutes. Plus, I knew she was mad about the whole situation."

"Was she mad at you?"

"Mortified might be a better word. I'm not sure who was more ashamed, me or her. That night with Dad, I scrunched down in the seat, trying to hide. There were people crowding the sidewalk, you know. Dad was quiet, like always. He asked me if I wanted to walk around and look in the store windows. I told him he must be joking, that I couldn't walk around, someone might see me. He said no one would recognize me and that I'd see the decorations better that way. But I said no.

"Kaufmann's window had an animated display, and I raised my head a little. I saw a snowman wave one arm. He had a black top hat tilted to one side and a red scarf around his neck. There was fake snow swirling around the snowman and the sleigh filled with presents next to him. I saw a bunch of little kids press their tiny mittened hands and noses on the glass. The whole scene was so sweet, like a Christmas card. Growing up, Mom and Dad would take us out after dark and drive around neighborhoods to see the lights. Afterward, we'd go home and string popcorn for the tree. I think Dad wanted to give me a little of that. It was really nice of him to come out on a cold winter night, just for me. But honestly? It only made me feel worse."

I apologized to Rebecca for my tears and self-indulgence. She reassured me that it was okay to cry, it was expected. Even so, I felt unworthy of her help. Finally, after a year of my apologizing, Rebecca asked me to please try to stop. It was one of the ways she helped me. I had to be conscious of the habit and work at making the change, not only in my behavior but, more importantly, in my mind. It was as challenging as lifting weights. Holding back on apologies gave my self-esteem the boost it needed. Not entirely convinced, I listened to her when she explained, "You are here because you need to be. And I am here to help you. There is no need to apologize or feel sorry for me."

Growing up, I went to Confession monthly, as required by my church. In the dark, closet-sized confessional, I'd kneel at the window facing a screen, behind which sat the priest. I'd list my transgressions in a mechanical voice: lying to Mom about brushing my teeth one morning; taking an extra piece of bacon when no one was looking; hitting my sister for being mean to me. It was as unpleasant as visiting the dentist, nerve wracking and fake. But with Rebecca, I confessed in daylight to someone who listened, reflected, accepted. These confessions were working. Little by little, the layers fell away, and I began to feel smoother.

33

The wooden stairs were bare and worn, and they creaked with each footstep on my way up to Rebecca's room. From the time I left home, I thought about what I wanted to talk about that day, but nothing came to mind. It was my usual routine, and mostly I had no inkling until I sat down on that couch. Rebecca carefully closed the door, trying not to disturb the massage therapy next door, then opened the window a crack, lending fresh air to the musty room.

Our routine had become a carbon copy that repeated itself at each appointment. I'd lay my purse on the floor, sit the water bottle on the coffee table, shed my coat, and toss it on the teal-colored couch. Then I'd sit down, grab a few tissues, and lean back. Always, there was chit-chat prior to the "real" talk, as if we needed those minutes to roll up our sleeves before excavating a deep mine. Ordinarily, I'd be perturbed at such monotonous repetition. But in my therapy, it was comforting, knowing that Rebecca and the couch would be there, accepting my secrets, tears, and nightmares.

As usual, I talked for the first three quarters of an hour, watching the clock. After forty-five minutes, I sighed, sat back and said, "Now you talk." This, too, was our usual routine.

Outside on the side street below, full dumpsters crashed to the pavement, and the truck gears ground as another one was lifted. A backup alarm screamed, high pitched and slow, loud enough to hear three blocks away.

Rebecca waited for the commotion to quiet. Her eyes fixed on mine in a way that caught me.

"What's wrong?" I asked. "Did I say something that I missed?" I chuckled at my words, but her expression was somewhat alarming.

"No, nothing's wrong." Then in a quiet voice so soft that I wasn't certain I heard right, she said, "Maybe it's time to find this person."

My head jutted as I leaned forward, puzzled. "This person? Like who? Do you mean Gavin?"

"No, I mean . . . ," she hesitated.

"The baby?" My voice went up an octave.

"Yeah," she said, her face serious, her eyes unblinking.

I stared at the worry stones, thinking of how soft they'd feel on my upper lip and on my cheeks. I wanted to hold them in my hand, run them over my forehead. If only they had some magical power to make things better. Decisions. My past. This pressure on my chest that never let up, no matter what I did or how much therapy I had.

"Find her?"

I thought this was behind me. But Rebecca had struck something hot. My face flushed. "Really? You think I should?"

"Do you want to?"

Her face showed no hint of emotion, none of the familiar expressions: sweet tilt of the head, or funny-looking, screwed-sideways mouth. She looked straight at me, holding my gaze, giving the feeling that we were inches apart, her hands on my shoulders. But she was still across the room, by the tall window.

"I don't know." The idea unnerved me. "What if she's dead?"

"What if she isn't?" Rebecca said with a gentleness that allowed me to breathe in.

I rubbed my rough lip with the side of my finger, feeling a scab where the dry flesh had torn. "But what'll I do if I find her?"

"I don't know. What do you want to do?"

I couldn't process her words. My child was lost to me, as much as my dead mother. My child—the one nobody talked about—my baby was gone, as if she never *was*, given away as if I never cared, as if her birth meant nothing to me. She had been buried along with my tears, the tears no one saw, but here she was in this space with Rebecca, more real than she'd been since she was lifted out of my arms.

"Well, I guess, mostly let her know me. It must be horrible not ever knowing who you came from." I took a quick breath.

"Or maybe being a mother who never knew her daughter?"

"Yes," I said and grew quiet. Then I said, "I can't imagine another daughter in my life. I suppose she'd have her own life, hopefully a good one, with kids, and a home. To tell you the truth, I don't know what I'd do."

"Well," the pace of Rebecca's voice quickened, "it's not something you *have* to do. But you might consider it. Take your time; it's your decision. Just mull it over."

The clock showed my hour was up. As usual, we both stood and set up our next appointment time, tapping on our screens, checking calendars. I slid my arms into the raincoat, reached for the door handle, fumbled for my car keys.

I shuffled out of Rebecca's office to the narrow hallway, past a sign that read, "Quiet please. Massage in progress." Down the steep wooden steps, my hand gripped the old worn railing. At the foot of the stairs, I switched my leather bag to the opposite shoulder, at the same time banging into the entryway table. The lamp rocked, and the green silk shade tilted sideways, toppling something near the lamp. A crash. I snapped to attention. Pieces of hobnailed milk glass scattered over the water-stained wood floor.

I knelt and began to pick up the shattered pieces of what had been a lovely old vase. Rebecca in front of me then, reaching out, taking them. She said, "Don't worry about it. I'll fix it. It'll be okay, not the same, but that's all right."

"I'm sorry, Rebecca. I'll pay for it. I mean it. Whatever the cost."

My blue Subaru sped along the six-lane highway toward home. Traffic moved ahead of the speed limit, each vehicle a few feet from the bumper ahead. On the car radio, Chris Isaak sang "You Can't Do a Thing." I kept up with the cars around me and steered onto the lower level of the double-decker bridge, crossing the river.

My mind raced. I trust Rebecca. *Is it really okay to search, like actively search, not simply put my name on lists and hope she'll find me?* I considered how it would be to find MaryLynn, wondered what she would be like. *Would she hate me? Would she like me? Would I like her?*

Traffic slowed. I tapped the cruise control and maneuvered out of the fast lane. I looked in my rearview mirror and saw the mouth of a tunnel I couldn't remember driving through. *How did I get here?*

In Pennsylvania, the adoption papers. My name on the bottom line, agreeing. As sharp as yesterday.

Up the hill, almost home, stones rattled the car's underside. I slowed on the gravel road and turned into the driveway. From the house, our dogs raced at top speed toward me.

By this time, our beloved Irish setter and golden retriever had made it to the end. We mourned our loss and had only Effie, my Parson Russell. But before long, we'd adopted two terriers rescued from the sidewalk of LA and our house filled once again with energy.

The dogs panted next to the car, waiting to begin our game. I passed them and pressed on the gas, zooming up the long driveway. The rearview mirror reflected the dogs rocketing behind the car: Effie, white with brown-tipped tail was in the lead; followed by Lulu with her brown fur blowing back, ears flapping; then Bingo, the puppy, short-legged with turned-out feet, working hard to keep up.

Daisies, poppies, and Queen Anne's lace bloomed over the hillside along the drive. The car rolled past my lavender rose tree with gangly branches, sparse spotted leaves, its trunk tilted over from years in the same pot. In spite of its bedraggled appearance, the rose tree persevered and still produced large fragrant flowers. I checked the mirror again for the pups catching up to me when I pulled into the garage.

Our century-old home overlooked the valley's patchwork of vineyards, alpacas, lavender, and Christmas tree farms. On that clear day, Mount Hood's white majesty showed along the eastern horizon. The living room's bay window faced the side yard with the many shades of Oregon greens: brilliant grass, dark pines, firs, redwoods, delicate moss, bright algae along the wet driveway edges.

During the long drive home, something in me had softened. Doubts and objections thinned until my thoughts cleared and settled on the solid truth. My mind was made up. I would look for her. I couldn't wait to begin. I launched into the odyssey; even before taking off my coat, I grabbed my laptop.

Charlie sat in the living room watching the local news, same as he did every midday. Bingo now laying next to him with her head on his lap with eyes half open, Charlie scratching behind her ears.

"I've made a decision," I said.

"Oh?"

I knew Charlie wouldn't care one way or the other. If he did have an opinion on a dilemma, he was an expert in nudging me toward what he thought best. Like learning to scuba dive. But finding my daughter—it was *my* thing, not his. Still, he was the first one I told and saying it out loud was a big step.

"I'm going to try and find my daughter," I said.

He looked away from the television. "You sure you want to do that?"

"I am," I said. "Rebecca suggested it. At first I wasn't sure. But then I thought more about it on the drive home. I think it's time."

"Good luck," he said. "I hope it works out like you want."

≈   ≈

On the loveseat, I leaned back against the arm, stretched out my legs, and opened the computer. My fingers to the keys, in the Google search bar, I typed: *how to find a child who was given up for adoption.* Sponsored replies popped up. Websites for searching, lists to join, articles, and blogs to read. Some registries had a fee, but most were free. It was 2015 and I had been retired for three months. I had the time. Thus, I began my search.

34

Catherine Vogeley, January 23, 1969, place of birth, Pittsburgh, Pennsylvania, Catholic Charities, I typed again and again, on different websites. I found blogs written by people like me. Some were heartbroken, usually adopted children whose parent had passed away or refused to communicate. There were stories from the elated with top-of-the-mountain outcomes, and my cohorts who waited to be found. My waking hours were spent reading others' accounts of searches and reunions. Grateful. Relieved.

Our families came together and everyone hugged.

She looks like me!

I never knew I had a sister.

She was schizo.

We couldn't stand each other.

Mom loved me, but her family didn't.

She slammed the door in my face.

She changed her phone number.

Afraid.

Angry.

Rejected, again.

What does she want after all these years?

꙳   ꙳

Years ago, Bertie and Opal had married wonderful men, and each had two healthy children. I was "Nana" like my grandmother and had discovered the unexpected, unimaginable joy of grandchildren. I'd made a vow to visit them every three or four months: I wanted my grandchildren to know their Nana. During one of my visits, I waited for a sliver of alone-time to talk to my daughters about the search. Opal was happy for me, hugged me, and gave her love and support. Bertie was more reticent, defensive, wondering if this was a good idea; she said she worried about my well-being. Bertie's response stymied me, but I vowed to accept whatever my daughters felt.

My siblings emailed back and forth with love and hope for a positive outcome. Charlie stood by, listened with a sympathetic ear, but maintained distance from the search. I even put a note on Facebook about the search. I thought of it as an unveiling. I needed to tell it. Wasn't I being fake if I didn't? Why shouldn't my friends and family know? I wanted to push shame back, to admit to the world what happened so long ago. That I had a secret and anyone who wanted to know about it could ask. Some people did. My two nieces were especially interested. My friends wished me well on the search. The telling was only important to me. Everyone else had their own problems. That was not to say that I was bitter. But realistic. What happened was truly mine and what I made of it.

Every day at five o'clock Charlie poured two glasses of wine and we meandered over the well-tended lawn to the pergola over which wisteria draped, its two-toned lavender blooms forming a canopy around us. We coordinated the landing, first me, then Charlie, holding our glasses high to keep from spilling. We pushed off and toasted to something in our day that we enjoyed. To sunshine! Happy Friday! To a scrubbed porch floor! To silly dogs! It was a precious ritual when we took time to focus only on each other, talking over thoughts on house projects, plans for our next camping trip, current events, and sometimes, my visits with Rebecca.

Charlie listened, never interrupted, and did not give advice but encouraged me to do whatever I needed to do for as long as I wanted. Occasionally he asked a question for clarification but did not probe nor criticize. Charlie's personality may be described as detached. Yet, he is unfailingly present and steady, always ready to help. He is the husband who fixes leaky faucets, builds a platform under the bed to raise the head for my night-time stomach trouble and then years later takes it apart when requested without an inkling of complaint. I backed his brand-new pickup truck into a mailbox and broke the tail light, felt horrified, and apologized profusely. Instead of getting mad, he joked about breaking-in the new truck. Generous of spirit. Trustworthy. Kind.

ᵔ ᵔ

Through the Pennsylvania Department of Health, I came upon a link to "Adoptions" that described options open to adoptees looking for medical histories, non-identifying information, and the wish to search for biological parents.

A notarized Biological Parent Registration Identification Form went into the mail. Orphan's Court of Allegheny County, Fifth Judicial District of Pennsylvania. Letters to the court requesting more information, forms then faxed or mailed, a petition for release of information from the adoption record. Weeks passed without further action. I wrote checks, and with each one, I hoped I was closer to finding her. A fee to the Pennsylvania Vital Records division, $20 for the birth certificate, $10 processing fee, $18 for shipping. They notified me weeks afterward, the birth certificate was unavailable. I did not feel discouraged. In fact, my enthusiasm grew with each new opportunity. I kept trying. I would not give up.

One day after showering, I opened my laptop, my daily habit now, to look for MaryLynn. On this day, I typed "Roselia, Catholic Charities" into Google search. Dots whirled clockwise. An image of Roselia appeared with large silver letters mounted against light brick: "Roselia Foundling and Maternity Hospital." Memories lit up the corners of my mind. In that moment, I felt the same anticipation, gladness, sadness, and fear I had the day when Mom and Dad walked with me through the doors below that sign.

Roselia was a refuge for me at a time when I had no other place. The nuns had been kind and the girls friendly. But the heartbreak behind that entryway still felt as real.

A button on the left column shouted: CONTACT US. I clicked and entered a brief note with name and dates, asking for help. I had a fleeting sense of disbelief that I was, in fact, searching, putting my name on records, bringing my secret history into daylight. I'd come to a point in my life when there were no obstacles. The wound had filled in to skin level, and the epithelial cells had begun to leapfrog over one another. *A woman has a right. A right to decide for herself what is best.*

One morning, I opened my email and saw a reply from Audrey, a Roselia adoption coordinator, who assisted with modern adoption cases. Audrey's note said that she was unable to help with the search. The current Roselia program was designed to support homeless pregnant women needing assistance and training in life skills. Audrey apologized and included the name of a social worker with whom I could speak, if necessary. I thanked her for her kindness and disregarded the social worker suggestion. I already had a therapist close to home. One more dead end, I thought.

❧   ❦

It was a fall evening when night arrived early, and the Oregon rainy season had begun; the living room blinds over the bay window closed out the darkness. The *Jeopardy* host on TV held cards in hand, contestants frantically tapping thumbs to answer buttons. Charlie lit the kindling in the fireplace. The warm glow felt comfortable, while outside wind whistled and rain clanged against the downspouts. Charlie rolled up his flannel shirt sleeves, folded his reading glasses into his breast pocket, then leaned into the fire, blowing at the base, growing the flame. Sap popped like a gunshot, and Effie ran from the room.

On my laptop, I typed in the adoption registry address as I did several times a week, and the site opened to the list of those searching. Impossibly small print and narrow lines of the database, unreadable at 100 percent view. The information was disorganized, not alphabetized or divided into regions of the country. I scrolled through pages. Finally, I located my name. In the last column on the right, an envelope icon occupied the tiny cell. My breath caught.

Charlie crossed the room and picked up his computer. He said, "What's up?"

"Oh, nothing," I said, nonchalant, afraid to consider the possibility out loud. "I have a message on this registry. It's probably telling me I have to renew my membership."

On the brown corduroy sofa, Bingo laid next to me, her warmth against my body, muzzle on my thigh. Her light brown fur and pliant ears welcomed my fingers, the tiny skull cupped by my curved palm. Her eyes closed, limp, entirely trusting.

Charlie pulled reading glasses from his shirt pocket, logged onto his computer, and tapped the keys. Charlie's face had the serious downward shape of an older man, and with Lulu curled up next to him, they could have been a Norman Rockwell painting.

Bingo's legs twitched, then muffled *ruffs*. I stroked her neck and ears. She calmed.

I pointed the cursor's arrow at the envelope and clicked.

Dear Cathryn, I was born on July 23, 1969, at Mercy Hospital in Pittsburgh. My mother was housed at Roselia. I wonder if there's any chance the month might have been mistakenly published and your daughter was actually born in July rather than January. If not, I apologize for the intrusion. But if so, please contact me as soon as possible. I'm hoping we have a connection. Maura

But July 23 was not January 23. No matter how much I wanted it to be different, I hadn't won. My heart ached for this Maura. Disconnected from her roots, searching and hoping. I wanted to be the one for her. I wanted it even more for her than for myself. No one deserved to be cut off from their birth parents without information, pictures, or history. And, I could admit now, no one deserved to be cut off from their child, without information, pictures or history.

I wrote back to Maura: *I'm sorry, I wish there were a mistake, but the dates are correct.* Maura and I emailed several times while she searched. Maura did eventually locate her mother with the aid of a DNA ancestry company, 23andMe.com. Her mother had died of colon cancer. That information led Maura to get a colon exam in which a precancerous lesion was discovered.

Maura was the first of several adoptees to contact me with hope there'd been a mix-up in the records. But none of them was my daughter.

Out-of-wedlock pregnancy, shame, and secrecy. Hundreds of thousands of women went through similar circumstances in the fifties and sixties. But not everyone searches, and the facts remain secret. Most reunions begin with the child searching for the birth parent. *Is it the shame that holds birth parents away?*

Starts and stops, filling out forms. Putting the search away for a time to let the process work. I questioned myself, my motivations, my expectations. *If I found MaryLynn, how would it be when we met? What if she were a criminal, a drug addict, a woman without boundaries?* I wanted to stay open and welcome whomever she was. *If I found her, who would I be without this lead weight that I'd dragged with me for most of my life?* I realized that I had allowed my heartache to define me. Would my shoulders go down, my posture straighten, my nighttime teeth-grinding stop, my smile come easily, my heart lighten?

Maybe she, Bertie, and Opal would get along, become friends. I wondered if her family and mine could be close, if her parents would thank me for giving them a chance to parent. *Naturally we'd be friendly. Why not?* Our most precious gifts were children. And we had that very much in common. *Besides, could anyone have too much love?*

The preoccupation with my search did not wane. As long as there were options, I kept looking. I hooked up with an adoption search angel through Facebook. When she learned the relinquishment was in Pennsylvania, she apologized and said the closed-adoption states were impossible. Perhaps it was time to let it go, knowing my information was out there for her to find. *After all, Maura found me.* I was running out of ideas.

❧ 35 ❧

January brought blustery weather. Under the wisteria, the heavy bronze windchime moved about, making a deep resonant sound that calmed my nerves. Windy days meant chills inside, too. Even though our old farmhouse had been modernized, the cold leaked through unseen cracks. A soft alpaca blanket lay over my feet on the loveseat. Once more, an idea: Google "search agents." Nearly every link turned out to be related to business, marketing, and employee search. Those aimed at adoption search were the same registries with which I'd already listed, but then a Florida agency came up. It was the only one that looked legitimate.

Locate Anyone Anywhere Fast. You Will Be Amazed. Contact Us Now!

10,000+ amazing reunions • Free evaluation • TV coverage • Get answers you deserve • Highlights: Operating Since 2001, Multiple Payment Options Available

This one hunted for missing family members, particularly adoptees and birth parents. Reviews of the agency varied. I contacted the agency.

The more I looked, the more my need to find her grew. In the beginning with Rebecca, I wanted to find MaryLynn to give her my background and apologize for giving her up.

But as days and months passed, my quest morphed into what felt like a compulsion. I had bottled energy that kept pushing me forward. The closed adoption laws protected biological mothers who wanted to keep the past secret, and adoptive parents who wanted to own their child without interference. *But what about the child? Where was her say in all of this?*

I worried that if I didn't hurry, one of us might die. *Was she even alive?*

The next morning, a call—a Florida number—came in.

A shrill, overly enthusiastic, woman introduced herself as Charmin.

"I got your note, Cathy, I'm so glad you reached out. Can you tell me a bit about your request and background of the issues?"

I paced the kitchen floor and said, "I'm Cathryn. I've been searching for my daughter who was adopted in 1969 through Catholic Charities in Pittsburgh." I recognized my voice, but the words were from someone else. They didn't fit with me, the one who kept that secret.

"Cathy, I know we can find your daughter. We need you to sign some documents of agreement and commitment to your search and that's it. You'll be on your way. Of course, we'll need photocopies proving your identity."

"Hold on. Are you suggesting that your agency can locate my daughter?" My heart sped up. This was the first time I'd heard anyone offer hope. "I'm sure you're aware of the Pennsylvania laws that adoption records are sealed for ninety-nine years?"

"Yes, I am. It means we'll need more time for the search."

This was it. I'd touch my daughter, look into her eyes, and tell her I was sorry. I was sorry for letting her go, for giving her away; I'd tell her I loved her. I'd ask her to forgive me.

I thought I had owned my choice to place her for adoption. But I wanted her now. I had to tell her I was sorry. I needed her forgiveness.

I said, "How does this work exactly? Can you describe the process?"

A large cat slinked along the blacktop outside the kitchen window, graceful and proud, with its head held high. How odd, I thought. Cats were a rare sight on our property, having been chased off by our canines. *That is an unusual cat. Look at how it walks.*

"Sure," her energetic enthusiasm began to irritate me. "The way this works, Cathy, is first we'll mail you documents to be signed. You send photocopies back to our agency. Then we begin the search." Charmin's voice became robotic, a loud infomercial, exclaiming the merits of the service.

Suddenly, I recognized the animal. I had never seen one in the wild. The fur was brownish gray and covered with black spots. A pointy tuft of hair topped each ear at the tip.

"When we find your daughter, we'll notify you. You'll receive updates along the way. The process is normally over within eight to twelve months. The turnaround time may be two to sixteen months. Your records will be kept on file for two years in the event that we aren't able to locate her."

"But how will you do that when no one else can? I mean how can you get into the sealed records?"

"Oh, don't you worry, we have ways."

"Ways?"

"We have access to records and information that most people can't get."

That was no house cat. It was a bobcat, a threat to other small animals like ours. My terriers were safe inside. I'd never seen one in the wild and watched it stroll into the woods, beyond our property.

Charmin and I spoke several times after that. The cost was close to two thousand dollars, paid in cash or check only, no credit cards. There were no rebates if the individual wasn't located. When I heard there were no statistics on their success rate, my confidence lagged. But I was running out of ideas. I wrote out two-columns of pros and cons, unable to decide whether or not to sign a contract. The cons column decided it. I told Charmin I couldn't use their service.

∞ ∞

On the second floor of the garage, Charlie had built a room for me to practice yoga and meditation. My goal was to calm and center myself, and practice Iyengar yoga. Yellow and orange paint, Kwan Yin the goddess of compassion, on one wall. I couldn't follow the TV yoga master. I tried doing yoga on my own but quickly became distracted, unable to concentrate.

In the little forest by the road, we'd constructed a labyrinth, an idea taken from a Zen retreat the year prior. We used a string to mark off the circle, and I laid baseball-sized stones in a pattern for walking meditation. Each morning, I raised my arms together and looked straight up through the treetops, swooped my arms in an arc to the forest floor, then straightened. Three deep breaths, and one foot forward, attention to each inhale and exhale. When that didn't help settle my mind, I said: "left, right, left, right," with each slow movement. Slow walking gave me a few minutes of peace.

Some days, I felt like I was losing my mind. Opal and Bertie talked about past events, visits I'd made and places we went. I had no recollection of what they described. This happened enough that I began wondering if something was wrong with me. One time at Macy's, the clerk asked for my street address.

"It's 11130. No, that's not right. It's 31130." I took a deep breath.

The saleswoman watched me, her face crunched with skepticism.

Finally, I said, "13310. Yes, that's it. I know it now." I laughed and rolled my eyes, "Flakey!"

The clerk laughed, too. She typed the address into the computer then turned to me. "Is there a northwest with that address?"

It sounded familiar. But no, that was not my place. Maybe it was Opal's. *I think she has NW on her address.*

I said, "No, I don't think so."

The woman frowned and said, "Are you sure?"

"Oh, yes, of course there is," I said. "I was joking."

I'd been lifted up and set down off-kilter. My preoccupation was irrational. I began questioning myself. *This is nuts. I'm losing it. It's because I can't sleep.* The nightmares. Always the same—running in an airport, late, trying to find my gate. The gate closing. The agent, "I'm sorry. You are too late."

A few weeks after the Florida agency experience—early evening after dark and after the kitchen had been cleared of dinner plates, with food covered and stored—the TV screen showed that week's photos of first birthday babies. As usual, I opened my laptop and scrolled through social media posts and ads, when a dancing panda cartoon came up, and with it a new idea: utilize the networking website that connected professionals to enhance job opportunities. I logged onto the site and in the search bar, I typed *Gavin Makis*. Maybe he could help with the search. The name came up, *Gavin Makis, Attorney at Law*. After my divorce in the nineties, I'd contacted Gavin. At the time, we talked as if no time had passed. He was still a smart aleck, sarcastic, soft-spoken. We'd talked about the child we had. I asked him if he'd want to meet her someday. He'd said, after a long hesitation, "Yes. I would." Back then, we got together for lunch. He was no longer the boy I'd fallen in love with at sixteen. After twenty years, I knew what I wanted and had a discerning eye. I no longer felt attracted to him. And now, almost fifty years after MaryLynn's birth, I mustered the nerve to contact him again.

I sent a message:

Cathy here. Gavin is this you?

He responded a few hours later. **Hi Cath. Yes, it's me. How're things?**

Great, thanks.

I learned that he still lived in Pittsburgh, where he worked as a criminal attorney. He'd been divorced after two years of marriage. I wrote, **Wow, that was a short one.**

Yup, that's all it took.

Wondering if you know of someone reliable who I might hire (you?) to search birth records for the adoptive parents, for the baby I surrendered thru Catholic Charities, born on January 23, 1969. I'm feeling more and more ready to meet her and give her the "story" if she needs to hear it.

I'll try to find a way to help. My mind is clear that what was done was done in the best interest of the child. I don't know if this is a good idea. Regardless of my personal misgivings, and out of respect for you and the pain I caused you, I will do what you ask. Always, Gavin

We agreed to talk the next week at ten a.m. Pacific time. When the day arrived, I decided to make the call away from the house. My past was separate from my present life. It was an unusually bright and breezy day in March with the freshness of coming spring. I walked through the community park that had trails through forested wetland, grassy knolls, a children's swing set, and a pond with Canada Geese. A handful of active people enjoyed the sun in the park as well.

I hustled along the park trail and slid on the muck at the edge of the grass. *Glad I wore my rubber clogs.*

09:45, according to my watch. A fist of pressure twisted in my stomach. I rooted through my pack for a protein bar. No bar, but I found a small TUMS container, *even better.* Up on a grassy knoll, a large man in a Hawaiian print shirt lumbered too slowly, missing the disk sent his way by a friend. The disk bonked against a post and rolled in the opposite direction. He ambled after it, made a wide stance, reached down, and lifted it.

09:55.

A wooden bridge spanned the wetland. Below, a great blue heron slept, majestic in the quiet, oblivious to the complications of human lives. I stopped. The bird's head hid under a wing with a bit of white at the top, from which a few delicate feathers curved. Effortlessly, the animal rested on one leg. The stillness calmed me. I began walking again, passing the disc players once more. The man missed it every time. Keep trying, I thought. Don't give up.

10:00. I stepped off the path into wet grass. My chest tightened and my breath quickened. *Should I wait till 10:02? Or is it better to call exactly at ten?* Time did not heal all wounds. I dialed the number.

"Gavin Makis speaking."

"Hi, it's Cathy."

"Cath, how's it going?" His voice was still buttery with a distinctive Pittsburgh accent, familiar.

"So, what'd you find out?" I asked.

His voice flattened, lost its energy. "Oh. Right." A pause. "Listen, Cathy, I don't think this's going to work. Everybody said pretty much the same thing."

"Come on. You're right there in the same courthouse, aren't you? Can't you use some work-around? Don't you have friends in the records department?"

"Yeah, sure I do. I got my friend in records to check. He told me, 'You aren't going to get anywhere with this.' He said, 'forget about it. Those things are locked up. It'll be another fifty or so years before anyone can look at them.' My buddies all said, forget it."

Oh, for fuck's sake.

"Seems like I hear birds or something. Where are you?" he asked.

"Where? I'm at a park, walking."

"Really? Oh, hey, I was working on a deal up in Bellingham, Washington. That's near you, right?"

"Well, sort of. It's on the same side of the country as me."

"Anyway, they wanted to build a road next to the railroad up there. The environmental hotheads were going nuts, and some businesspeople were going to sue, trying to stop it. I finally told the guy, 'Yeah, sure, we can put in a trail alongside. Then the bird-watchers can have a ball. You know, they can do their thing, make love to the hummingbirds or whatever the hell the tree huggers do up there.'"

He went on, offending my sensibilities. Around the base of an old fir tree, a cluster of narcissus bloomed, each extraordinary with a pastel cup and white petals. *Mom was right, he was a smart aleck.*

"Hey. Cath, are you still there?"

"Yeah. I'm here. I don't see what that has to do with the subject."

I heard him take a deep breath.

"Yeah, okay. I thought you'd be interested. You know. Since you live in the Northwest."

I leaned closer to the flowers, inspecting the fancy cup-and-saucer design with tiny, curved petals protecting powder-covered stamens. "I'm only interested in whether or not the records can be opened."

"Cathy, what are you doing? What do you think's going to happen? I mean a *lifetime* has gone by."

"Listen, if you don't want to be a part of this, that's your choice. But help me find her. I owe it to her to say I'm sorry, and I want to find her. I can't help it."

"Sure, sure. I know."

I examined the flower's individual parts, each one having its own delicate structure. A coaster of thin white petals under a melon-colored cup with frilly edges. A stand of dainty threads in the center. Exquisite in its perfection.

"I think you're making a big mistake," Gavin said.

"How come?"

"You know, this could turn out badly."

"Like what? Like how? I want to hear what you think. What could happen?" I pushed up from the grass, using my free hand.

I sucked on my water bottle but got no results, empty as it was. I walked to the fountain at the sidewalk's end. The fountain didn't work. My stomach cramped.

"Okay. I can see your mind is made up. I don't think it's a good idea. It could backfire on you."

"Listen, if you find anything different about the adoption records, can you let me know? If you aren't interested in finding her, I understand, and that's your business. But if you can help me, that'd be great."

"Hey, listen, I got to go," he responded. "Nice talking to you."

"Yeah, sure. Bye, Gavin."

"Take care of yourself. Bye."

Rebecca sat across the room. Her large eyes protruded so that she resembled a wide-eyed storybook character. My arm draped over the couch armrest. The scent of lavender filled the hallway and leaked under the door. The room had become as familiar as my own recliner.

I leaned back against a sofa pillow. I'm getting better, I thought. I'm sleeping better. Drinking less.

Absentmindedly, I moved Mom's garnet ring up and down, back and forth, on my right hand, feeling the gold, soft as infant's skin. The oval stone was dull and scratched but still precious to me. The normally blackish opaque stone shone red in the light, dark as port wine. For as long as I could remember, the ring was on Mom's right finger.

"How are things going with the search?" Rebecca asked.

I moved my eyes from my hand to Rebecca's kind face. "Well, actually not so great." Shoulders up, my hands moved on my legs toward my knees. I breathed deeply and stuck out my thumb, counting off each blind alley as I listed it. "My name is on several adoption registries." The index finger went up. "I've asked Gavin. Remember, he's an attorney in the county where the baby was given up?"

Rebecca nodded.

"Anyway, he says the same thing as the court. Records are sealed for ninety-nine years." Now with two fingers up, I said, "I've contacted Pennsylvania records division for documents. They won't release a birth certificate to me. I've talked to Roselia adoption people, who say the records are sealed. I've talked to orphan's court clerks and search agents, no progress. I've registered on multiple internet adoption search sites and Facebook groups." All fingers up, I had no more to add and dropped my hand. "You know? I don't know what else to do."

"Mmmmm," Rebecca said and nodded.

"There's nothing left."

Society had spoken: *you cannot know this person walking this world with your DNA, the one who grew in you, your own flesh and blood.*

Don't hold your child. Don't look at your child. You will never be able to let her go.

I leaned back again and tapped my hand on the armrest, head tilted. My thumb twisted the ring around. I never sat still. "I want to find my daughter. If it's meant to be, it'll be. If not, well, I gave it my best."

I picked up my water bottle and sipped. "I don't know what else to do. So, rather than eat up my insides, I'm letting go. I'm putting it out to the universe. And you know something? Since I decided, I feel a lot better."

Waiting, praying, talking, crying, meditating, exercising, thinking, believing, blinking awake through the night, wishing for sleep, and living through days of exhaustion. I'd reached a dead-end and had to accept it. There was a calming with letting go, a feeling that came so slowly I didn't know it happened until that day with Rebecca when I realized: *I didn't cry today for the first time since starting therapy. I'm better, lighter.*

☙   ❧

Light filled my bedroom on a glorious morning. Sea green walls and a moonlight-colored ceiling surrounded our white, four-poster bed. I dressed in jeans and a silk shirt to meet a friend for coffee. The view from the sleeping porch high over the valley gifted me with the last of the morning fog. Winter pansies along the porch railing smiled up at me with their bright yellow and purple pixie-faced petals. Sunshine always fed me, but that day, I felt an unfamiliar lightheartedness. *Was it freedom? Had I truly laid down the awful bag of rocks?*

I took a deep breath, stretched side to side, pondered my blessings. Across the valley, a neighbor's two white cows stood motionless, silent, heads to the ground: live ivory statues. Seldom did I hear their sounds, but now and then, one of them would bellow. That morning, I heard a long miserable moo that caught my attention, and I raised up on my tiptoes to see. But the white cows had not moved from where I'd last seen them; nothing had changed. *Maybe I imagined it.*

But when I opened the mirrored jewelry box, something had indeed changed. Not anything in the box, but something in me. Mom's garnet ring laid in a velvet groove among earrings and other things. Her ring that I knew and loved; it went along during afternoon soap operas. It was there as she pulled fish sticks from the broiler, took sheets off the clothesline. In her sleep, it was there; it rode along for diaper changes. For spankings. Through cake making and gift wrapping. When her hands gripped the steering wheel on Sunday mornings, the ring squeezed between her finger and the smooth plastic underneath. The yellow chiffon for my prom dress brushed the garnet when she held fabric under the sewing machine needle, and when she pinned the side seam, her ring tickled my bare skin. After Mom's passing in 1979, Jeannie claimed the ring but loaned it to me now and then. In dollars, it wasn't valuable, but for me, it was Mom. I wore it whenever I needed a little extra strength.

But now the garnet seemed to glare at me, or was it me who glared. It was small and inanimate, simply a stone—a stone that held her DNA. I stood there for what must have been a full minute. I couldn't touch it. I closed the jewelry cabinet and walked away.

It was an unfamiliar feeling, this anger toward Mom. Up till then, I couldn't fully admit that she was selfish and cruel. That she could have helped me in so many ways but chose not to. Later, I understood that by walking away from the ring, I regained the last bit of power I'd given away. I felt anger toward Mom for the shame, her revulsion toward me, disregard for my hurt; her part in the outcome with Gavin, turning me away from him, denying my need for him.

Rebecca helped me to see Mom as a person: not merely my mother, but a Catholic woman trying to get along in the world she knew, doing her best and probably suffering with her own guilt, unaware of how to be with me, afraid of softening toward me or driving me to promiscuity. My anger did not disappear, but over time the edges of my feelings softened. She had been gone for thirty-seven years, but I would welcome the chance to talk to her, to ask her how it was for her, and give her an opportunity to explain. She had begun asking me on her death bed if I was okay—when it was too late to answer me honestly or provide any answers—but I had never been able to ask *her* anything. I wanted to understand.

In hindsight, I know that as a fragile teenager I needed trustworthy loved ones. And so, the years following my pregnancy were spent trying to outrun my fear of abandonment, which tangled up with my feelings of guilt for abandoning my little girl.

                   ❧   ❧

Mid-March sun mixed with rain. I worked at the breakfast table, hands on the computer keys. Next to me sat a three-gallon, clear glass jar with notes, dubbed "the happy jar," a failed New Year's resolution from the previous year, meant to capture one happy thing each day. There were about two dozen Post-It notes, every one of them was blank. The happy thoughts I'd written faded in the sun and disappeared with time. *The irony of vanished happy notes.*

Above the hills a rainbow had formed, a full arch of red, orange, yellow, green, blue, and violet. Brilliant against the dark rain clouds, it seemed like a bridge between heaven and earth.

A thought occurred to me. There was an email from Catholic Charities about a year ago. There was a name, a social worker. Back then, I didn't need a social worker and never followed up. Maybe, just maybe there was more to that. I typed Catholic Charities in my Gmail search bar and waited. Finally, the note from Roselia came up.

I re-read the email from Elaine, a caseworker at Roselia, about a contact at Orphans Court. During the year since Elaine had sent the email, I talked many times to Leacy Brown, the court clerk, without results. But there, there in the email . . . the social worker's name and number.

Lucy White's information is Grant St, Pittsburgh, PA 15219
    She is part of the Adoption Department, Orphans Court Division
    Our adoption specialist is Marcia Dietz and her direct line is (412)XXX-XXXX
    Good Luck with everything. Elaine Cosely **Caseworker for Team Hope — Roselia Apartments**

It was a long shot. This Marcia social worker was a last chance. Pen and paper next to me, I dialed Ms. Dietz's number and waited. I noticed the happy jar pastel notes were not all blank. There was one that showed a heart with tiny stars of asterisks surrounding it. Inside the heart, Opal had written, "I love you Mom!"

Ms. Dietz answered.

I said, "Hello, I'm a birth mother looking for my daughter adopted in 1969. I understand the records are sealed. But I'm hoping things have changed in these modern times and that it might be possible to find her."

"Give me a moment here. All right, go ahead with your information. Let's have your name, birth date—yours, and the baby's."

If my mouth had a switch, it could've produced the data robotically, as I'd repeated the information so many times.

"Hmm. There is a good chance."

"Sorry? A good chance?"

"Uh huh, a good chance we can find the information," she said, matter-of-factly.

"Wait. What? Are you serious?" I said, almost shrieking. I stood and walked to the kitchen window, then back to the chair. "You can look at my records?"

"Well, sometimes," her voice went distant.

"Sometimes?" Silence. "Are you still there?"

"Sorry, I had to unwrap lunch, a hoagie today. Hope you don't mind."

"No, you go right ahead."

"Anyway, yes, sometimes we can."

"I am amazed. Are you sure? Why? How?" My elbow cramped from the tension, so that I put her on speaker and held the phone palm up, stretching out my arm.

"Well," she said, "the laws changed. The restrictions loosened in 2011. People can find each other in adoption cases with certain steps."

I sat, limp against the back of the chair. "Oh, my God," I whispered. "What do I need to do?"

Marcia chuckled. "I guess, for now, try and be patient. We'll start on this tomorrow."

"Start tomorrow?"

"I think so. It depends. We may need to look through records on microfiche. 1969 was a long time ago. I'm not sure, but we'll see."

"*Microfiche*? Holy cow, I haven't heard that word for years. I remember going through those old journal articles in school. So, a guestimate would be?"

"Hold on, Cathy. We'll do our best. You sit tight. I'll call you as soon as I find anything."

"I don't want to sound pushy, but if you could say it will be days, weeks, or months, that would be a help."

"We're talking maybe a week at the most. Okay? We'll talk soon."

"A week is nothing. Believe me. Thank you."

I felt giddy, trying to hold onto myself, like the feeling of flying up from my seat on a roller coaster, with gravity suspended. I could've touched the sky.

❧ 38 ❦

March 17, 2016

The gate closed behind me while our dogs watched from the other side. I walked out of sight, arms pumping. Our pooches kept me grounded, the way energetic children can keep you going. I loved these puppies, substitutes for my faraway family. They'd be waiting in the same spot when I crested the hill thirty minutes later, and they'd race back and forth along the fence till I reached the gate.

The road was a series of grades up and down, culminating in a high spot that curved and dropped sharply to the main road. A few businesses lined the unpaved road, making a lot of traffic during certain seasons. The road wore in corduroy ruts during those periods and made driving bumpy, but walking was actually better with the humps. They gave me something to push against on the steep parts.

I started down the hill. Gravel rolled under my hiking shoes, and my feet slipped. To the right and along the fence, a field of white alpacas grazed, silent, moving only to lift a head and stare, their lower jaws sawing side to side. The hill curved around their field, and my feet slipped on the gravel again. Past the beehives, I checked for activity around the white boxes. Only a handful per box, but then two scouts flew at my head. I flapped my hands, then realized the bees were already gone.

I turned to retrace my steps at the bottom of the nearly vertical hill. Too hot then, I pulled on the jacket's zipper tab and opened it.

My phone jangled in my pocket. I checked the number. A Pennsylvania area code.

"Hello?" I said.

My foot caught in a divot. I tripped and went down hard onto one knee. My phone flew, and stones dug into my palm. I grabbed for the phone as a car neared, its tires chewing into the gravel.

"Hello?" I said again and stood, moved to the side of the road.

"May I speak to Cathryn Vogeley?"

Breathing hard, I said, "Yes, this is she."

The car moved past slowly as the driver called, "Hey, are you all right?"

I nodded and twittered my fingers, embarrassed.

"Hi, Cathryn, my name is Adrienne. I've been assigned your case by our agency, Family Design. Is this a good time to talk?"

"Yes, yes, I've been waiting to hear from you," I said. *It's happening, it's truly happening. Don't be too excited. Nowhere to sit. Don't fall in a gulley.* I held my scraped palm against the phone, pressing it tightly to my ear.

"I am a search agent, as you may have guessed. We have contracted with Roselia to locate your daughter. How are you doing?"

"I've waited so long for this. I have to tell you. I am so excited; I can hardly stand it."

Adrienne chuckled while I recovered. "Yes, I can imagine this is a big event for you. It's been a lot of years. We'll send you forms to complete. Personal info, consent, and such. Once you return the forms and everything is in order, we'll make contact." Adrienne's voice had a lilt—relaxed, professional. No western Pennsylvania accent.

"Make contact? Has she already been found?" My heart stopped; this couldn't be real.

"I haven't personally located her address, but given the data from Roselia, I have no doubt your daughter will be located. The information is available."

She is real. Suddenly the ancient story I carried inside took form. She is real. The full-cheeked infant sleeping in my arms forty-seven years ago. I'd spent my life forgetting her, trying to leave her behind. Trying to pretend she never happened.

"There is a fee. It's three hundred dollars. Once we have your payment and papers, we can begin. I'll be sending a letter along with the details as well. By the way, in case you can't meet the financial obligation, there may be assistance, as long as you qualify. So, that's it. You'll return the materials, include a check, and we'll get started."

A tanker truck bumped and passed on its way to a dairy farm. The wheels thunked into a pothole and caught my attention. On the truck's side, a cartoon Guernsey with a white diamond on the forehead, curly eyelashes, and a wide smile. A neighbor followed behind and steered around the deep hole. I waved. The world was still clicking, thunking, roaring, crunching while I was at the edge of a gravel road in Oregon hearing news of my first child. *Fill out some forms and send a check. That's it?*

I thought of the past year. The Florida search agency had charged a sizeable amount of money, without any adjustments, if the search failed. I thought of the myriad of adoption registries, Facebook sites, and blogs. The maze where I wandered finally had a way out.

Alpacas galloped along the fence, tiny hooves whose only sound was swishing grass through which they passed. The smallest one, pure white with pink feet and nose, nuzzled against its mama.

"I will send a check. And then?"

A mourning dove flew low to the ground, picked up a twig, and took flight again. Next to the alpaca shelter, a mama killdeer flapped in the ground, distracting predators from her chicks.

"Then, we locate the address and mail a query letter, let your daughter know her birth mother is searching and give her the option of connecting."

The words repeated in my head: *let your daughter know her birth mother.*

When Rebecca suggested the search, I thought, I don't need another daughter. I have two already. What would I do with her? Back then, I was still breaking through that protective layer, so well built and solid. It had been peeled off now, exposing me and her: the daughter I wouldn't allow myself to think about. My first child, as much my daughter as Bertie and Opal, who I loved more than anything in the world.

Adrienne said, "Now, I don't want to discourage you. But I need to say that sometimes a person declines or doesn't respond. You need to be prepared for that possibility. Connection can be rocky."

I'd heard that on the adoption search forums. But I had no reservations. My heart ran to her, nothing slowed me down.

"How long's that take? I mean, normally? I mean, after you get the paperwork and check?" Standing still, I'd cooled down and chilled. I zipped up and walked toward home.

"Usually, it's between one and two weeks, but it can take months, depending on the recipient's feelings. Remember, this is *a process*," she said. Her demeanor was compassionate, experienced.

Over the following weeks, it was impossible to hold my attention steady. *Read a book?* Not even a magazine article. My memory became even more unreliable. I drove in the opposite direction from where I wanted to go. I couldn't sleep.

∾   ∾

Late one morning, when I was alone in the living room flipping through social media, an email arrived. I opened Gmail with my normal cynicism. *Probably an ad or spam.*

Instead, Adrienne's name showed in the preview line. I moved the cursor and held my breath.

Click.

My daughter was located. Letters had gone out to her and her adoptive parents announcing my wish to connect. My mind raced as if I'd found buried treasure in my backyard. *What if something goes wrong? What if the letters are thrown into recycling without being opened?* Adrienne assured me the letters would be re-sent if needed. And if the second round didn't elicit a reply, she would try contacting by phone.

I was asked to compose a letter to be sent by the search agent in case I never got to say anything else. I'd have this one chance. "Remember," Adrienne wrote, "it's possible that she may not want to connect. If that's the case, we want to be respectful of that decision."

I closed the computer and wandered down the hallway to the kitchen. Two windows at the far corner faced Mount Hood, but that gray day, clouds obliterated the view. NPR on the radio discussed the homeless problem in Portland and the opioid crisis. *What will I do if my daughter is a street person, a drug addict? Anything is possible. What if, instead, she is a governor's wife? Or a governor herself?*

Write a letter? I want to get this right. Don't overwhelm. What do I need to tell her? What is most important? What do I say? I need some chocolate.

In the end cupboard, easy to reach above Quaker's Original Oatmeal, was a stash of "emergency" O'Henry candy bars that Charlie stocked for such occasions. The chocolate nutty caramel soothed my anxiety. The candy bar was in two sections, and I stowed the second half in the loose wrapper, placing it in the back of the shelf. Before I walked two steps from the counter, I'd eaten the second half.

My daughter, whose life was shaped by strangers, people chosen by Mrs. Chau, a social worker with poor English.

Reaching into the refrigerator, I pulled out the milk carton and poured a small glassful. Then back to the shelf; I ate a second candy bar.

Fingers to keyboard. A voice cautioned, "You should wait. Give this time. Don't rush. Compose thoughtfully. This may be the only opportunity you ever get." But restraint lasted only a brief moment. I could not wait another second. Something might happen: a massive stroke, a heart attack, a gas explosion. I wrote a note, read it once, and hit send, unwilling to revise or polish.

4-13-2016

To my long-lost child,

I want to tell you that I've always regretted having to give you up. You were conceived during a time when there was no acceptance of an unmarried mother. It was shameful to become pregnant before marriage . . .

I've hoped and prayed that you were well loved and appreciated by your adoptive parents and siblings. Please know that I did the best that I could do for you at the time.

For many years, I was unable to allow myself to think about you and all that happened. Recently I retired and have had lots of time to think and process the events. After years of therapy, I've decided to try to locate you and let you know me if you want. If not, I understand. I hope that you can forgive me.

All the best,

Your birth mother

Over the next week, I checked my email constantly. Even at night, I rolled over and hoped for news, anything related to her. At stoplights, I'd pick up the phone to check for a note from Adrienne. The obsession grew, until I needed relief and walked down the hill, or had dinner with friends—anything to get away from the constant checking. Almost two weeks passed. Eventually, I avoided email, despising the inbox without Adrienne's reply.

April 26, 2016

Cathryn,

I received a call from your daughter late today. She was emotional. She never thought someone from her biological family would contact her after so long. She has always known she was adopted. I read your letter to her. She was pretty blown away and asked if she could take a couple of days to let the idea of her biological mother trying to contact her gel. I have scheduled a phone call to speak with her on Friday. She asked a lot of questions and I answered them as best I could. . . . She would like to know what you would like to gain from contact with her. I told her that to my knowledge, you wanted to make sure she was happy and healthy and that you would be willing to have contact if she was okay with that. I also made sure she knew that she was under no obligation to release information, but that you would be open to anything she would like to provide. I want to let you know that I felt it was a very positive call. Emotions run high when I tell people out of the blue that their biological parent has asked me to contact them, but she was very willing to talk to me again. Please look at this as progress, and if there is any information you would like me to pass on I will.

Thank you for putting your trust in me, and it is my honor to be a part of your journey.

I replied: *Omg. Adrienne. I wonder if you have any idea what your words mean to me. I cannot express my gratitude enough. This is so huge for me and I'm sure for her. I've been constantly checking my email and nearly sick to my stomach with anxiety. I was shocked to see your name. I couldn't read your note fast enough. Dear God in heaven thank you Adrienne. I know it's past your work hours. I so appreciate you writing so late.*

Bertie and Opal were happy for me. Opal offered to go with me if her half-sister wanted to meet. Bertie maintained distance. She couldn't relate to a sister fathered by another man. I made an announcement to my siblings. "Congratulations," people said. I talked to friends about my search-and-find. Gavin did not reply to my texts with the news of connection.

After several weeks, I received a short email forwarded by Adrienne. My baby, now a middle-aged woman, wrote:

> . . . *You have asked if I can forgive you, but there is nothing to forgive. I know you did the best thing for you and for me at the time. . . . I don't blame you—I admire and thank you for giving me life. Helena*

We exchanged long emails during the first few months. She is highly educated and is a full-time mom of three young girls, living across the country from me. At her bidding, I sent a recorded message, so she could hear my voice. I've shared photos of myself, Bertie and Opal, my grandchildren, siblings and extended family, my parents and grandparents, Gavin's high school yearbook picture.

Our exchanges became my stories of her beginnings, answered by her sympathy for my predicament during my pregnancy in the nineteen sixties. Almost like a therapist, she pulled it from me, and like a client, I let the memories spew out. I shared with her that I was taking writing classes and working on my story. She wanted to read everything I wrote. Afraid it might be too much for her to manage, I hesitated. But she insisted nothing would be too much, that she was a grown woman and could handle anything.

I asked questions, too. *How was her childhood? How did she feel now?* Helena wrote about her parents, who were loving, college-educated people of Germanic and Italian heritages— exactly as I'd requested. Hers was a home of plenty, where she was an only child, the center of her parents' world. I'd imagined her as happy in her parents' spotlight.

Yet, a spotlight can be too bright, suffocating. That first year of our connection, Helena revealed what I considered startling, almost shocking. She was angry about her beginnings; about how decisions that didn't include her were made on her behalf, robbing her of siblings, heritage, family. She felt peculiar growing up, like a curiosity to those who discovered her parents weren't biological. Helena's father asked her not to talk about it with anyone. "It's nobody's business," he'd said.

I'd thought of her as a well-loved gift to her parents. That she'd be special to them, unlike my formative years when I was the third in three years, feeling in the way and costing my parents money in clothes, food, and school supplies. I'd spent my life feeling ashamed, only to discover my daughter, whose circumstances seemed opposite, was ashamed, too, as if we were two sides of the same coin. But how does a child given up for adoption ignore the fact of being given away, even if they land in a loving home?

Helena had written that she and her husband were Catholic, and their daughters attended Catholic school. She asked if I was still Catholic, did I go to church, did I believe in God. Fair questions, but not ones I could answer easily. I replied, cringing as I wrote that I do believe in God, not in the traditional religious faith, but in the sense of an omnipresence of peace and love. That God is not a judge of our failings but there for us; a supreme being for whom words and definition are impossible; that I believe in the universality of suffering and of joy. That Buddhists' beliefs of love and harmony parallel my own philosophy. She asked if I am a Buddhist; do I participate in services at a temple. I answered that I do not belong to any formal religion. That sometimes I miss the Catholic liturgy with the pageantry, music, litanies, incense, vestments, bells, etc. In truth, my Christian background will always be a part of me. But I believe the heroes of love and forgiveness, those around whom religions have been developed, are basically the same: charismatic men who represent the omnipresence of our God and the importance of goodness in the world.

Helena wrote about having wished (as a child) for a large family. My siblings and spouses, children, and grandchildren total thirty and so I shared photos of our family reunions. She commented on resemblances to her children, but expressed no interest in meeting them. Neither Bertie, Opal, nor Helena had interest in contacting each other in spite of offering to share emails.

It was 2017, when millions of women in America and around the world marched in solidarity for women's rights. Sexual harassment emerged as the number one news story, with TV personalities, actors, and authors taken down. But it was my year to finally let go and let the world be as it was.

During the fifteen months since connecting with Helena, the initial frenzy of emails dwindled. I have seen clear photos of her beautiful children, but only one fuzzy picture of Helena. I've never heard her voice.

I'm willing to wait as long as it takes. It may never happen.

Every day, before rising, I'd look for a note from Helena. At first, when she didn't reply to my last message, I felt dread and the familiar squeeze in my throat. *That was the last time I'll hear from her. Did I say something wrong?* Then, a whistle signaled a text from her, a light breezy message, asking how I was, texting about driving her three girls to and from activities. But it wasn't enough. I wanted to meet, to put my arms around her, to look into her eyes, to say I love you, to say I'm sorry. I offered to fly to the East Coast near her home, where we could meet in the airport, then I would fly back to Portland in the same day, sparing her from explanations to her parents, children, or anyone else.

But she couldn't.

For months, I wrestled with myself and my thoughts. Ruminated on my goal: to let her know me, and to ask her for forgiveness. *That wish was satisfied. She is choosing not to be a part of my life. I must respect that.*

The emails became texts then those, too, dwindled to nothing.

⦃   ⦄

The emotional rush that came with finding Helena took me by surprise and swept me far beyond my rational objective. I had needed to tell her who I was and to answer her questions. I had to remind myself over and over that the choice of letting me in her life was up to her and that whatever that decision was, I would respect it. I laid awake at night, thinking of her.

I'd thought that finding her would fill the hollow ache inside me. But there was still something missing. Some defect existed in me, an inadequacy, which, right or wrong, I blame on my birth when Mom's patience, energy, and generosity were stretched beyond her limits. I wondered if I'd ever accept and love myself as I am.

⦃   ⦄

The answer came that summer in August when, under the open sky in central Oregon, everything lined up. I was ready, and so was the universe.

I stood behind the trailer, motioning back, then left. Charlie maneuvered the camper into our space. I shouted, "Okay. You're perfect!" He shut down the truck engine and dropped out of the driver's seat. His blue ball cap ever-present, white T-shirt and shorts, socks with sandals.

That's my Charlie, I thought. Handsome as can be, nerdy as most engineers, and smart as hell. The eclipse was my idea, and he arranged for a spot in the path of totality. He came along only for me. We leveled the camper, pulled out the metal steps, rolled out the awning, and unfolded our tilt-back lounge chairs.

Thousands of others across the makeshift campground attended to similar duties. I wondered about the crowd. Never having been to a big festival, I thought of Woodstock and Burning Man. But, no, this was a sedate and respectful crowd. No nakedness, drunkenness, loud music, sex, weed, needles, or anything remotely wild. Most were families and older couples like Charlie and me. Polite and considerate, people even picked up their own trash and used the recycling bins.

Arid central Oregon. The chances of clear August skies were about the best in America. The treeless land and surrounding flat terrain provided an unobstructed view of the sky. Rows and rows of tents and awnings filled one section, and in the other, hundreds of RVs and trailers parked close together in the hot sun. All reservations had a place in the field, where over six thousand attendees were expected. No one came for a camping experience. The place lacked trees, trails, campfire grates, bike paths, streams, and the fragrance of the great outdoors.

❧　❧

The night was cold enough that we ran the camper's heater. But the next morning, the desert sun turned the air hot. The entire eclipse would last over two hours, about sixty minutes to the full eclipse. Totality would be only two minutes long. A wide-brimmed, cotton hat shaded my face, and the light beach cover-up shielded my fair skin. Through my protective cardboard glasses, the sun was a little round breath mint. Murmurings began up and down the rows of RVs at 9:06 a.m. when the eclipse commenced. A neighbor pointed at the sun. Someone said, "It's starting; look at that."

The sun reminded me of the Apple logo, a disk with a bite at the one o'clock position. I felt mildly disappointed. This was supposedly a huge event. But the sun looked tiny through my two-dollar glasses. Downright unimpressive. Well, I thought, I'm here now. It'll be fun to tell my friends about it.

I stared at the sun, head hanging back. My neck cramped. I held onto my head with my right hand, and it cramped, too. An hour is a long time to stare up at the sun, I thought. Finally, I walked to the lounge chair under the awning and threw the wide-brimmed hat on the table.

The sun will move, I thought, and sat in the lounge chair, picking up the novel I intended to finish. Every few minutes, I replaced the cardboard glasses, checking the moon's advancement.

I glanced toward the neighbors' group-camp of five middle-aged men. The night before, after dark, they set up camp about ten feet away from ours. We'd talked with them and learned that they were scientists from San Diego up to central Oregon for the eclipse. Sina, a professor of astronomy, set up his telescope, computer, camera with filters, and tables. He was a short man with glasses and a faint accent that may have been Persian. Walking to their camp in the cold desert air, I folded my arms across my front for warmth, intending to say hello and ask him about his project. Sina scuttled about, never stopping to look at me, although he was pleasant, friendly. He adjusted and readjusted the telescope and computer on a folding table.

I asked him questions and he engaged readily. I confessed, "Honestly, I don't know much about stars or constellations. But I'm here, because I heard it's a big deal."

"What do you think you'll see?" Sina asked, leaning into the scope's eyepiece.

I said, "Well, the moon gets between the earth and the sun, blocking out the light. It's supposed to get dark, but I don't know exactly how dark. Totality will last a little over two minutes. And I've heard that's when you can take off the special glasses if you want. But is that right? I mean, I don't want to ruin my eyes. Is it truly safe to take off the glasses?"

He stopped fiddling, and from the light of his computer screen, I saw his puzzled expression. "Yes, yes, there's nothing to worry about with totality."

"I really don't want to hurt my eyes. Are you sure it's safe?"

"Oh yes, of course! Don't you know? Totality is it! Totality is everything. It's the reason everyone is here from across the world." He threw his hands out to his sides. "The rest of the eclipse is okay. But there is nothing that compares to totality. You will look at the sun." His voice went up an octave. "You will look *right at it.*"

"Oh," I said, astonished at his passion on the subject. "No, I didn't know that totality was *everything.* What'll happen exactly?"

His tone hushed. "When the sun is almost completely covered, the temperature will drop. And it'll become dark."

"How dark?" I asked. "Do you mean midnight-type pitch black?"

Sina wiggled the wire connections between the instruments. "No, not that dark, but enough so that the planets and stars will show. There will be a red glow and a halo of rays shooting out from around the black center."

I didn't get it. I expected to see the moon cover the sun. The fact that hundreds of thousands worldwide would travel to Oregon is what made me want to come. I didn't know why it was such a big deal. The bit about being life-changing? It's a moon, and it's a sun.

My insides felt jittery. An hour of anticipation seemed longer in the middle of a desert. I couldn't absorb the words in my book and gave up, slipping the book next to me. Charlie puttered around the campsite, adjusting the awning, checking the refrigerator's temperature.

A truck with wide tires inched through the makeshift roads between campers and sprayed water on the ground to control the dust. A small circle of young children squatted in the ruts made by the truck's tires. With little mud-covered palms, they flattened scoops into pies, which they stacked like burgers. Nearby, families of varying ages sat around large tables under canopies, drinking coffee. A little girl ran ahead of her father yelling, "You can't get me." The giant gathering possessed an unusual energy, full of life and expectation. Everyone smiling and talking fast, as if anticipating a first-born child.

Around ten o'clock when the sun was only a sliver of light and the air had cooled, we strolled past the other campers to an open field of wild carrots, to make sure we'd have a clear view of the sky. Little by little, others joined us. A semicircle of couples holding champagne glasses. Children and parents held hands; many stood in the lane between the campers, avoiding the deep tracks left by the water truck.

The moon's shadow crawled over the mountains in the distance and reached us. The air became cold as night and I shivered, wishing I'd brought a sweater. But I couldn't look away from the sun. The crowd stilled. A black dome formed over us while the horizon stayed dimly lit. The darkened sky transformed into clear night with plainly visible stars. A man held his little girl, pointing up to a constellation the name of which I don't recall. A few spoke in reverent whispers as if in a church sanctuary.

Nightfall in midmorning. Cold under a desert sun.

Death might be like that, too. When the light goes away, and breath stops. When every chance for a good life is past. When death takes the despair and dissolves the scars until you're away, floating free.

I still thought about death often, but in a softer, more accepting way, nothing like the day when I held the gun. The gnawing wish to get it over with was mostly gone.

The moon covered the sun completely to joyful shouting, *oohs* and *ahs*. I pulled off my glasses. The sun's corona radiated into the blue-black dark with explosions of light shooting into the sky; like a perfectly round pupil, like the center of an eye encircled by a thin, glistening white ring. My breath shortened, then came all at once. My eyes wetted; tears ran down my face.

For the next two minutes, totality took me away from the field, away from myself to a place of pure connection with the essence of life, my life, all life. It took me away from the years of tears and heartache, anger and despair that I'd wrestled with, feeling lost and alone. I suddenly felt as if God had reached down and cupped my face in His hands; a feeling washed through me and I allowed myself to open, to let the truth sink in without words or prayers or thoughts. Before that moment, I was a jigsaw puzzle without its last piece, incomplete, always hoping for something, to be right, to be okay, to be best, to be enough. Under the eclipse, it was as if those pieces that were me expanded to fill the empty space on their own. *I am no different than anyone else. I have a right to be here on this earth. I am* enough.

Charlie reached for me, and we wrapped ourselves together, each wiping our eyes, not speaking.

A moment later the moon slid over to the other side of the sun and totality ended. I replaced my flimsy glasses, took Charlie's arm for support, and we walked back to the campsite while others scattered as if in a concert crowd when the music stops and the lights come on. Across the way, jacks banged. An awning retracted with a loud grinding noise. Truck doors slammed; an engine roared. Then, a crash, as lawn chairs landed in the neighbors' truck. Slow-moving RVs rolled by.

My lounge chair waited, and I collapsed into it, feeling as limp as a wrung-out sock. Charlie messed around the campsite, pouring coffee, setting out a plate of doughnut holes, adjusting his chair next to mine. "Coffee?" he asked.

"Sure," I said, looking up at his kind face. But I sat there in a daze and didn't reach for the mug. My starch was gone, my energy depleted, like when I worked out hard, collapsing with exhaustion and feeling complete.

Except I hadn't done anything but stand in a field and look up.

❧ Epilogue ❧

2021

Helena once described meeting me would be like ripping off a Band-Aid. So far, the Band-Aid remains intact. She sends a text on my birthday, a brief note wishing me well. And I do the same for her. I can only conclude that she is content with her life, preferring the safety of her small family to the risk of rejection.

My euphoria under the total eclipse has stayed with me. It wasn't by magic that I transformed, but the result of years of work, as well as the strong bond with my loving husband. I've come to understand my life as a tapestry of choices and, more importantly, circumstances that made me who I am, a completed masterpiece, a woman who is finally comfortable in her own skin.

The details of my account are unique to me, but broadly speaking, the experiences are uncannily similar to others' stories. Well over a million women gave up children during the "Baby Scoop Era."[*] The practice of closed adoption was cruel and unjust, leaving deep scars that for many have never healed. I wrote this story for my sisters in loss who truly understand, and for their children. It is my hope that my memoir will inspire others to forgive; forgive themselves and the world as it once was.

---

[*] Wilson-Buterbaugh, K. (2017) *The Baby Scoop Era: Unwed Mothers, Infant Adoption, and Forced Surrender.* www.babyscoopera.com

❧ Acknowledgments ❧

With sincere thanks to:

My first writing instructor, Jennifer Lauck, without whose insistence this story would not have been written; for years of classes, for her patient instruction as I learned to create scenes and story structure.

Joanna Rose who taught me the beauty of word sounds and rhythms.

My sister Barbra Vogeley McDill who read the multitude of revisions with grace and encouragement.

Charlie Young, my loving husband whose stoicism provided stability during my discovery process.

My writing group, Myrna Guisdorf, Allan Seigel, Glenda Goodrich, Elyse Garret, John Lucas, and Christine Dreier, who propped me up when I wanted to give up. To the many generous beta readers who offered important feedback and to the Facebook Binders group of women writers for their support and information. To my editors, Clarissa Voracek and Jocelyn Carbonara whose expertise and support were exactly what I needed.

About the Author

Cathryn Vogeley was born in Pittsburgh, Pennsylvania during the post WWII baby boom. She grew up in a suburban community among a tumultuous family of seven. Cathryn is the daughter of a devout Catholic and third of Irish triplets. As a girl she was fascinated by the nuns with their long black habits, veils and wimples that allowed only the skin of their hands and the front of their faces to be visible adding to the mystery of a body under all of that fabric. But she matured into a teenager and the curiosity dissolved when she enrolled in nursing school and met the boy who would change her life.

Cathryn Vogeley practiced nursing over the first forty-five years of her career. She earned a Master's degree from Kent State University as a clinical nurse specialist. Her mission has always been healing. Cathryn has raised two daughters and is grandmother to five young grandchildren. Cathryn makes her home in the wild and wonderful Pacific

Northwest where she lives with her husband and three terriers. She enjoys writing, traveling to see family and to tropical places for scuba diving.

Cathryn is a keen observer with a sensitivity toward the injustice, the ridiculousness, and the beauty of the world. Her urge to write was born from her desire to bring such stories to the forefront; to bring alive the nitty-gritty of our lives and the profound affect one person can have on another.